Drumbeat™ 2000

MW01253010

Drumbeat Terms to Get Familiar With

Asset: Anything you use to make your Web pages. Images and styles are two examples. You store and sort assets in the Asset Center (see Chapter 3).

Attic: The upper-right area of the Drumbeat screen, above the layout area.

Attributes Sheet: Contains information about whatever element is selected. You reach it by clicking a tab in the upper-left area of the Site Management area. It's not just a passive list — you can use it to make important changes.

Basement: The lower-right area of the Drumbeat screen, beneath the layout area.

Content Table: A container for a set of related stuff you want to have available. It's organized in rows and columns and lives in the attic.

Contracts, interactions, activations: Self-contained segments of JavaScript that are on hand to make elements on your pages interactive. Applied to more than one element, a contract is known as an interaction. Applied to a single element, it's an activation (even though it probably interacts with the user of the page). Chapter 16 is all about contracts.

DrumNotes: Helpful guidance notes and site files, provided by the makers of Drumbeat and available at http://drumnotes.drumbeat.com.

Preview tab: The little tab, down in the lower-left corner of the layout area, that allows you to do an "instant publish" and see a page as Internet Explorer would see it right there in the layout area.

Recordset: A representation of a dynamic data table. You can set up icons for your recordsets in the basement and apply interactions between them and the visible page elements.

SmartElement: Any page element, whether it's visible or not. You can inspect (and often change) the properties of any SmartElement on its Attributes Sheet.

Snapshot: The Drumbeat version of the Save As option. An extremely useful backup if things go horribly wrong later.

Starting Points: Prefab Drumbeat sites that can be used to get you started on your own designs.

Shortcut Keystrokes You Can Use

Keystroke	Function or What It Does		Keystroke	Function or What It Does
F1	Help (in browser window)		Ctrl+O	Open an existing site
F7	Spell checker		Ctrl+P	Prints site report
F12	Opens the site in the selected browser		Ctrl+PgDn (toggle)	Makes scrollbars visible or invisible
Ctrl+A	Selects all		Ctrl+S	Takes a snapshot (a safety copy of your site)
Ctrl+B (toggle)	Expands or contracts basement			
Ctrl+D (toggle)	Expands or contracts attic		Ctrl+Spacebar (toggle)	Expands or contracts Site Manager and Asset Center
Ctrl+F	Find			
Ctrl+H	Replace		Ctrl+W	Returns to Layout mode from Preview mode
Ctrl+K	Assigns link			
Ctrl+L (toggle)	Expands or contracts the Layout		Ctrl+Y	Preview mode
Ctrl+N	Opens new site		Ctrl+Z	Undo

Drumbeat™ 2000 For Dummies®

Cheat Sheet

Forms SmartElements

Icon	SmartElement	Description
	Checkbox	Binary element (on/off or yes/no value).
	Dropdown list	Can be populated manually, or from a Content Table.
	Edit Box	Standard text-input form element. To turn it into a multiline edit box (equivalent to the HTML form option TEXTAREA), check Multiline on its Attributes Sheet. If it's a password field, check Password to replace characters with asterisks as they're typed.
	Form Button	Form element to which you can give the status of Submit, Reset, or plain ol' Button.
	Hidden Form Field	Appears in the basement; its text is set and read by means of interactions with other SmartElements.
	Image Button	Container for a multiple image, usually used for a rollover button. You can activate it to submit the form. Not available for sites rated Generic.
	Image Checkbox	Drumbeat's own invention: a container for a set of three images that behave as a check box form element. Image 1 is the unchecked state; Image 2 is the mouseover state; Image 3 is the checked state. Not available for sites rated Generic.
	Image Radio Button	Another Drumbeat invention: a container for a set of three images that behave as a radio button form element. Not available for sites rated Generic.
	List Box	Similar to a drop-down list but with drag "handles" for you to expand it to show as many list items as you want. Also allows multiselect.
	Radio Button	Standard radio button type of form element. Meaningful only if part of a set.

Helpful Buttons That Change Their Appearance

- In Site Manager: Insert Page, External Page, PageSet, Frameset
- On main toolbar: Publish All Pages, Publish Selected Pages, Publish Selected Sections
- On main toolbar: Browser List
- On main toolbar: Arrange Elements (11 choices)
- On Content Table toolbar: Add Row/Column

Helpful Buttons That Don't Change Their Appearance

- Add Assets
- Context-sensitive help
- Locate Assets

Copyright © 1999 IDG Books Worldwide, Inc. All rights reserved.

Cheat Sheet $2.95 value. Item 0624-2.

For more information about IDG Books, call 1-800-762-2974.

The IDG Books Worldwide logo is a registered trademark under exclusive license to IDG Books Worldwide, Inc., from International Data Group, Inc. The ...For Dummies logo is a trademark, and For Dummies and ...For Dummies are registered trademarks of IDG Books Worldwide, Inc. All other trademarks are the property of their respective owners.

...For Dummies®: Bestselling Book Series for Beginners

TM

References for the Rest of Us! ®

BESTSELLING BOOK SERIES

Are you intimidated and confused by computers? Do you find that traditional manuals are overloaded with technical details you'll never use? Do your friends and family always call you to fix simple problems on their PCs? Then the *...For Dummies*® computer book series from IDG Books Worldwide is for you.

...For Dummies books are written for those frustrated computer users who know they aren't really dumb but find that PC hardware, software, and indeed the unique vocabulary of computing make them feel helpless. *...For Dummies* books use a lighthearted approach, a down-to-earth style, and even cartoons and humorous icons to dispel computer novices' fears and build their confidence. Lighthearted but not lightweight, these books are a perfect survival guide for anyone forced to use a computer.

"I like my copy so much I told friends; now they bought copies."

— Irene C., Orwell, Ohio

"Quick, concise, nontechnical, and humorous."

— Jay A., Elburn, Illinois

"Thanks, I needed this book. Now I can sleep at night."

— Robin F., British Columbia, Canada

Already, millions of satisfied readers agree. They have made *...For Dummies* books the #1 introductory level computer book series and have written asking for more. So, if you're looking for the most fun and easy way to learn about computers, look to *...For Dummies* books to give you a helping hand.

IDG BOOKS WORLDWIDE ®

DRUMBEAT™ 2000 FOR DUMMIES®

by Gayle Kidder and Stuart Harris

Foreword by Alan Cooper

IDG Books Worldwide, Inc.
An International Data Group Company

Foster City, CA ◆ Chicago, IL ◆ Indianapolis, IN ◆ New York, NY

Drumbeat™ 2000 For Dummies®

Published by
IDG Books Worldwide, Inc.
An International Data Group Company
919 E. Hillsdale Blvd.
Suite 400
Foster City, CA 94404
www.idgbooks.com (IDG Books Worldwide Web site)
www.dummies.com (Dummies Press Web site)

Copyright © 1999 IDG Books Worldwide, Inc. All rights reserved. No part of this book, including interior design, cover design, and icons, may be reproduced or transmitted in any form, by any means (electronic, photocopying, recording, or otherwise) without the prior written permission of the publisher.

Library of Congress Catalog Card No.: 99-65841

ISBN: 0-7645-0624-2

Printed in the United States of America

10 9 8 7 6 5 4 3 2

1B/RQ/QZ/ZZ/IN

Distributed in the United States by IDG Books Worldwide, Inc.

Distributed by CDG Books Canada Inc. for Canada; by Transworld Publishers Limited in the United Kingdom; by IDG Norge Books for Norway; by IDG Sweden Books for Sweden; by IDG Books Australia Publishing Corporation Pty. Ltd. for Australia and New Zealand; by TransQuest Publishers Pte Ltd. for Singapore, Malaysia, Thailand, Indonesia, and Hong Kong; by Gotop Information Inc. for Taiwan; by ICG Muse, Inc. for Japan; by Intersoft for South Africa; by Eyrolles for France; by International Thomson Publishing for Germany, Austria and Switzerland; by Distribuidora Cuspide for Argentina; by LR International for Brazil; by Galileo Libros for Chile; by Ediciones ZETA S.C.R. Ltda. for Peru; by WS Computer Publishing Corporation, Inc., for the Philippines; by Contemporanea de Ediciones for Venezuela; by Express Computer Distributors for the Caribbean and West Indies; by Micronesia Media Distributor, Inc. for Micronesia; by Chips Computadoras S.A. de C.V. for Mexico; by Editorial Norma de Panama S.A. for Panama; by American Bookshops for Finland.

For general information on IDG Books Worldwide's books in the U.S., please call our Consumer Customer Service department at 800-762-2974. For reseller information, including discounts and premium sales, please call our Reseller Customer Service department at 800-434-3422.

For information on where to purchase IDG Books Worldwide's books outside the U.S., please contact our International Sales department at 317-596-5530 or fax 317-596-5692.

For consumer information on foreign language translations, please contact our Customer Service department at 1-800-434-3422, fax 317-596-5692, or e-mail rights@idgbooks.com.

For information on licensing foreign or domestic rights, please phone +1-650-655-3109.

For sales inquiries and special prices for bulk quantities, please contact our Sales department at 650-655-3200 or write to the address above.

For information on using IDG Books Worldwide's books in the classroom or for ordering examination copies, please contact our Educational Sales department at 800-434-2086 or fax 317-596-5499.

For press review copies, author interviews, or other publicity information, please contact our Public Relations department at 650-655-3000 or fax 650-655-3299.

For authorization to photocopy items for corporate, personal, or educational use, please contact Copyright Clearance Center, 222 Rosewood Drive, Danvers, MA 01923, or fax 978-750-4470.

LIMIT OF LIABILITY/DISCLAIMER OF WARRANTY: THE PUBLISHER AND AUTHOR HAVE USED THEIR BEST EFFORTS IN PREPARING THIS BOOK. THE PUBLISHER AND AUTHOR MAKE NO REPRESENTATIONS OR WARRANTIES WITH RESPECT TO THE ACCURACY OR COMPLETENESS OF THE CONTENTS OF THIS BOOK AND SPECIFICALLY DISCLAIM ANY IMPLIED WARRANTIES OF MERCHANTABILITY OR FITNESS FOR A PARTICULAR PURPOSE. THERE ARE NO WARRANTIES WHICH EXTEND BEYOND THE DESCRIPTIONS CONTAINED IN THIS PARAGRAPH. NO WARRANTY MAY BE CREATED OR EXTENDED BY SALES REPRESENTATIVES OR WRITTEN SALES MATERIALS. THE ACCURACY AND COMPLETENESS OF THE INFORMATION PROVIDED HEREIN AND THE OPINIONS STATED HEREIN ARE NOT GUARANTEED OR WARRANTED TO PRODUCE ANY PARTICULAR RESULTS, AND THE ADVICE AND STRATEGIES CONTAINED HEREIN MAY NOT BE SUITABLE FOR EVERY INDIVIDUAL. NEITHER THE PUBLISHER NOR AUTHOR SHALL BE LIABLE FOR ANY LOSS OF PROFIT OR ANY OTHER COMMERCIAL DAMAGES, INCLUDING BUT NOT LIMITED TO SPECIAL, INCIDENTAL, CONSEQUENTIAL, OR OTHER DAMAGES.

Trademarks: For Dummies, Dummies Man, A Reference for the Rest of Us!, The Dummies Way, Dummies Daily, and related trade dress are registered trademarks or trademarks of IDG Books Worldwide, Inc. in the United States and other countries, and may not be used without written permission. All other trademarks are the property of their respective owners. IDG Books Worldwide is not associated with any product or vendor mentioned in this book.

is a registered trademark under exclusive license
to IDG Books Worldwide, Inc. from International Data Group, Inc.

About the Authors

Gayle Kidder is a long-time hack with more than 20 years' experience writing for books, magazines, and newspapers on topics as diverse as science, theatre, art, travel, fiction, computers, and the Web. With her left brain and right brain in constant war with each other, she has made a more respectable living from time to time as a technical writer and editor, most recently as technical writer and editor for Elemental Software. She lives in San Diego, California.

Stuart Harris is a software designer and author and, somewhere in his deep dark past, a former BBC TV documentary producer. He is expert in HTML, dHTML, JavaScript, and Perl and proficient in other languages, of both computer and human varieties. He, too, lives in San Diego.

ABOUT IDG BOOKS WORLDWIDE

Welcome to the world of IDG Books Worldwide.

IDG Books Worldwide, Inc., is a subsidiary of International Data Group, the world's largest publisher of computer-related information and the leading global provider of information services on information technology. IDG was founded more than 30 years ago by Patrick J. McGovern and now employs more than 9,000 people worldwide. IDG publishes more than 290 computer publications in over 75 countries. More than 90 million people read one or more IDG publications each month.

Launched in 1990, IDG Books Worldwide is today the #1 publisher of best-selling computer books in the United States. We are proud to have received eight awards from the Computer Press Association in recognition of editorial excellence and three from Computer Currents' First Annual Readers' Choice Awards. Our best-selling ...For Dummies® series has more than 50 million copies in print with translations in 31 languages. IDG Books Worldwide, through a joint venture with IDG's Hi-Tech Beijing, became the first U.S. publisher to publish a computer book in the People's Republic of China. In record time, IDG Books Worldwide has become the first choice for millions of readers around the world who want to learn how to better manage their businesses.

Our mission is simple: Every one of our books is designed to bring extra value and skill-building instructions to the reader. Our books are written by experts who understand and care about our readers. The knowledge base of our editorial staff comes from years of experience in publishing, education, and journalism — experience we use to produce books to carry us into the new millennium. In short, we care about books, so we attract the best people. We devote special attention to details such as audience, interior design, use of icons, and illustrations. And because we use an efficient process of authoring, editing, and desktop publishing our books electronically, we can spend more time ensuring superior content and less time on the technicalities of making books.

You can count on our commitment to deliver high-quality books at competitive prices on topics you want to read about. At IDG Books Worldwide, we continue in the IDG tradition of delivering quality for more than 30 years. You'll find no better book on a subject than one from IDG Books Worldwide.

John Kilcullen
Chairman and CEO
IDG Books Worldwide, Inc.

Steven Berkowitz
President and Publisher
IDG Books Worldwide, Inc.

Eighth Annual
Computer Press
Awards ≥1992

Ninth Annual
Computer Press
Awards ≥1993

Tenth Annual
Computer Press
Awards ≥1994

Eleventh Annual
Computer Press
Awards ≥1995

IDG is the world's leading IT media, research and exposition company. Founded in 1964, IDG had 1997 revenues of $2.05 billion and has more than 9,000 employees worldwide. IDG offers the widest range of media options that reach IT buyers in 75 countries representing 95% of worldwide IT spending. IDG's diverse product and services portfolio spans six key areas including print publishing, online publishing, expositions and conferences, market research, education and training, and global marketing services. More than 90 million people read one or more of IDG's 290 magazines and newspapers, including IDG's leading global brands — Computerworld, PC World, Network World, Macworld and the Channel World family of publications. IDG Books Worldwide is one of the fastest-growing computer book publishers in the world, with more than 700 titles in 36 languages. The "...For Dummies®" series alone has more than 50 million copies in print. IDG offers online users the largest network of technology-specific Web sites around the world through IDG.net (http://www.idg.net), which comprises more than 225 targeted Web sites in 55 countries worldwide. International Data Corporation (IDC) is the world's largest provider of information technology data, analysis and consulting, with research centers in over 41 countries and more than 400 research analysts worldwide. IDG World Expo is a leading producer of more than 168 globally branded conferences and expositions in 35 countries including E3 (Electronic Entertainment Expo), Macworld Expo, ComNet, Windows World Expo, ICE (Internet Commerce Expo), Agenda, DEMO, and Spotlight. IDG's training subsidiary, ExecuTrain, is the world's largest computer training company, with more than 230 locations worldwide and 785 training courses. IDG Marketing Services helps industry-leading IT companies build international brand recognition by developing global integrated marketing programs via IDG's print, online and exposition products worldwide. Further information about the company can be found at www.idg.com.   1/24/99

Authors' Acknowledgments

Lots of people at Elemental Software helped us at various stages in this book. First on the list to thank is Jim Bates, for his boundless energy for solving problems and making all the resources at his fingertips available to us, and particularly for helping get the CD materials together. Thanks to Gary McAnally and Brad Beith in QA for reviewing some of our materials and making sure the examples worked. A big thanks to Sam Mathews for putting together the installable packages for the CD (at a very stressful time). Julie Thompson and Amit Kishnani were invaluable resources when it came to dealing with the developing JavaServer Pages version of Drumbeat. Thanks to Rick Crawford, for help with some SmartElements; Justin Palm, for providing some custom scripts; and John Keller, for advice and help on DrumNotes. And a special *merci beaucoup* to our co-worker and office mate Natalie Calkins, for putting up with the muttering and fussing from the other side of the room during this project and being supportive and understanding about the double workload. We thank you all, and wish you and all the rest of the Elementalists good luck as the little company that could moves on to its future with Macromedia.

We also owe big thanks to our daughter, Alexandra Rapp, for help with some of our page designs; to Joey Large, for the artwork used in the Drumbeat Action Auction examples; and to our friend in the fine arts, Ann Reilly, whose artistic contribution enhanced our scripting examples. And while we're talking art, thanks to that fine leopard from the zoo in French Guiana who stood in at the last moment for a reluctant San Diego orangutan.

Publisher's Acknowledgments

We're proud of this book; please register your comments through our IDG Books Worldwide Online Registration Form located at http://my2cents.dummies.com.

Some of the people who helped bring this book to market include the following:

Acquisitions, Editorial, and Media Development

Project Editor: Rebecca Whitney

Acquisitions Editor: Gregory S. Croy

Technical Editor: Heidi Bautista (consultant bautista@mint.net)

Media Development Editor: Marita Ellixson

Associate Permissions Editor: Carmen Krikorian

Editorial Manager: Mary C. Corder

Media Development Manager: Heather Heath Dismore

Media Development Coordinator: Megan Roney

Editorial Assistant: Beth Parlon

Production

Project Coordinator: E. Shawn Aylsworth

Layout and Graphics: Brian Drumm, Angela F. Hunckler, Barry Offringa, Brent Savage, Janet Seib, Kathie Schutte, Michael A. Sullivan, Brian Torwelle, Mary Jo Weis

Proofreaders: Christine Berman, Mary Lea Ginn, Joanne Keaton, Marianne Santy

Indexer: Liz Cunningham

Special Help
Brad Beith; Constance Carlisle, Suzanne Thomas

General and Administrative

IDG Books Worldwide, Inc.: John Kilcullen, CEO; Steven Berkowitz, President and Publisher

IDG Books Technology Publishing Group: Richard Swadley, Senior Vice President and Publisher; Walter Bruce III, Vice President and Associate Publisher; Steven Sayre, Associate Publisher; Joseph Wikert, Associate Publisher; Mary Bednarek, Branded Product Development Director; Mary Corder, Editorial Director

IDG Books Consumer Publishing Group: Roland Elgey, Senior Vice President and Publisher; Kathleen A. Welton, Vice President and Publisher; Kevin Thornton, Acquisitions Manager; Kristin A. Cocks, Editorial Director

IDG Books Internet Publishing Group: Brenda McLaughlin, Senior Vice President and Publisher; Diane Graves Steele, Vice President and Associate Publisher; Sofia Marchant, Online Marketing Manager

IDG Books Production for Dummies Press: Michael R. Britton, Vice President of Production; Debbie Stailey, Associate Director of Production; Cindy L. Phipps, Manager of Project Coordination, Production Proofreading, and Indexing; Tony Augsburger, Manager of Prepress, Reprints, and Systems; Laura Carpenter, Production Control Manager; Shelley Lea, Supervisor of Graphics and Design; Debbie J. Gates, Production Systems Specialist; Robert Springer, Supervisor of Proofreading; Kathie Schutte, Production Supervisor

◆

The publisher would like to give special thanks to Patrick J. McGovern, without whom this book would not have been possible.

◆

Contents at a Glance

Cartoons at a Glance

By Rich Tennant

page 9

page 187

page 373

page 285

page 89

Fax: 978-546-7747 • E-mail: the5wave@tiac.net

Table of Contents

Foreword

1nventing the future

The relentless demand for more active, more responsive Web sites that accept and deliver complex information and functionality has forced a segmentation of the workplace. The visually skilled Web designers have been relegated to a position secondary to that of the more technically capable programmers. This has the unpleasant side effect of forcing more unnecessary technical concessions on the user because the programmer has more influence over Web sites than the site designer does.

The solution to this problem, of course, lies in giving the site designer better tools. New tools that are strong enough, capable enough, and sufficiently adaptable to the rapid maturing of the Web will let the site designer create those responsive Web sites without having to defer to the idiosyncrasies of the programmer's way of thinking. We need a Web development tool that offers the site designer the same level of ease of use they are familiar with in a composition tool for *static* Web sites, but also to empower it for the needs of the next century. It needs the strength and sophistication to interface directly with all mainstream corporate and departmental database programs, to easily specify generic pages en masse yet create them individually and specifically for each visitor to that site, and to encompass complex, two-way interactions so typical of e-commerce sites and corporate intranets.

Drumbeat 2000 is precisely that product. It brings an unprecedented level of functionality to the webmaster's screen without forcing him or her to be a code wonk. Complex, dynamic web site functionality can be expressed in terms like "shopping cart" and "view" instead of in terms like "if-then-else" and "do-while." In just the same way that the Web brings computing power to the user masses, Drumbeat 2000 brings site development power to the site designer.

The goal of every interaction designer, when designing a complex and powerful product, is to ensure that the only training the user needs is training in that user's own business domain. A well-designed accounting program should be immediately usable by the trained accountant, without any additional computer training. Likewise, a web development tool should be immediately usable by a skilled visual web designer. His or her training in understanding and specifying branded, commercial interaction should be entirely sufficient to use the program without any additional training in programming languages or server conventions.

You now hold in your hands a book that introduces a program that does just that. It lets you get started immediately constructing web sites that until now required a high level of programming skills. With this book, you can easily convert your vision into reality in far less time and with far less technical obfuscation than ever before.

Other books and other web design tools have offered a quicker path to simple, static web sites, but Drumbeat 2000 offers that same quick path to complex, dynamic web sites that are backed up with sophisticated databases and that offer enormous power and capability to the casual web user.

The future of computing is on the Internet. Read on, and you will have a hand in inventing that future.

Alan Cooper

Introduction

*W*elcome to our little corner of the computer bookshelf. It's been rather crowded in this section lately, with all those books telling you how to build fabulous web sites that are guaranteed to be snazzier and smarter and to make you a million bucks in no time. Whatever.

That's not what this book is about. This book is all about how to make your life easier while you're building those snazzy web sites while taking advantage of all the latest web technology. Drumbeat 2000 is primarily about building database-driven web sites — and it helps you do it faster than does any other product on the market.

Drumbeat makes building database-driven web sites that use Active Server Pages (ASP) or JavaServer Pages (JSP) technology easy. And you don't even have to do any coding.

Who You Are and Why You're Reading This Book

We figure that you already have a handle on why you should be building web sites with databases and why you think that you should know about Drumbeat. If you've picked up this book, chances are that you've already built your share of web sites. You've picked up a little JavaScript, a little ASP or JSP, some Java, and maybe Cascading Style Sheets (CSS). Or, maybe you're a whiz at creating web graphics and a little shaky on the technical side. You probably don't have time to find out about all the things you think that you should know. Or, if you're already up to speed, maybe you just don't have time to do all those projects yourself. You need a tool that will help you get there faster.

Drumbeat could just be the tool for you. But, whoa! Have you looked at it? Cool interface, lots of powerful features — but how do you figure it all out?

It's the ...*For Dummies* series to the rescue! What would you do without it?

Which Version Is for You

You have a decision to make right away if you want to install Drumbeat. The CD includes two separate 30-day trial versions of the program. Your basic decision is whether you want to create Active Server Pages or JavaServer Pages. If you're not planning to build either ASP or JSP pages, it doesn't matter which version you use, but you probably should choose the ASP version because it's the original flavor of Drumbeat.

What's the difference? Active Server Pages (ASP) is Microsoft technology, designed to run on the Microsoft Internet Information Server (IIS) — although you can use ASP on other servers, too, with the proper supporting programs. ASP has been around for a couple of years and is popular for creating server-side applications on the Web. You can use any ODBC-compatible database with the Drumbeat ASP version.

JavaServer Pages is Sun technology and is much newer. JSP is designed to be a cross-platform product and to run on a variety of web servers (not just on Windows IIS). You do have to have JSP server application support installed, however. JavaServer Pages are more robust and scalable for large-scale applications. The Drumbeat JSP version is the first WYSIWYG program available for creating JSP. Because the program is so new, the version on the CD works with only IBM WebSphere and DB2 databases. This version of Drumbeat may be expanded to cover other databases and servers soon, however. You can check the Macromedia web site for updates.

Both versions of Drumbeat work essentially the same way. With the JSP version, however, you must have direct access to a WebSphere server to publish JavaServer Pages. You cannot publish and browse your pages in development on your own machine. With ASP, you can publish and browse on your own machine using Personal Web Server (a scaled-down version of IIS for workstation use). Whichever version you choose, be sure to check for updates on the Macromedia web site (www.drumbeat.com).

How This Book Is Organized

This book is divided into five parts. Parts I and II introduce you to the basic web-site-building tools in Drumbeat. Parts III and IV concentrate on building database-driven web sites, with examples included on the CD. Part V, the ritual Part of Tens, contains a bunch of cool stuff to help you in building your killer web sites.

Part I: Creating a Web Site

This part of the book helps you familiarize yourself with the basic concepts of building a whole web site with Drumbeat. Chapter 1 gives you a quick, hands-on tour of the Drumbeat workspace, showing where to go to accomplish the different tasks you need to do as you build a web site. Chapter 2 quickly takes you through all the stages of page and site design — from creating pages to previewing them to publishing the site to a server. Chapter 2 also describes SmartPages. Chapter 3 explains how to organize all the assets you use to create a site and keep them at your fingertips in Drumbeat — even if they're scattered all over your computer, the local network, or even an ISP's hosting machine.

Part II: Adding Design and Style

Part II shows you how to use all the tools Drumbeat provides for designing, creating, and styling web pages quickly and easily. Chapter 4 describes how to use templates to make design work efficient and site-wide changes fast and easy. In Chapter 5, you find out how to create and use styles throughout your site, to make text and even buttons and images sporty, using the Drumbeat Style Builder and Cascading Style Sheets. In Chapter 6, we explain what Content Tables are in Drumbeat and how you can use them to streamline the design and execution of your site. The clever way that Drumbeat cuts through the confusion of creating frames is described in Chapter 7. Chapter 8 is devoted entirely to tips and tricks for adding jazzy effects and cutting design time in half — or more. Chapter 9 looks at PageSets, a nifty and efficient way to design multiple pages from one template. The content may come from any organized collection of objects or be fully database driven.

Part III: Creating Server-Side, Database-Driven Pages

In this part, you can get quickly into the process of building your own server-side, database-driven pages. Using the DataForm Wizard, you can build Active Server Pages or JavaServer Pages in a few minutes. Then, you can customize the forms to make them more functional. In Chapter 10, you get the basics of designing and using databases, hooking up to your database, and building SQL queries in Drumbeat to access the database. Chapter 11 introduces the Drumbeat DataForm Wizard, which makes building Active Server Pages or JavaServer Pages as easy as baking a cake from a box. You can use the sample database provided with the Book Samples on the CD to follow along. Chapter 12 describes form elements — such as edit boxes, list boxes, check boxes, radio buttons, and form buttons — and how to use them in Drumbeat, whether you use the DataForm Wizard to make your database pages or build them by hand. Chapter 13 discusses how to make your forms smarter by adding form validations or password protection, by making them fire off e-mail, or just by using nicer image buttons to submit your form.

Part IV: It's Not a Web Site — It's a Web App

Part IV is designed to help you understand how all the pieces of your site can fit together to make not just a simple web site but also a fully customizable web application. Chapter 14 takes you on a little journey through a web application built to show sophisticated search and filter operations. Chapter 15 describes the scripting features in Drumbeat and how to use them to create your own reusable point-and-click interactions or to make snippets of custom script. A web application that uses personal customization features is the focus of Chapter 16. The application uses login, session objects, and cookies to track user information.

Part V: The Part of Tens

The Part of Tens is where all the cool things are — mostly shortcuts to some useful things you can use to add pizzazz to your web site. Chapter 17 is a collection of *DrumNotes* (look on the CD in the back of this book for a pocketful of DrumNotes), which are minisites that demonstrate techniques you may want to add to your own web site. Chapter 18 features a collection of Drumbeat *interactions,* which are canned pieces of JavaScript you can add to your site with a simple point-and-click action.

Appendixes

Appendix A is the place to start if you're new to databases and want to get the basic concepts down.

Appendix B tells you all about the other goodies on the CD.

On the CD

This is your lucky day. You can find lots of cool things on the CD to help you build web sites that will inspire envy in your cyberfriends, starting with a 30-day trial version of Drumbeat — either the Active Server Pages or the JavaServer Pages edition (which was brand-new at the time this book was published). To make your learning curve easier, we've included several of the demo sites used as examples in this book (with all necessary files included) in addition to an assortment of "official" DrumNotes — minisites that demonstrate popular techniques you can copy.

How to Use This Book

You can read this book any way you like: from front to back or middle to front or with your cereal bowl balanced on the page to keep it open. You bought it — it's yours. If you're already familiar with Drumbeat and bought this book to learn how to do particular chores, check the Table of Contents or the index and jump right to those sections. You'll find cross-references to other sections that may be useful to you. If you're not familiar with Drumbeat, however, we recommend that you read the first couple of chapters first to get yourself feeling at home in the environment.

If you've never built a database-driven web site, you should definitely read Chapter 10 and Appendix A to familiarize yourself with databases and then read and follow the examples in Chapters 11, 12 and 13 — and then you'll be well on your way. If you're not building database sites, you can probably skip most of Parts III and IV.

Sample site files are included on the CD to help you work through some of the examples in the book. You're free to use them as you please. Or ignore the sample files, and just try to apply to your own site the principles in the examples.

Conventions Used in This Book

Here are a few things it may be helpful to know, to save you the time it takes to figure them out later.

In normal text, phrases in bold indicate things you should type, like this: On the Attributes Sheet, give the image button the name **ClickMe**. (In the numbered steps, which are in bold, it's the opposite.)

Words or phrases shown in `monospace` font indicate either computer code or choices you see on-screen, as shown in this example: In the Interactions Center, find and apply the interaction `First: When First is clicked go to the first page in PageSet`.

Instructions often tell you to select multiple objects, such as when we say "Select the edit box on the Layout and the recordset in the basement." You can select multiple objects in Drumbeat in two ways:

- ✓ **Ctrl+click or Shift+click:** Click the first element, and then Ctrl+click or Shift+click the next one and others subsequently. The difference between Ctrl+click and Shift+click is a *toggle:* If you Shift+click an element that's already selected, you can deselect it. When you Ctrl+click an element, it stays selected (until you release the Ctrl key and click something else).

- ✓ **Marquee-select:** This term carries over from graphics programs. To marquee-select several objects at a time, simply hold down the mouse button and draw a box on-screen, starting from an empty spot. Every time the outline of the box touches an element, it's included in the selection.

Right-click menus are numerous in Drumbeat. You click the right mouse button frequently to pop up menu choices, and some of these menus even have submenus, called *cascading* menus.

Some Drumbeat buttons also have a little dropdown arrow beside them. The arrow signals that the button in question has several possible variants. You click the dropdown arrow to show a small menu of choices. It lets you decide, for example, whether you want to browse a page with Netscape 4.6 or Internet Explorer 5.0. The appearance of the button stays with the last selection you used. If your buttons don't look precisely like the ones shown in the figures, it's just because you've been making different choices along the way. When a button has a choice like this, we often tell you to, for example, "Click the dropdown arrow on the Browse button, and select your browser."

If dialog boxes have an OK button in them, we figure that you're smart enough to know that you need to click it after you've made your choices. You wouldn't believe how much fatter this book would have been if we had written "Click OK" every time that was strictly necessary. Ditto for the Next button, which is common in a series of dialog boxes, like you see when you're working with a wizard. If we omit that step, it's because we think that you're smart enough to know what to do.

Icons Used in This Book

Directs you to shortcuts, insider info, and things to make your life easier. Having worked with Drumbeat as closely as we have for as long as we have, we know about many of these things.

Gives you more detailed explanations if you feel that you just have to know the hairy stuff. If you don't care as long as it works, skip the places marked by this icon.

 Reminds you of things you probably already know but sometimes forget. Everyone forgets the basics sometimes!

 Lets you know that something bad may happen if you don't heed these warnings. Your radiator may overheat, or your web site won't publish properly. We hate when that happens.

 Indicates content relevant to the discussion on the CD in the back of this book. In some cases, you can follow along with the examples in the book with the sample site files we provide.

 Points out information that's different or specific if you're using the JavaServer Pages Edition of Drumbeat. ASP users can skip them.

 Decodes the gobbledygook that's involved whenever terms are new or confusing.

 Gives you handy references to other ...*For Dummies* books you can pick up for more information about a particular topic.

Part I

Creating a
Web Site

The 5th Wave   By Rich Tennant

©RICHTENNANT

"Hold your horses. It takes time to build a
home page for someone your size."

In this part . . .

In this part of the book, you'll see how Drumbeat gives you the tools to set up your web site structure and manage all the pieces you use to put together your site. Make yourself at home in the Drumbeat work environment as you design your first Drumbeat site using all the great tools at your fingertips. And we'll show you how easy it is to publish, revise, and republish your site.

Chapter 1

Exploring the Workspace

. . . .

In This Chapter

▶ Organizing your site with pages and templates

▶ Setting basic page attributes

▶ Using images and other assets

▶ Behind the JavaScript curtain

▶ Locating the database action

▶ Five favorite buttons and five ways to customize your screen

. . . .

*O*pening a new piece of software is kind of like opening a Christmas present from your slightly dotty Aunt Agatha, who ran off to Katmandu when she was young and whom you've known only from an occasional letter or Christmas card. It's exciting and baffling all at one time — there it is, all out of its shiny wrappings and fancy box, but what is it? What do you do with it?

Drumbeat is no exception to the software "dazzle" factor. A great deal of stuff is crammed on that initial screen, and lots more is lurking behind the scenes. Drumbeat is such a jam-packed program that it'll probably take you a long time to discover all its hidden dialog boxes and mini-interfaces.

In this chapter, you get acquainted with the interface, by exploring the areas you see, and discover some you don't see right away but that are important. Because we assume that you're a reasonably experienced web site developer, the questions you're most likely to have are

✔ "How do I do the things I normally do when I'm building a web site in this new environment?"

✔ "How do I get at those things that make Drumbeat special — the reasons I decided to try it out in the first place?"

We don't show you how to use the more advanced tools just yet, although if you're experienced in tasks like database connectivity and JavaScripting, you see where it happens and then can try out your own stuff if you're ready. Drumbeat is not just another HTML editor — it's a powerful tool for the development of Active Server Pages and JavaServer Pages, with tools for connecting to databases and powerful scripting features that create everything you need for a web application in a hands-off, code-free environment.

Wizard, Be Gone!

When you open Drumbeat, you're faced with a simple initial choice: Create a new site or open an existing site. If this is your first time, you're obviously creating a new site. Before you click that OK button too fast, though, let us give you some strong words of advice: Turn off the Use Wizard option and banish the Wizard. (Figure 1-1 shows you how.)

Figure 1-1:
Banish the
Wizard by
unchecking
the box.

If you fall under the Wizard's spell, you may have to walk through not one, but two separate Wizards (the New Site Wizard and the Publish Settings Wizard) with a minimum of 18 separate dialog boxes — more if you make certain choices along the way. When you're just starting out in your exploring, you don't need to be confronted with this blizzard of choices. Be assured that there's nothing in the Wizard you can't set later within Drumbeat and no choice you make is ever irrevocable. Just about everything you can imagine about your site, you can change instantly on a whim within Drumbeat, including

- ✔ The browser you want to target initially
- ✔ The server application support the site needs (if you're publishing ASP or JSP)
- ✔ Where to put your site when you publish
- ✔ The folder structure for your site

And Drumbeat has lots more, so save all those irritating technical questions for later.

If you turn off the Wizard and click Create a New Site, you face just one dialog box with some fairly manageable choices, as shown in the New Site dialog box in Figure 1-2.

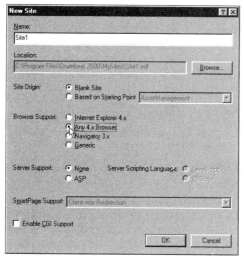

Figure 1-2:
Choosing
basic
options for a
new site.

Other than suggest that you rename the site to something more interesting than Site1, we recommend that you leave everything set to the default settings for now. The only thing you may want to change is the Browser Support option. If you're a Netscape jockey and don't even have Internet Explorer on your system, click to switch the browser support to Any 4.x or Navigator 3. (Be aware, however, that if you choose Navigator 3, you can't play with everything in the Drumbeat toy box because you're limited to only the features supported in Netscape 3.) While you're on the Drumbeat learning curve, we highly recommend that you use the Any 4.x option — then you can play with all the toys and check your results in both browsers.

If you know what you're doing with Active Server Pages and are properly set up for publishing, you can choose ASP for server support. For ASP, you must have either access to a Microsoft Internet Information Server 3.0 or later or Personal Web Server running on your local machine. If you have the JSP version of Drumbeat for IBM WebSphere, you can choose WebSphere support. You don't need either of these settings yet for the exercises in this chapter, so if you don't know what we're talking about, keep the Server Support option set to None.

What You See and What You Don't

What you see when you first open Drumbeat, and before you've gained enough confidence to rearrange things as you please, are four main areas plus the expected menus and toolbars along the top. As with many Windows programs, you can now customize and rearrange the toolbars. In addition, the appearance of some of the buttons changes according to the most recently used option on the button. The four areas, as shown in Figure 1-3, are

- **Site Management Center:** You can perform certain tasks on its three tabs:

    - **Site**: Create your site structure and add pages.

    - **Templates**: Inspect and create templates for page design and assign pages to them. (For more info, see Chapter 4.)

    - **Attributes**: Set the attributes or properties of elements, as well as pages and templates, you use in the layout area.

- **Asset Center:** After you figure out how to use this feature, you can see how all the "stuff" you use on your web site is conveniently organized on it for you. (Chapter 3 covers the Asset Center in detail.)

- **Layout and Preview area:** You assemble your page in this WYSIWYG pane. You can also switch it to look at a quick, browser-style preview.

- **SmartElements toolbar:** Just look for the skinny thing in the middle with all the buttons. They represent a few of the most useful and popular components you use in designing your site. We give you a proper definition in the section "Adding text and links," later in this chapter.

What you don't see are many of the more powerful features of Drumbeat:

- **Content Center:** Use Content Tables to store frequently used assets, including data from CSV (comma-separated values) files and ODBC databases. (For more info, see Chapter 5.)

- **Interactions Center:** You can use this feature to apply pre-scripted activations or interactions to elements on the page. We introduce the Drumbeat concepts of activations and interactions gradually throughout this book. (A complete explanation of them, and the contracts that power them, is in Chapter 15.)

- **SQL Query Builder:** Set up access to your databases by creating or importing SQL queries.

- **Element Library:** All the rest of the SmartElements that don't fit on the SmartElements toolbar live in the library, including features such as applets, plug-ins, ActiveX controls, and design-time controls.

- ✔ **Contract Manager:** Inspect, edit, or create from scratch those contracts that underlie the interactions you see in the Interactions Center.

- ✔ **Script Center:** Write custom bits of client-side JavaScript here. You can also create server-side scripts in VBScript (in the ASP version) or Java (in the JSP version).

We can't cover all these features in one chapter (if we could, we would have either a very long chapter or a very short book), but we take you on a whirlwind tour of them by setting up some introductory web-building tasks.

Templates tab

Site tab   Attributes tab   SmartElements toolbar   Layout and Preview area

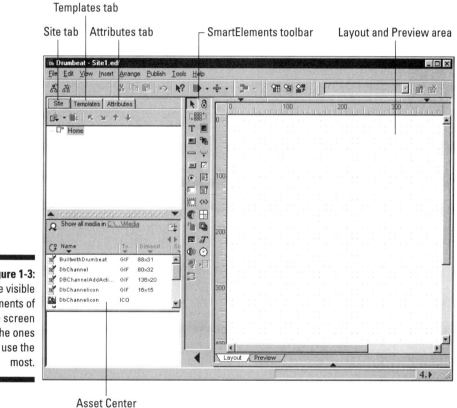

Figure 1-3:
The visible elements of the screen are the ones you use the most.

Asset Center

Setting the Stage

The collection of three tabs in the upper-left corner of the Drumbeat screen make up the Site Management Center. You spend a great deal of time there because it's the logical center of the site, where you create your pages and organize everything.

When you open a new site in Drumbeat, you see on the Site tab one initial page, labeled Home. It's the default starter page. You can't delete this page because you have to have at least one starter page on your site, although you don't have to use it. You can rename it Marrakech or something else more exciting, if you think that "Home" is dull and unadventurous. Whatever you name them, you'll certainly want to add pages.

To add a page:

1. **Click the Site tab, if it's not already selected.**

 2. **Click the Insert Page button, the little blue icon with the plus sign (+) on it.**

Voilà! A new page appears on the screen, temporarily named Page2. Click the Insert Page button a couple of more times and add two more pages — drearily named Page3 and Page4. Notice that all three pages appear in a neat list, indented below the Home page.

Click the Page2 label, and then click Insert Page again. Page5 now appears indented below Page2. It's not hard to get the idea. You can create a complete site tree that reflects the organizational structure of your site by adding pages wherever you want. We know, we know — you're *dying* to give these pages more imaginative names.

To rename a page:

1. **Click the page you want to rename and press F2.**

2. **Type the page name.**

Although this quick Windows trick works in Windows Explorer as well as in most Windows programs, you can do it another way in Drumbeat by right-clicking the name of the page and choosing Rename from the pop-up menu, as shown in Figure 1-4. Notice that the right-click menu also lets you insert pages below the selected page.

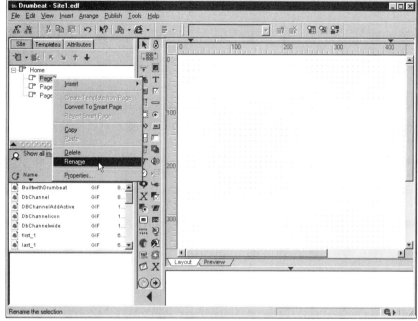

Figure 1-4:
Rename
pages by
either
choosing
from the
right-click
menu or
pressing F2.

If you want to move pages around or promote or demote them in your site structure, those blue arrows at the top are the tools for the job, as shown in Figure 1-5.

Click Page5 and then click the arrow that points northwest. The Page5 label appears at the same level as the rest of the pages. Click the southward arrow to move it down, and the southeastward arrow to indent it in the site structure. It then becomes subordinate, to the page directly above it in the file structure, as shown in Figure 1-6.

Figure 1-5:
The page
arrows.

Figure 1-6:
Make pages
subordinate
to other
pages to
create a
detailed site
structure.

Before all this navigational changing makes you seasick, let's move on to something more colorful. One of the first things a web developer who's familiar with HTML does is create some background and link colors — which are usually included in the BODY tag of the HTML file. To do that in Drumbeat, you have to take a look at the other tabs in the Site Management area.

Setting backgrounds and link colors with templates

Click the Templates tab, just for a quick peek at it. Notice that the tab has one default template, the master template, as shown in Figure 1-7. You can't delete this element either (and, unlike with the Home page, you can't rename it).

Figure 1-7:
The
Templates
tab.

All the pages you create on the Site tab also appear on the Templates tab, and they're all below the master template in the site structure. Notice, though, that the pages are in a different order than on the Site tab — they're arranged alphabetically, with no regard to your site structure. That's because the concept that rules here is design, not logic. So far, all the pages belong to the master template. To set the link colors for all the pages in the site, you can set link colors on the master template, and all the pages then inherit the same link colors.

Click the master template to select it on the Templates tab, and then click the Attributes tab. The options on the Attributes Sheet for the master template are exactly equivalent to the attributes you would set in the BODY tag of your HTML file, including background color, background image, and link colors. Drag down the bar below the Site Management Center (with the two blue arrows on either side) to expose the full set of attributes. Figure 1-8 shows the content of a typical Attributes Sheet for both templates and pages.

Figure 1-8:
Background
and link
colors are
attributes of
both tem-
plates and
pages.

To set a background color:

1. **Click the white color box next to the Bkgnd option.**

2. **Choose a new color from the basic Windows color palette, or click Define Custom Colors to expand the selection.**

If you use RGB values for colors, you can enter the RGB values in the expanded custom colors dialog box and add the color to your custom colors for the site.

The link options correspond to the link color attributes in HTML. The difference is that you use styles (rather than just colors), as you do for all text elements in Drumbeat. Four default styles for links are available that you can use to designate only link colors.

To select link colors:

1. **Click the dropdown arrow next to the Link Style edit box.**

2. **Scroll to find the LinkColor style, as shown in Figure 1-9.**

Figure 1-9:
Click to
change the
link default
color.

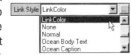

Use the default styles in the following table to get started:

Table 1-1	Drumbeat Conventions for Link Styles	
Option	*Drumbeat Style*	*HTML Attribute*
Link Style	LinkColor	LINK
Visited Link Style	VLinkColor	VLINK
Active Link Style	ALinkColor	ALINK
Hover Link Style	HLinkColor	HLINK

You're probably wondering just what colors these are, and you'll no doubt want to change them to your own custom colors eventually. You can create your own custom styles, including link styles, in the Style Builder. Chapter 5 shows you how.

Adding text and links

Everything in the layout area in Drumbeat resides in a container of some sort. Images have image containers, text blocks have text containers, buttons have image button containers, and so on.

To add text to a page, you first have to create a text container. In Drumbeat terms, you use a Text SmartElement.

SmartElement is just one of those weird Drumbeat terms you get used to. SmartElements are cool because they already contain the necessary knowledge to adjust their code for different target browsers. After you start using SmartPages (another Drumbeat term) to produce pages for different target browsers, you see how this feature comes in handy. The same SmartElement can produce different code for different browsers, and you don't have to worry about the various browser idiosyncrasies.

To add text to a page:

1. **Select the Text element on the SmartElements toolbar and drag the element to the layout area, or click the layout area where you want to place the Text element.**

2. **Adjust the size and position of the text container if you want, and type your text.**

   The Text Formatting toolbar pops up on the screen.

3. **When you finish typing, click outside the text container.**

4. **Refine the size of the text box by simply dragging it to the size you want with the handles. Or, use the Width attribute on the Attributes Sheet to give the text box a precise width.**

   The height of the box adjusts automatically to accommodate the text.

5. **Position the text box where you want it by dragging-and-dropping or by using the Left and Top attributes on the Attributes Sheet.**

   You can Ctrl+click several elements and position them all together. Another technique is to include a set of elements in a "box" drawn around them with the mouse, starting from an empty spot in the layout area. In this process, known as *marquee-selecting,* the box only needs to touch an element in order to include it.

The Text Formatting toolbar can get annoying sometimes because it seems to always pop up on top of the text element you want to edit. (It's kind of like the cat trying to sit on your keyboard when you're typing.) You can simply move the toolbar aside by dragging it by the title bar. (Don't try dragging the cat off by its tail, however!) A good idea, if you're doing a large amount of text work, is to anchor the toolbar to the bottom of the screen. Just drag it to the bottom bar, and it stays put.

Although you can use the text toolbar to format the text, we suggest that you don't, just yet. Most of the time, you want to assign a style to the whole text container. Any formatting you apply in-line with the Text Formatting toolbar overrides that style property in the container style. You may want to use it to apply italics or boldface on words or phrases, for example.

To apply a style to a text element:

1. **Select the text container (or select several at a time), and click the Attributes tab.**

2. **Choose a Style from the Style dropdown list, as shown in Figure 1-10.**

Create text links with the Assign Link button on the Text Formatting toolbar. To create a link:

1. **Select the text within the container you want to link, and click the Assign Link button on the Text Formatting toolbar, as shown in Figure 1-11.**

2. **In the Link dialog box, select a page in the site tree to link to, as shown in Figure 1-12.**

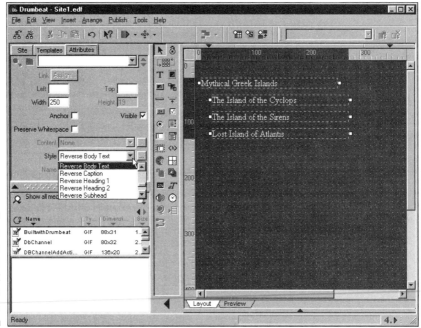

Figure 1-10:
Apply a new text style to several text boxes at a time.

Figure 1-11:
Create a text link with the Text Formatting toolbar.

Undo a link with the Undo Link button, or edit the text of the link with the Link Text button on the Text Formatting toolbar.

Note that you can also create links to URLs and lots of other options, but let's keep it simple for now.

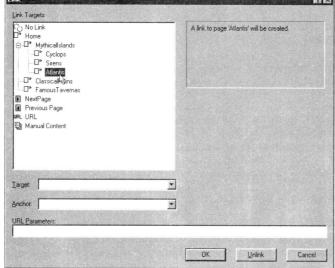

Figure 1-12:
Choose the
page you
want to link
to or other
link options
in the Link
dialog box.

Finding your stuff

Directly under the Site Management Center is an area named the Asset Center. When you first load Drumbeat, it holds a few little Drumbeat images that aren't very useful. The genius of the Asset Center, however, is in the way you can organize it to show just *what* you want *when* you want it. It's rich enough that it deserves a chapter of its own (Chapter 4). One of the first things you'll want to use it for is to display the images you have for your site.

Under some installation scenarios (particularly if you install over an earlier version of Drumbeat), you may not have any default images showing in the Asset Center. You can add the default media file C:\Program Files\Drumbeat 2000\Media by using the following procedure:

To add a folder of images (or other stuff) to the Asset Center:

1. **Click the Add Assets button (the folder icon with the plus sign to the right) and choose Media Folders, as shown in Figure 1-13.**

2. **Click Add, and then browse to locate the folder that contains your stuff.**

   If you don't have anything to use just yet, you can use some clip art included with Drumbeat. Navigate to the Drumbeat 2000\Media folder on your hard drive and choose one of the theme folders you see there. Greek Ruins is selected in Figure 1-14; it's the one we use in some of the examples in the rest of this chapter.

Figure 1-13:
Add to your
project the
folders that
contain your
site assets.

3. **Click OK, click OK again, and then click Done to get back to work.**

Figure 1-14:
Choose the
asset folder
and whether
you want
to add
subfolders.

Notice that the Asset Center refreshes itself and now contains much more
stuff — mostly images you can play with. Select one on the Asset Center list,
and you see a thumbnail image of the image in the asset viewer, in the lower-
left corner of your screen. Press the arrow keys to move up and down and
preview the images. You see, toward the bottom, two "tile" images that are
meant to be used as background images. Select the Home page, from either
the Template Manager or the Site Manager, and add a background image.

To add a background image: Select the image you want from the Asset Center
and hold down the Shift key as you drag it to the layout area.

Click the Attributes tab while the page is selected, and you see that the
Bkgnd Image box is checked and the BkgndContent box says `File`. If you
click the ellipses button, you can see the file path. You can assign the background image in this way on the Attributes Sheet if you want, although
Shift+drag is much quicker.

You can use a masthead image in Greek Ruins, too; it's named ar2_mast_image.
Find it by scrolling in the Asset Center.

To add an image to the page: Select the image in the Asset Center and drag
the image to the page.

While the image is still selected, click the Attributes tab, and you see the attributes of the image you can use, as shown in Figure 1-15. You can position the image exactly where you want it by using the Left and Top attributes, add a border of a specific size, give the image a meaningful name, and assign ALT Text (text displayed as a ToolTip or by users who aren't displaying images).

Rollover tricks made easy

Another useful little SmartElement is the Image button. This element lets you create a rollover button quickly and easily, with all the scripting included. In the Asset Center, find two images that are different versions of the same button. The Greek Ruins media folder contains several: Home, Next, Previous, Back, Search, as well as several plain buttons. (All the clip art folders in Drumbeat include similar themed images.) We used the plain button to create our own button images in Photoshop.

A *rollover* button changes its appearance when a user's mouse pointer is placed over it. To create a rollover button:

1. **Select the Image Button on the SmartElements toolbar and drag it to the layout area.**

   (Be careful — this one looks much like the Image element and the Image Map, although its function is quite different.)

Figure 1-15:
A background and masthead image added to the layout area, with the attributes of the masthead image revealed on the Attributes tab.

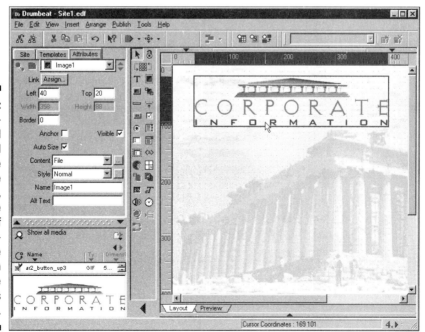

2. **Select an image in the Asset Center and drag it to the button in the layout area.**

   The first image you drag on the button is the "on" image — the one you see when the mouse is placed over the button.

3. **Select a second image and drag it to the button. This image is the "off" image.**

To see the content of the image button, right-click the button and choose Show Content Order. In the dialog box that pops up, you can see the two images that are stacked in the Image Button, as shown in Figure 1-16, and you can change their order, if you want.

Figure 1-16:
The images in an image button can be switched to control the rollover behavior.

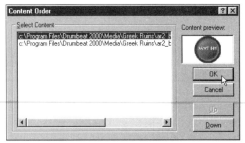

To see the rollover effects, you have to publish and preview the page.

First, add a link to the image. You use this method to add a link to any element in the layout area, except for hypertext links within a text element. To create a link on the Image Button:

1. **Right-click the Image Button and choose Assign Link. (Or, while the image is selected, click the Assign Link button on the Attributes tab.)**

2. **In the Link dialog box, choose the page you want to link to.**

Viewing pages through the browser's eyes

Clicking the Preview tab just below the layout area automatically publishes the page and lets you view the page as it would appear in the browser. If you click the Preview tab, you can try out the new rollover button.

If your images have ended up in the wrong order, you can return to the Layout tab and change their order, as explained in the preceding section.

After you've previewed the page, don't forget to click the Layout tab again to display the layout area.

If you don't have Internet Explorer on your system, the Preview function isn't available. You can publish your pages by clicking the Publish button on the toolbar. (Pressing Ctrl+U does the job, too.) To test the links you've created, you need to publish the rest of the pages in your site anyway, which you can do with the Publish button, as shown in Figure 1-17.

Figure 1-17:
Publish any
number of
pages.

After publishing the site, click the Browse button or click the dropdown arrow next to it and choose the browser you want to use to view your page, as shown in Figure 1-18.

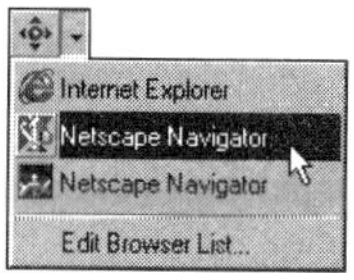

Figure 1-18:
Browse
your site
with any
browser.

Creating Cookie-Cutter Pages

Maybe you don't really want to give all the pages in your site the same background color and the same color links. Another section of your site may have different background colors, a different background image, and different link colors to make it distinctive. Templates make creating a new look for a whole section easy.

To create a new template:

1. **Click the Templates tab and select the master template.**

2. **Right-click and choose Insert➪Template (or choose Insert➪Template from the main menu), as shown in Figure 1-19.**

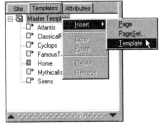

Figure 1-19:
Insert a new template under the master template.

Rename the template the same way you do pages: Select the Template and press F2 or choose Rename from the right-click menu.

The new template is subordinate to the master template, so it's inheriting its background and link colors from the master template. Click the Attributes tab, and you see that all the attributes for this template are disabled for now. The attributes for a page would be similarly disabled. To change inherited attributes on either a page or a template:

1. **Select the template or page, and then click the Attributes tab.**

2. **Click the Inherit icon in the upper-left corner of the Attributes Sheet.**

   In the Inherit Attributes dialog box, you can choose which attributes you want to be inherited from the parent template and which you don't.

3. **Uncheck the attributes you don't want to be inherited from the parent template, as shown in Figure 1-20.**

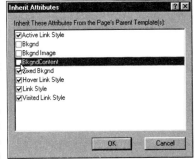

Figure 1-20:
Disinherit page attributes from a template to assign them individually.

When you click OK, the attributes for the template you've unchecked are enabled, and you can then set them the way you want on the Attributes Sheet. You can now choose a new color for the background of this template. We changed our background color from dark blue to yellow, although you may choose to assign a background image too.

Assigning pages to templates

Click the Templates tab and assign a couple of pages to this template so that you can see how it works. To assign a page to a template:

1. **On the Templates tab, select the page.**

2. **Hold the mouse button down and drag-and-drop the page on the template. The result is shown in Figure 1-21.**

Figure 1-21:
Drag-and-
drop a page
on a new
template.

Notice that the page that was dark blue has turned light yellow. Logically, of course, it would have made sense from the outset to make two separate templates — a blue template and a yellow template — and let the master template hold only those elements you want on all pages in the site.

Looking Behind the Scenes

Drumbeat is not just another HTML editor. As smart as some of the tricks we describe in this chapter are, they barely scratch the surface of the program's capabilities. Let's take a look at some of the things we cover in lots more detail later in this book that you may be curious about now, including

✔ Using interactions

✔ Scripting

✔ Connecting to databases

The JavaScript circus act

Point-and-click interactions are a big time-saving feature of Drumbeat. By simply applying point-and-click interactions, you can create a raft of both client- and server-side scripting without ever having to bother with creating the code yourself. Here's a quick circus trick you can do to see how it works:

1. **Drag any image you want from the Asset Center to the layout area.**

   Add your own folder of images if you have one you want to play with, or use one from the clip art folder.

2. **Select the image, right-click it, and choose Possible Activations from the pop-up menu.**

   Bingo! The Interactions Center opens above the layout area. In the Interactions Center is a list of possible interactions you can apply to this image.

3. **Select the one in the Element Movement category that reads** `Fly in when page loads`, **as shown in Figure 1-22. Double-click the selection to apply it.**

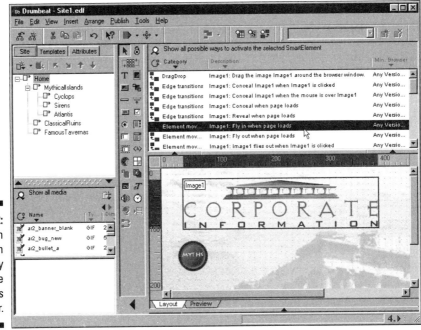

Figure 1-22:
Find an interaction to apply in the Interactions Center.

Because this "interaction" has only one participant (the image), it's really an *activation* rather than an interaction. A Parameters dialog box pops up, giving you the possible parameters that go with it. You can choose whether you want the image to fly in from the right, left, top, or bottom of the screen and the speed at which it moves.

4. **Make your parameter selections, as shown in Figure 1-23, and then click OK.**

Figure 1-23:
Choose
parameters
for the inter-
action.

Preview the page to see it work. If you use the Preview option, you see how it works in Microsoft Internet Explorer. Prove to yourself that it works in Netscape 4.x too, by clicking the dropdown arrow on the Browse button and selecting your Netscape browser.

Checking out your site in both browsers requires that your browser preference be set to Any 4.0. If you didn't take our initial advice about that, you can change it now. Choose File⇨Preferences⇨Site and change the browser preference to Any Version 4.0.

Editing scripts

If you're a JavaScript jockey and want to check — in just a few mouse clicks — the script Drumbeat created in the preceding section, you can take a look at the underlying scripting action in the Contract Builder:

1. **Choose Tools⇨Contracts from the main menu.**

   The Contract Manager appears. For now, both the Category and Browser dropdown lists are probably set to All.

2. **From the Category dropdown list, select Element Movement; from the Browser dropdown list, select Any Version 4.0.**

3. **The first contract on the list happens to be the one you just applied:** Fly in when page loads. **Make sure that it's selected, and then click the Actions tab.**

4. **In the second edit box (the one on the right) at the top, select the onLoad event so that the top line with the edit boxes now reads** When the Document onLoad event is triggered.

In the text box shown in Figure 1-24, you can see the complete JavaScript applied with this interaction.

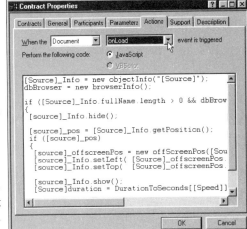

Figure 1-24:
Check the
script of an
interaction
in the
Contract
Manager.

Click the Parameters tab and you see the two parameters you used to apply the interaction: From and Speed.

If you can't keep your hands off, you could edit the script here and save it, although we recommend that you don't because you will overwrite the existing interaction. You can make a copy of the interaction and edit it instead. (See Chapter 15 for more information.)

Another place you can your hands dirty with scripting is in the Script Center. Although we don't go into that subject here, you can have a quick peek if you close the Contract Manager and click the Script Center button on the toolbar.

The Script Center opens in the same space that was previously occupied by the Interactions Center. On the left is a scripting pane and on the right, a convenient scripting tree that lists the properties, methods and events you can use, as shown in Figure 1-25. (For more information about the scripting tree, see Chapter 15.)

Figure 1-25:
Develop
your own
scripts in
the Script
Center.

Organizing content

One more component lives in the same space above the layout area as the Interactions Center and the Script Center: the Content Center. The three buttons on the toolbar above the attic, as shown in Figure 1-26, control which one is displayed at any time.

Figure 1-26:
These buttons control
the display
in the attic.

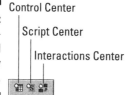

Control Center

Script Center

Interactions Center

Nothing is there yet because you haven't created any Content Tables. Figure 1-27 shows a Content Table we created by importing a CSV file and then adding another column in which we dropped some images.

Figure 1-27:
A Content
Table in the
Content
Center.

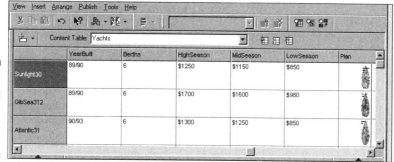

	YearBuilt	Berths	HighSeason	MidSeason	LowSeason	Plan
Sunlight30	89/90	6	$1250	$1150	$850	
GibSea312	89/90	6	$1700	$1600	$980	
Atlantic31	90/93	6	$1300	$1250	$850	

Content Tables are an efficient way of organizing assets you use frequently in your site. They all can be referenced from one central location so that changes in the Content Table are instantly reflected throughout your site, wherever those elements are used. (Chapter 6 goes into this subject in detail.)

Content Tables can also hold data from external CSV files or from database queries, which can be used to create PageSets and data-driven pages. (Read more about that subject in Chapters 9 through 13.)

Accessing a database

Speaking of databases (and we did, in the preceding section), we're willing to bet that that's why you've come to this party. Databases are accessed through SQL queries. You can build your SQL queries in Drumbeat or access existing queries built in your database application. To see where the database action happens:

1. **Click the Add Assets button and choose Queries. The Query Manager opens.**

2. **Click New to create a new query, as shown in Figure 1-28.**

Figure 1-28:
Adding a
query.

The SQL Query Builder opens. If you have database sources you have already set up by creating a DSN for them on your system, you can find them on the Data Source dropdown list. You find a few there anyway because, during installation, Drumbeat creates DSNs for the all databases used in the Starting Points. Select one and you see the database structure in the Tables and Columns windows. Select a table to see the columns in that table. (If you're new to database setup, you can read all about it in Chapter 10.)

If you're a SQL whiz, you can try typing a SQL statement to access your database and use the Test button to see the results. You can also use the SQL Wizard to create simple SQL queries.

To be able to use any database content in your site, you have to change your site preferences for database publishing.

You can change your site preferences as well as your publishing settings at any time within Drumbeat. Change the browser target or server support options, and then simply republish your site to have it take effect.

To change your site preferences for database publishing, choose File⇨Preferences⇨Site. In the Site Preferences dialog box, for Server Application Support, select ASP from the dropdown list.

If you're using the JSP version of Drumbeat for IBM WebSphere, choose WebSphere for server support.

Five Favorite Drumbeat Buttons

This section describes five buttons you use repeatedly in Drumbeat. Each button is really several buttons in one because dropdown menus, as shown in this section, enable you to choose specific options or filter for exactly what you want.

Poke the Locater Assets button, (see Figure 1-29) and you're confronted with a plethora of choices. Filter your assets by type of asset, file size, browser compatibility, or Location.

Figure 1-29:
The Locate
Assets
button.

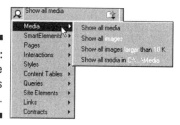

And there's more! The query displayed in the Asset Center is shown in the phrase next to the button. Any word shown as underlined can be clicked to change the filter for even more options.

Use the Add Assets button (see Figure 1-30) to

Figure 1-30:
The Add
Assets
button.

- ✔ Add new media folders
- ✔ Access the SmartElement Library to find more SmartElements, including ActiveX controls, applets, plug-ins, design-time controls (DTCs), and COM objects
- ✔ Access the Style Builder to create new styles
- ✔ Create and edit database queries
- ✔ View contracts (which control point-and-click interactions) and edit and create your own

Use the Publish button (see Figure 1-31) to publish one or more pages in your site with one click. The dropdown menu enables you to choose the nature of the publish operation:

Figure 1-31:
The Publish
button.

- ✔ **All Pages:** All pages in the site
- ✔ **Selected Pages:** The selected page (the one in the layout area) or group of pages selected in the Site tab site tree
- ✔ **Selected Sections:** The selected page plus any subordinate pages in the Site tab site tree

The last option you used is the default option on the button. The button changes its appearance to show the current default. Ctrl+U is a convenient shortcut to publish using your last choice.

Click the Browse button (see Figure 1-32) to browse your site in any installed web browser after publishing. The last web browser in which you chose to view your site is the default option on the button. The F12 keyboard shortcut uses your last choice.

Figure 1-32:
The Browse
button.

Drumbeat automatically detects the browsers on your system during installation and adds them to this list. If you add new browsers later or want to change the list, just choose the Edit Browser List option.

Click the Arrange Elements button (see Figure 1-33) to arrange a whole group of elements in the layout area at one time. Here are a couple of examples:

✔ Select several text boxes, click the Arrange Elements button, and select Align Left to line them all up evenly to the left.

✔ Select several navigation buttons, click the Arrange Elements button, and select Space Evenly Down or Space Evenly Across to space them out equally between the first and last buttons.

Figure 1-33:
The Arrange
Elements
button.

Five Smart Ways to Customize Your Workspace

The Shutter button on the bottom of the SmartElements toolbar automatically expands the layout area to the full width of the screen, as shown in Figure 1-34. Click again to return it to its preceding size. Or use the keyboard shortcut Ctrl+Spacebar to toggle between them. Adjust the layout area to any width by dragging the splitter bar on either side of the SmartElements toolbar.

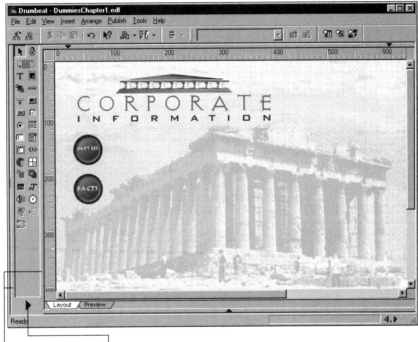

Figure 1-34:
Click the
Shutter
button to
expand the
layout area.

Slider bar   Shutter button

The small, blue arrows (one up, one down) on the splitter bar between the Asset Center and the Site Management Center control the size of each area. The left arrow snaps the Asset Center wide open, as shown in Figure 1-35, or contracts it to its preceding size. The right arrow does the same for the Site Management Center. You can drag the splitter bar to any stop you want.

Expand Asset Center

Adjustable slider bar ┌ Expand Site Manager

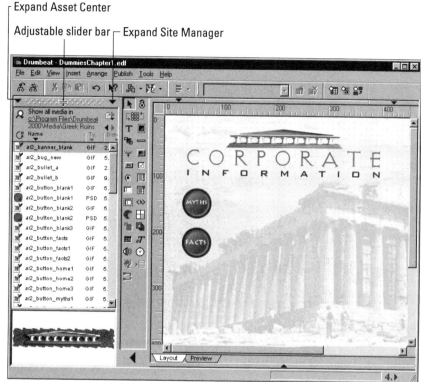

Figure 1-35:
Expand the
Asset
Center
or Site
Manager
to the full
height of the
screen.

The small, blue arrows on the splitter bar just above the layout area, as
shown in Figure 1-36, snap open the area known as the *attic,* where you can
display either the Content Center, the Interactions Center, or the Script
Center. Ctrl+D is a convenient keyboard shortcut that toggles the display.

Open/close attic button ─┐

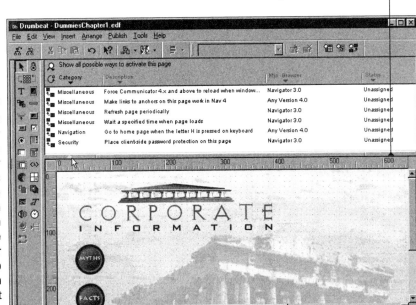

Figure 1-36:
Open or
close the
attic or
adjust its
size to the
maximum in
combination
with the
Shutter
button so
that you can
see the text
of interac-
tions.

The single blue arrow on the splitter bar below the layout area, as shown in Figure 1-37, snaps open or shut the basement area, where nonvisual elements of the page, such as database components, hidden form fields, and audio files are represented. Although you can't adjust the height of the basement, it sprouts scrollbars if its content overflows the fixed height. Ctrl+B is a convenient keyboard shortcut.

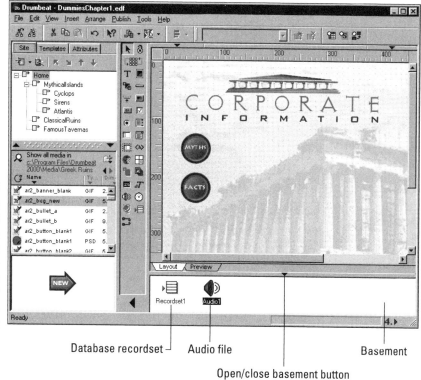

Figure 1-37:
Nonvisual
elements
displayed in
the base-
ment can be
exposed or
hidden.

Database recordset ⌐ Audio file   Basement

Open/close basement button

Whenever you're doing a great deal of text work, you can anchor the Text
Formatting toolbar, as shown in Figure 1-38, so that it stays put and doesn't
get in your way. Choose from the View menu which toolbars you want to display or hide.

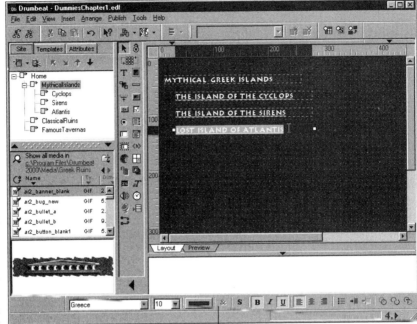

Figure 1-38:
The Text
Formatting
toolbar is
anchored to
the bottom
of the
screen.

Text Formatting toolbar

Chapter 2

Setting Up a New Site

. . . .

In This Chapter

▶ Choosing options for a new site

▶ Building the site structure

▶ Using different kinds of pages

▶ Bringing it together with links

▶ Getting ready to publish

▶ Ten steps to ASP publishing

▶ Creating browser-specific pages instantly

. . . .

*I*n Chapter 1, we advise you to skip the Publishing Wizard if you're new to Drumbeat and just get to work. In this chapter, however, we start you out at the beginning and explain what all those options you can choose for your site mean. Then we set up a new site in Drumbeat and show you how to organize it the way you want, link it all together, and prepare to publish.

Warning: This chapter was written on an absolute sugar high. As a result, we show you the absolutely fastest ways we know of to accomplish the tasks at hand, including the kinds of tricks that only experienced Drumbeat users know, which would take you months to discover yourself.

Creating a Site

Every time you kick up Drumbeat, you have two choices: Create a new site, or work on a site you've already created. Whenever you decide to build a new site, you have two basic options:

🗸 Create a new site from scratch, using a blank slate.

🗸 Use a Starting Point.

Drumbeat provides a number of *Starting Points,* which are fully functioning sample sites you can use to develop your own site or from which you pinch ideas and discover new techniques. You can also create your own Starting Points (by simply saving a site file in the Starting Points folder). Your personal Starting Point can be like a site template, with all your standard or favorite options (link colors, styles, templates, and Content Tables, for example) already included.

You can find documentation that tells you how to use each Starting Point that ships with Drumbeat: Look in the folder for the Starting Point in the Drumbeat program files. For example, the documentation for the UserLogin Starting Point, if you installed Drumbeat in the default location, is in C:\Program Files\Drumbeat 2000\StartingPoints\UserLogin\Documentation\ UserLogin.doc.

Depending on the version of Drumbeat you have, when you open a new site based on a Starting Point, you may see a message that the site database isn't compatible with this version of Drumbeat. Just click Yes to respond to the message "OK to convert?" The same thing happens when you open one of your own sites after you upgrade your version of Drumbeat. It won't ruin your work, but if you're worried about it, just make a backup before you open the file.

Drumbeat files have the extension .edf. Unless you change the default location, they're located in C:\Program Files\Drumbeat 2000\MySites.

Two separate dialog boxes (that means two sets of options) cover your choices for any site:

- ✔ **Site Preferences (choose File⇨Preferences⇨Site):** Choose the server support (if you're publishing ASP or JSP) and initial target browser support.
- ✔ **Publish Settings (choose Publish⇨Publish Settings):** Use its various tabs to control the location to which files are published.

You don't have to worry about the second set of options until you're ready to publish your site, so we talk about them in the last part of this chapter. But before you start building your site, we go over in more detail some of the site preferences we blithely skip over in Chapter 1. You're confronted with these choices whenever you create a new site.

Setting preferences

The basic publishing instructions for Drumbeat are stored in your site preferences. To get to them, choose File⇨Preferences⇨Site. The same set of options you see in the site preferences are presented in the New Site dialog box (if you don't use the New Site Wizard) or the first few screens of the New Size Wizard (if you do). Only four options are shown:

- ✔ Browser support
- ✔ Server application support
- ✔ SmartPage support
- ✔ Server scripting language

One of the great things about developing your site in Drumbeat is that you can be as wishy-washy as you want. You can change your mind about any of these things a dozen times or more as you're developing your site.

What if your boss or your client changes his mind in the middle of a project and wants you to downgrade your site to Netscape 3? Don't pound the walls. Just change the browser support settings and republish (and tell him that you worked all night). You can even change server-side scripting from JavaScript to VBScript in an instant. Drumbeat takes care of rewriting all the code for you.

Choosing your browser

The type of browser support you choose is the basic browser for which you want to design your site. It's typically the browser you expect the majority of your site visitors to be using. If you need to create browser-specific versions for other browsers, you can do so later, after you've done all the major design work. See the section "Creating a SmartPage," later in this chapter.

At other times, you may want to design for the highest common denominator (to show off your skill) or the lowest common denominator (to show what a fair, open-minded person you are). If you're running in a *contained* environment (an intranet where everyone has identical browsers on identical machines), your choice is simple: Do as the clones do.

If you forget what type of browser support you've chosen for your site, you can always tell by the browser support icon that appears in the lower-right corner of the status bar at the bottom of the screen.

"Are you being served?"

Server application support boils down to a simple yes-no question: Are you being served? This question refers not to your web server, but rather to the support application for database publishing. Choose None for the Server Application Support option in the Site Preferences dialog box if you're not doing active database publishing.

If you're publishing Active Server Pages with ASP support or JavaServer Pages with IBM WebSphere (in the Drumbeat 2000 JavaServer Pages Edition), choose that option. If you're not using any databases, don't complicate your life and skip doing the ASP or JSP setup. You will then be publishing simple HTML pages (rather than ASP or JSP pages), which work on any server.

Selecting SmartPage support

Whenever you use multiple versions of a page for different browsers, you have to provide a way for users to be directed to the correct page for their browsers. The method used for that redirection is what you choose when you select your type of SmartPage support. (The SmartPage is the redirect page.)

In most cases, the option for SmartPage support is grayed out because Drumbeat has already made your mind up for you, along the following lines:

- ✔ If your server support is ASP or WebSphere, your choice is server-side scripting.

- ✔ If your server support type is None, the assumption is that you will use client-side scripting.

- ✔ If your server support setting is None *and* you enable CGI, you can choose client-side or server-side redirection. For more info about SmartPages, see the section "Creating a SmartPage," later in this chapter.

CGI is used in Drumbeat rarely and in only specific circumstances. Drumbeat includes only a few CGI SmartElements in the Element Library (which you'll probably never use). One reason you would choose to enable CGI is if you want to use server-side redirection on a site with no database server support. Another is if you have your own custom CGI scripts, such as e-mail form submissions you want to include. If you do enable CGI, you have to configure the path to Perl on your server on the CGI tab in the Publish Settings dialog box (choose Publish⇨Publish Settings). If you have the JSP version, the CGI option is not available.

Choosing a server scripting language

Server scripting language appears as an option in the Site Preferences dialog box only if you use database server application support (ASP or WebSphere). The choice is straightforward: If you use ASP support, you can choose either server-side JavaScript or VBScript.

The choice is entirely up to you. Drumbeat generates all the JavaScript or

VBScript behind the scenes for you anyway. If you want to write your own scripting or edit the scripts that Drumbeat generates, choose the server scripting language you're most comfortable with.

If you have the JavaServer Pages version of Drumbeat and choose WebSphere support, you have no choice: The server scripting language is Java.

Creating a Site Structure with Pages

Web site structures can be very simple or very elaborate. You can think of your site structure — the one you create on the Site tab — as a site map or an outline. Figure 2-1 shows the beginning of a web site being built for a company whose business is making and selling handmade chocolates. To understand your client better, of course, you probably should have them send along an assortment of their wares for sampling.

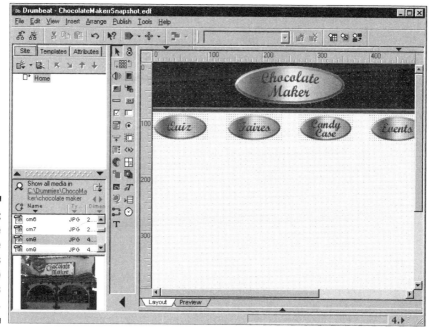

Figure 2-1: The chocolate maker is about to go in business on the Web.

The Chocolate Maker site you create has four sections:

- ✔ A candy showcase full of sinfully delicious temptations
- ✔ Information about the Renaissance Faires where the chocolates are primarily sold
- ✔ Information about other places where the chocolates are sold (harvest fairs, farmer's markets, and street fairs)
- ✔ A chocolate quiz with awards for knowledgeable chocoholics

Your first task is to create the site structure with these four sections. (For this site, site preferences are unimportant, and you can leave the Server Application Support option set to None.) You could take one of a half-dozen approaches to building this site. After a handful of dark chocolate raspberry truffles to get ourselves on an appropriate sugar high, here's the absolutely fastest way we found to do it:

1. **Click the Home page in the site tree to select it.**

2. **Press the Insert key four times (or click the Insert Page button if you prefer mouse action).**

3. **Press the down arrow to go to the first page. Then press F2 to rename the page. Type the name of the first section entry page, and then Return.**

4. **Press the down arrow to go to the next page, and then repeat the renaming process from Step 3.**

5. **Repeat Step 3 until all four sections are renamed.**

6. **With the first page selected, click Insert Page (or press Insert) to insert as many pages as you need for that section of the site under the entry page. Repeat the renaming action with F2 and press the arrow keys to navigate to the next pages.**

7. **Repeat this set of steps as many times as necessary to create pages for each section.**

Avoid using spaces in page names. Although Drumbeat and Windows allow spaces in page names, some servers and browsers do not. If you need to use spaces, you can give your page a different name for publishing on the Publish tab of the Web Page Properties dialog box: Right-click the page in the site tree and choose Properties. (See the section "Web page properties," later in this chapter.) The final site structure is shown in Figure 2-2.

You can add pages to your site from either the Site tab or the Templates tab. If you're more design-oriented and you already have some design templates worked out, you may prefer to add pages directly to a template on the Templates tab instead. Although the Insert Page button isn't available, you can use the Insert key to insert a page directly below a selected template. (See Chapter 4 for more information about working with templates.)

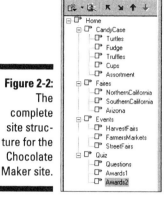

Figure 2-2:
The
complete
site struc-
ture for the
Chocolate
Maker site.

Using our method on the Site tab, you can add pages precisely where you want them in the site tree that represents the logical structure of your site. Use the blue page arrows at the top of the Site tab to move pages around in the site tree, or promote or demote them in the hierarchy if you want to rearrange things, as shown in Figure 2-3.

Using different kinds of pages

The preceding section deals with one only kind of page: the plain old vanilla — er, we mean chocolate — HTML page. You can see a few other options on the Insert Page button if you click the dropdown arrow on the button, as shown in Figure 2-4. Your options are Pager, External Pager, Pageset, and Frameset.

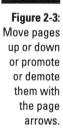

Figure 2-3:
Move pages
up or down
or promote
or demote
them with
the page
arrows.

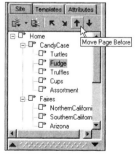

Figure 2-4:
The Insert
Page button
dropdown
options.

On the Templates tab, the corresponding options on the Insert right-click menu when you select a template are Page, PageSet, and Template. That's because you can't add external pages to a template. Framesets appear only on the Site tab and are an item all to themselves. (PageSets are explained in Chapter 9, and Chapter 7 is the frameset bible.)

Using external pages to keep your code intact

Maybe you're thinking that Drumbeat could be the ticket for maintaining *most* of your site. Its automation features are great, and you realize that you don't really need to get at the base code of every single page. However, you've spent weeks getting that one critical page on your site to look and work just the way you want. You don't want *anybody* getting his sticky little chocolate-covered fingers into the code and messing it up.

We understand how you feel. (How about a piece of walnut fudge, for sympathy?) Some things just don't lend themselves to external formulas, and no software program can be all things to all people (especially not to finicky programmers). The solution is easy: You can bring your page into the site as an external page. It then appears in your site structure, you can make links to it from other pages in Drumbeat, and you can even publish it from Drumbeat. Drumbeat leaves the code alone, however.

An external page may also be a page on the Web that you want to link to and include in your overall picture. Suppose that much of the chocolate maker's business takes place at Renaissance Faires, where seductive wares are sold by flirtatious maids laced into snug Elizabethan costumes (everybody knows that food and sex are related, right?) and that you want to include information about the faires on the site, without having to duplicate the work of keeping up with ever-changing event schedules. Because the Renaissance Pleasure Faire, where a big part of your business happens, has a nice little search engine visitors can use to search for upcoming faires, you want to bring that page into your site as an external page.

To create an external page:

1. **On the Site tab, click the dropdown arrow on the Insert Page button and choose External Page.**

2. **In the External Page dialog box, as shown in Figure 2-5, enter the name for the page. (The name you use for it in Drumbeat doesn't have to be the same as the page's real filename.)**

3. **Give the path or full URL to the page.**

If the media files (images and scripts, for example) are kept in a different sub-folder, you can provide that path, too, if the page is local (on your own machine).

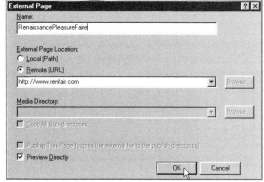

Figure 2-5:
Setting up
the informa-
tion for an
external
page.

If you bring a local file into your site as an external page, you can let Drumbeat publish it for you when you publish your site, by clicking the Publish This Page option. (The file is simply transferred intact to the publish location.) If you click Copy All Subdirectories, Drumbeat publishes any accompanying media as well. To include the media, however, you must specify the directory in which it's stored. (You can do this on the Publish tab in the Web Page Properties dialog box — see the section "Web page properties," later in this chapter.)

Click the External Page in the site tree and you can preview the page directly in Drumbeat. If the external page is a remote URL, you have to be connected to the Internet. If you're not, Windows prompts you with its usual message to connect. This message should clue you in to the fact that the Preview feature is just an embedded browser window.

The Preview Directly option, available at the bottom of the External Page dialog box or in the Web Page Properties dialog box (again, see the "Web page properties" section, later in this chapter) applies only if you're pub-lishing ASP or JSP pages. Whenever you browse your ASP or JSP site, the browser always starts at the specified default page. If you check the Preview Directly option, you don't have to work your way down to the external page via links to view it in Drumbeat.

Web page properties

Every page, no matter what kind, has a set of properties that can be edited. To see the web page properties:

1. **Select the page in the site tree (on either the Site tab or the Templates tab).**

2. **Right-click and choose Properties or choose Edit⇨Properties.**

The General tab merely tells you the name of the page and the target browser. Click the Publish tab to see the main properties you'll want to edit (as shown in Figure 2-6):

Page Title: The content of the <TITLE> tag, which controls what's displayed on the browser's title bar (the bar across the top). If you've changed the name of your pages in the site tree, as we did when we built the site structure, the new page name is not automatically reflected in the title of the page. You have to change this option in the Web Page Properties dialog box to avoid publishing web pages with title bars that say silly and useless things like Page2. It's especially important when your site is indexed by a search engine. You want your page title to reflect the content accurately so that if somebody with cybermunchies is searching for chocolate truffles, the search engine doesn't ignore your site.

Publishing Location: Publishes the page to a different destination from the rest of the site (if you have some reason to do so). Just uncheck the Use Default Destination option. If the publishing option is set to Staging, this line specifies the staging publishing location. If the option is set to Production, it's the production publishing location.

Published File Name: Publishes the file under a different name from the name used in Drumbeat and shown in the site tree, if you uncheck the Use Page Name As Published File Name option. This feature is useful if your page names contain characters your server can't handle (such as spaces) or if you have a filenaming convention that would be awkward in the Drumbeat site tree.

File Extensions: Lets you choose a different extension for the published file, if necessary. If you leave this option set to Automatic, the published file extension is .html for ordinary web pages, .asp for Active Server Pages, and .jsp for JavaServer Pages.

We sampled a few chocolate cashew turtles with caramel centers before coming up with this sugar-rush technique for creating proper titles for all the pages in the chocolate maker's site:

1. **Select the first page in the site tree and press Alt+Enter.**

2. **Click the Publish tab in the Web Page Properties dialog box.**

3. **Press the Tab key to go to the Page Title box, type the new page title, and press Enter.**

4. **Click an open area in the site tree, press the down arrow to go to the next page, and then repeat Steps 1–3 as often as necessary.**

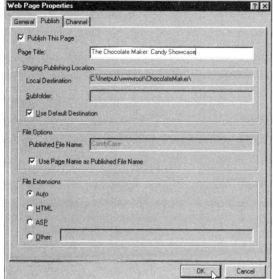

Figure 2-6:
The Publish
tab of the
Web Page
Properties
dialog box
contains the
main page
properties
you'll want
to edit.

If you use the mouse to click a page in the site tree, the page loads into the layout area. On the other hand, if you press the arrow keys to navigate to a new page, the page does not load into the layout area, so you can save the loading time when you're editing page names or properties for the site. Just click in an empty space in the site tree first, and then press the arrow keys.

Making connections: Creating links

The Chocolate Maker site is in business. All we need is a little piece of chocolate-coated English toffee for energy, and we're ready to show you how to link everything properly. The major navigational button images and logos for each section are the same for all pages in the site. So, the images were placed on the master template on the Templates tab earlier, along with a chocolate mocha cream background (refer to Figure 2-1). All that remains to be done is to link up the buttons.

Follow these steps to link the first button:

1. **Click the Templates tab, and then click the master template in the site tree.**

2. **Select an image button.**

3. **Right-click and choose Assign Link. (Sugar rush shortcut: Press Ctrl+K.)**

4. **In the Link dialog box, select the page to link to. Then click OK.**

In the example shown in Figure 2-7, a link is being created to the entry page for the chocolate-display section of the chocolate maker's site.

You can press the arrow keys to navigate the pages in the Link dialog box, too, if you prefer (although it may not be faster than a mouse-click.) Press the right-arrow key to expand the tree if you're on a page with a plus sign next to it, and the up- and down-arrow keys to move through the site tree.

Using relational page links

Relational page links are a nifty feature that is especially useful if you like to change your mind and rearrange your site as you work out its structure — or your boss does. *Relational* links are links using the Next Page or Previous Page option in the Link dialog box. Drumbeat makes the links according to the order of the pages in the site tree, as shown on the Site tab. If you move pages or rearrange them, Drumbeat remakes the links to reflect the new order in the new site tree.

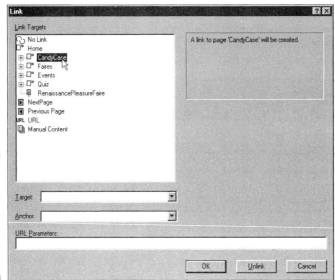

Figure 2-7:
Making a
link to a
page in the
site in the
Link dialog
box.

You can make it easy — in fact, irresistible — for visitors to browser through the different types of chocolate wares using relational links to create a series of links from one seductive chocolate temptation to the next. Follow these steps to create a series of links:

1. **On the Site tab, select the Turtles page.**

2. **Click and drag the Text element on the SmartElements toolbar to the layout of the Turtles page.**

3. **Type** Next Temptation **and click the Align Text Right button to right-justify the text.**

4. **Select the whole text and click the Assign Link button on the Text Formatting toolbar, as shown in Figure 2-8. (Sugar-rush technique: Press Ctrl+K).**

5. **In the Link dialog box, click to select Next Page, and then click OK.**

Figure 2-8:
Click this
button to
link text in a
text box.

Because the text is right-justified, drag the text box over to the right edge of the layout area. Then do the same thing all over again, this time creating a text box with the words **Previous Temptation**. Leave the text left-aligned and link it with the Previous Page link option.

To align the two text boxes to the same top position:

1. **Select the first text box, and then Ctrl+click the second text box. Or** *marquee select* **the two boxes (see the definition in the Introduction).**

2. **Click the dropdown arrow next to the Arrange Elements button and choose Align Top, as shown in Figure 2-9.**

To quickly duplicate the links on all the pages in the section:

1. **Select the two text boxes with links you created earlier.**

2. **Press Ctrl+C to copy the items (or choose Edit⇨Copy).**

3. **Select the next page in the section, click the layout, and press Ctrl+V to paste the items.**

4. **Drag the two text boxes together to the proper position.**

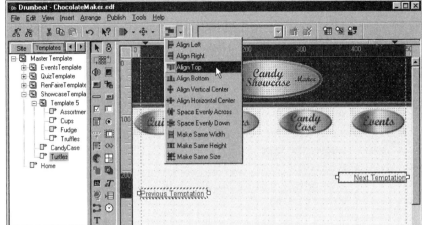

Figure 2-9:
Align the
text boxes
to the same
top position
by choosing
an option
from the
Arrange
Elements
menu.

Now you can move the pages around in any order you want and add new pages to the section for new chocolate creations, and the links maintain their integrity, always linking to the Next or Previous Page, as shown in the site tree. Notice that whenever you copy and paste elements from one page to another, the link information is also copied.

To get the text links on all the pages to appear in the same place, place guides on the template where you want the text boxes positioned. Drag the text boxes and snap them to the guides. An even better way to do this task (the sugar-rush way) is to put the link text on a separate template for these pages. Then you have to make the links only once.

Here are the rules of relational links:

- ✔ Next Page and Previous Page links work only between pages in the same section and at the same level in the hierarchy in the site tree, as shown in the Site Manager.
- ✔ Next Page and Previous Page links are endlessly looping within this level. That is, whenever you click a Next Page link on the last page in the group, the first page in the group is displayed.

Linking to URLs and other protocol

One of the easiest ways to make a link to a URL on the Web is to use an external page. This technique can save you a great deal of time and minimize the chance of errors being made when full URLs are typed. To create a link to an external page, all you have to do is select the external page in the site tree in the Link dialog box. The URL link is then automatically created.

If you use a large number of external links, you won't want to make external pages for all the possible web pages you want to link to on the site, though (or you could end up with a cluttered site structure). You may also want to make URL links other than the HTTP kind, such as links to an FTP site or an e-mail address.

To create a link to a URL:

1. **Select the text or image to be linked and select the link option:**

   • **Text:** Click the Assign Link button on the Text Formatting toolbar.

   • **Image:** Click the Link Assign button on the Attributes Sheet, or right-click and choose Assign Link.

   • **Both text and image:** Press Ctrl+K (the "sugar-rush" technique).

2. **In the Link dialog box, select URL.**

   A number of URL linking options become immediately apparent, as shown in Figure 2-10.

3. **Select the protocol to use.**

   An ordinary web link uses the default `http://`.

4. **In the URL box, type the address (for example,** www.chocoholic.com**).**

   Do not include the protocol prefix (`http://`). Drumbeat automatically adds it for you. You can see a sample entry in the figure.

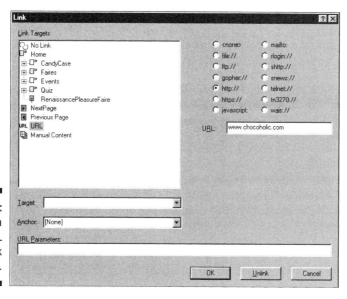

Figure 2-10:
Making a link to a URL in the Link dialog box.

The same procedure creates other types of links, such as e-mail or FTP links. Some examples are shown in Table 2-1.

Table 2-1	Sample Entries for Some Familiar Protocol Links	
Link Type	**Protocol**	**Sample URL Entry**
E-mail	mailto:	support@drumbeat.com
FTP	ftp://	192.215.247.19/QuickStart.exe
		www.drumbeat.com
		servername.drumbeat.com
Security	https://	www.host.com/

Using URL parameters

We can almost hear you experienced web site developers clearing your throats: "Ahem — what about parameters you want to tack on in order to add filter or search criteria?"

The answer's easy. Follow these steps to add URL parameters:

1. **Enter the main URL in the URL box and append a question mark (?).**

2. **In the URL Parameters box, add the rest of the query string.**

You can use URL parameters to link to CGI scripts you've created or to create links to stored procedures in your database or SQL parameters you've created for your queries to the database. (You can find an example of using a SQL parameter in Chapter 14, in the section about using dynamic SQL queries.) You may want to add a database to the Chocolate Maker site. That way, your chocolate maker client can add new chocolates whenever they want (as long as they send you a sample for approval first). If you use URL parameters to link to the pages for each of the different chocolate types, you can set up one link that works for all types, as shown in Figure 2-11.

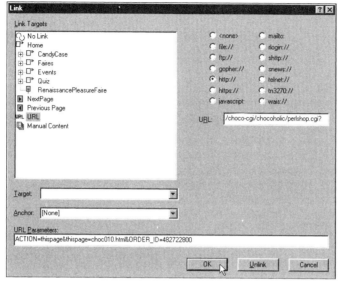

Figure 2-11:
Appending
a URL
parameter
to a link.

Publishing Your Site

It's time to make a few critical decisions about how you want to publish your site. Two sets of options cover your site setup and publishing choices (as described in the section "Setting preferences," near the beginning of this chapter):

   ✔ **Site Preferences** (choose File⇨Preferences⇨Site)
   ✔ **Publish Settings** (choose Publish⇨Publish Settings)

If you want to change your mind about the target browser for the site or change to ASP or JSP publishing after you have your database content lined up, go to the Site Preferences dialog box.

If you want to tell Drumbeat where to publish your site, set up the publish directories, choose a home page, or define the alias for an ASP or JSP site, use the Publish Settings dialog box.

Doing a double-take

Drumbeat enables you to have two separate publishing settings for the same site. This capability enables you to set up a staging site, where you can publish and test your files during development. When you're ready to publish live to the world, you can just switch to your production settings and publish. You can put this dual publishing feature to several good uses:

✔ If you're publishing on an in-house intranet, you can use your staging settings to publish to either your local machine or a limited-access network drive. Then use your production settings to publish where your boss or client can preview it or to "go live."

✔ If you're publishing remotely by FTP to your Internet Service Provider (ISP), you can use your staging publishing settings to publish to your local machine. Then set up remote access to transfer files by FTP when you're ready with your production settings.

✔ If you want to publish different test versions of your site, you can use the staging and production settings to go to different locations so that the settings don't overwrite each other.

To switch between staging and production settings, choose Publish⇨Staging or Publish⇨Production to check the option you want.

What you need to know about publishing

The Publish Settings options are identical for staging and production. To set the publishing options for the current selection (staging or production), just choose Publish⇨Publish Settings. For a basic site with no server application support, the important questions you have to answer in the Publish Settings dialog box are

✔ Where are you going? (General tab)

✔ Where do you want this stuff? (Media tab)

What's so smart about SmartPublishing?

SmartPublish is a Drumbeat publishing feature meant to save publishing time. Drumbeat keeps track of which pages have changed since you last published. Pages that have changed are marked as "dirty" in the site tree by a little blue arrow next to the page icon. If SmartPublish is enabled on the Publish menu, Drumbeat publishes only those pages that have changed since the last time you published.

You can make certain changes to a page (such as a change in a query to database content that is not native to Drumbeat) that do not tip off Drumbeat that the page has changed. When you attempt to publish, you may get a message indicating that the selected page cannot be published or has no changes. Rather than pull your hair out about it, just disable SmartPublish and everything will be fine. You may want to do that anyway, if you have a large site and want to control what's being published each time. Another way to kick Drumbeat into realizing that the page has changed is to make a minor change in the Layout and then undo it (by pressing Ctrl+Z or choosing Edit⇨Undo).

For a database-driven site with ASP or WebSphere support, add these questions to the list, which you answer on either the ASP or WebSphere tab:

- ✔ Who am I?
- ✔ Which way is home?

Where are you going?

You tell Drumbeat on the General tab where to publish your site. The default location to which Drumbeat publishes is C:\Program Files\Drumbeat 2000\ Publish\. Although you can use this default folder (or directory) if you want, you'll see, after you create several sites, that pages with the same name in different sites overwrite each other (especially if you never change the name of that ubiquitous Home page). The wise approach is to establish a separate folder for each site you publish. You can publish non-ASP or non-JSP sites wherever you want on your computer or on a network drive.

Folders, directories — it's all a bunch of confusing doublespeak these days, ever since Windows decided to copy the Mac convention of using the term *folders* rather than *directories*. They're really the same thing. You usually hear "directory" when people are referring to networks and servers (it's what your system administrator understands), and the Drumbeat interface reflects that. We occasionally use "directory" in this section when it seems more correct or matches the choices in the dialog box. Which is correct? Who cares? Just substitute the term you're most comfortable with.

If you choose ASP or WebSphere publishing, the default folder doesn't work. It must be changed to a folder you create in the root directory of the web server. If you're using ASP and testing your pages locally with Personal Web Server, that will be in the Inetpub/www root folder that PWS creates. Your folder, therefore (as shown in Figure 2-12), is liable to look like this: C:\Inetpub\wwwroot\ChocolateMaker\.

A similar folder exists on the Internet Information Server (IIS 3) on Windows NT, if you're publishing out to a network server. The easiest thing is to browse to the correct folder to set up the destination for publishing, to avoid typing errors in the path.

Going to a remote server

If you choose the option Publish to a Remote Directory on the General tab in the Publish Settings dialog box, you still have to provide a local directory as a temporary "intermediate directory" so that Drumbeat can gather all the stuff with the proper file structure before it transfers the files to the remote computer.

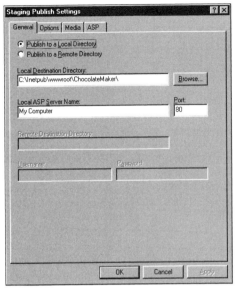

Figure 2-12:
The staging
Publish
Settings for
Chocolate
Maker for
publishing
and viewing
with
Personal
Web Server
on our own
machine.

Drumbeat uses an internal FTP client (ignore this term — it's a techie thing) to connect to the host server at publish-time and then transfers everything (pages, image, scripts — the whole kit and kaboodle) to the server. It even creates all the necessary folders for you. To set up the FTP transfer, you have to provide the same information in the Publish Settings dialog box as you do when you use your FTP application:

- ✔ **Remote Destination Directory:** The FTP host address
- ✔ **Username:** Your login name
- ✔ **Password:** Your secret code

If you don't want to save your username and password with your settings, you can leave them out and Drumbeat will ask you for them at the appropriate time after connecting to the server. Figure 2-13 shows the production Publish Settings set up to send the site to the remote server on the ISP.

Where do you want this stuff?

Drumbeat considers everything that's not a web page or a database to be media, including images, scripts, audio and video files, applets — what have you. On the Media tab in the Publish Settings dialog box, you can tell Drumbeat exactly where you want to put everything.

If you're the kind of person who prefers to keep everything in one place so that you don't have to remember where you put it, you can use the Drumbeat default media folder for everything. If you're the kind of person who loves the way those elaborate closet organizers keep everything tidy, you can choose separate folders for everything, as shown in Figure 2-14. You're not limited to the dropdown suggestions — you can type your own folder names. If you just want everything in one big heap (like your laundry), put a check in the Flat Directory Structure box so that everything publishes to the same root folder as your pages.

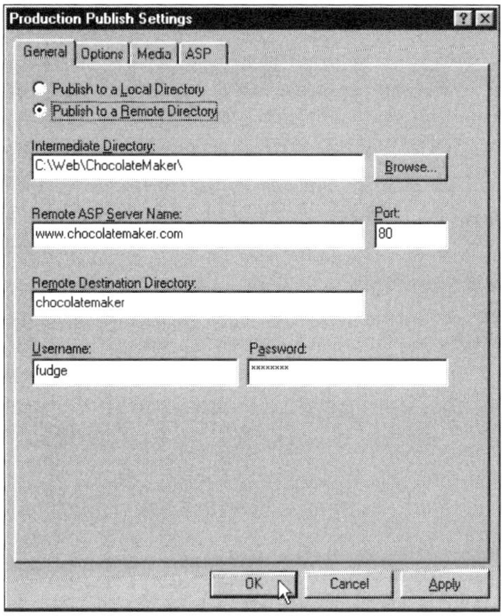

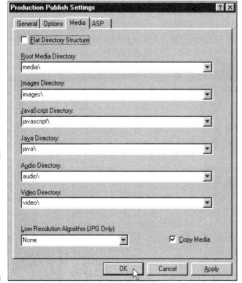

Figure 2-13:
The Production publish settings for publishing the site remotely by FTP.

Figure 2-14:
Choose separate folders for all the different types of files.

Unless you say otherwise, Drumbeat publishes all the media for your site (images, audio — the whole lot) each time you publish your site. If you're just tweaking the layout, you can save time when you publish by unchecking the Copy Media option on the Media tab in the Publish Settings dialog box after you've published the media the first time. Don't forget to recheck the box if you change or add any files!

Who am I?

If you've chosen ASP or WebSphere support in the site preferences (see the section "Setting preferences," earlier in this chapter), you have one more tab — the most important one — to fill out for the site. For the site to work properly, it needs to know two things: "Who am I?" and "Which way is home?" An ASP or JSP site always has a name it goes by on the server, which is known as the *alias* — that's the "who" part. It also needs to have a place to start from, or a *home* — that's the default page.

If you use the root web publishing folder of your server, the alias is simply the name of the folder you created there for your site. For example, if the path to your site (that you specified on the General tab) is C:\Inetpub\wwwroot\chocolatemaker, the Alias is chocolatemaker (see Figure 2-15).

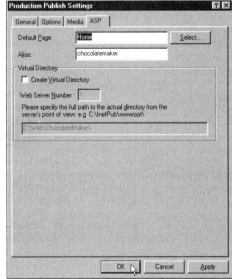

Figure 2-15:
Setting up the alias and the default page is important for ASP or JSP publishing.

In Windows NT, you can create a "virtual directory" to point to a location other than the web publishing root. If you create a virtual directory, the site's actual location is stored with the alias so that the server redirects to the proper location. You can create a virtual directory yourself in Personal Web Manager for

Personal Web Server or the Management Console for IIS. Drumbeat can create the virtual directory for you only if you're publishing to IIS 4 on Windows NT. (Thankfully, JSP users don't have to worry about virtual directories.)

For the JSP version of Drumbeat, you also have to provide the path to the servlets folder. For WebSphere, the correct path in the WebSphere folder on the server is WebSphere/AppServer/servlets.

Which way is home?

Whenever you browse server-side pages like those created by ASP and JSP, the browser always has to start from a home. It doesn't really matter where home is, although you do have to start somewhere. The Default Page option on the ASP or WebSphere tab shows this starting page. It can be the one labeled Home, or it can be any other page in the site. If you leave it set to Home and you're not using the home page in your site and you didn't put any links to other pages on the Home page, you may be somewhat bewildered whenever you try to browse the site and end up staring at a blank page. We've done this more than once ourselves, when we've forgotten to designate the default page (D'oh!).

You can change the default page to any page you want in the site. Just click Select and select the page in the site tree. While working on your site, you may want to change the default page to the one now in design, in order to browse directly to the page you're working on without having to click through to the page from the top.

ASP publishing in ten easy steps

If you've never published an ASP site, it probably sounds more complicated than it really is, so we cut it down to the essentials. All you have to do is follow these ten steps:

1. **With your site open, choose File⇨Preferences⇨Site.**

2. **For the Server Application Support option, choose ASP and click OK.**

3. **Choose Publish⇨Production.**

4. **Choose Publish⇨Publish Settings.**

5. **In the Production Publish Settings dialog box, enter the path to your folder you're publishing to on the server.**

   If you've created the folder properly, the path looks like this: C:\Inetpub\wwwroot\mysite.

   For the letter *C,* substitute the drive you're publishing to on your computer or your intranet. (See the section "Where are you going?" earlier in this chapter, for more information.)

6. **Select the ASP tab. For the alias, enter the folder name you're publishing to on Inetpub\wwwroot. In the preceding example, the folder is** `mysite`**.**

7. **For the default page, click Select and select the page you want to start from in the site.**

8. **Click OK.**

9. **Click the Publish button.**

10. **Click the dropdown arrow on the Browse button and select the browser that matches your target browser setting for the site.**

For the JSP version of Drumbeat, the steps for JSP publishing setup are pretty much the same, with only a few changes: In Step 2, choose WebSphere for the Server Application Support option. In Step 6, the path to the web publishing folder may be different — you have to check with your system administrator if you don't know it. You should also add the path to the servlets directory on the WebSphere server on the WebSphere tab. The path should be WebSphere/AppServer/servlets.

Personal Web Server (PWS) has to be installed and running for you to be able to browse your ASP site locally. If you have Windows 98 or Windows NT, you can install PWS from the Windows CD. (If you use Windows 95, you really should consider upgrading for ASP, although you can install PWS by following the instructions at the Microsoft site (where you can obtain it) or on the Drumbeat installation CD, if you have the full version.) After PWS is installed, you don't really have to worry about it — it's either running or not running, and it runs by default when you turn on your machine. You can assure yourself that it's running by checking for its icon (make sure that it doesn't have a red slash through it) on the system tray at the bottom of your Windows screen.

Creating a SmartPage

We web designers are, as we're sure you know, the primary victims of the "browser wars" that saddled us with two main semicompatible browser types, plus a host of older versions left in the wake as the ship of progress sailed on. Ensuring that your pages make sense in as many browsers as possible is now a major challenge, and impatient web designers often complain that it's more trouble than it's worth to create "low level" versions of their pages and then figure out the redirect scripting. Well, what if you could do all that at the click of a button?

"At the click of a button" is almost what Drumbeat offers, in the form of its SmartPage concept. *SmartPages* are pages that have multiple versions, with automatic redirect serving appropriate versions to users according to their browser type. To create a set of SmartPages:

1. **Design the page for the browser type you consider your primary target.**

2. **Right-click the page in the Site Manager, and choose Convert to Smart Page from the pop-up menu, as shown in Figure 2-16.**

   The SmartPage toolbar appears, as shown in Figure 2-17. It initially shows the browser type you designed the page for.

3. **Use the Create Page button to create a page for any of the other three browser types. Choose from the dropdown list the version of the page you want to create.**

4. **Inspect the page and make any needed changes.**

5. **Publish the page.**

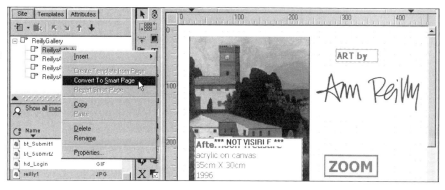

Figure 2-16:
Right-click a
page in the
site tree to
convert
it to a
SmartPage.

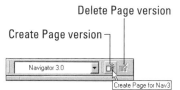

Figure 2-17:
The
SmartPage
toolbar.

Although Drumbeat takes care of the page redirection, you do have a choice of whether to have the redirecting done at the client or at the server.

Client-side redirection

Because redirection at the client is the Drumbeat default setting, you don't have to do anything to choose this option. The core of the client-side redirection system is a conventional JavaScript routine that senses a user's browser type and instantly replaces the redirect page with the appropriate page. You have to keep a couple of clever gimmicks in mind, however:

✔ How do you suppose that a browser which doesn't read JavaScript gets redirected by JavaScript? Aha — magic! No, seriously, a META instruction refreshes the page to the generic version after two seconds. If the JavaScript has taken no action after two seconds (it usually acts within about half a second), the META refresh takes over.

✔ One problem with "dumb" redirects is that your pages don't get catalogued properly by Internet search engines. Drumbeat places searcher-friendly stuff on the redirect page, including hyperlinks designed especially for robots to follow.

Client-side redirection has the advantage, therefore, of being compatible with all server types and being friendly to search engines. Its disadvantage is that inevitable half-second delay while the redirect is being calculated. Plus, if you worry about network traffic, you're taking up twice the bandwidth you need.

Server-side redirection

Redirection at the server uses CGI (the Common Gateway Interface) to run a logical program on the server, which detects the user's browser and serves up the appropriate page. If you think that you're publishing mypage.html with server-side redirection, you're also publishing a script written in the Perl language that handles the redirect logic.

Because the Perl script acts virtually instantaneously, no delay occurs and *only* the appropriate page is ever sent from the server. Friendliness to search engines is entirely a question of how you design the individual pages.

The disadvantage is that this system is tricky to set up. By no means do all ISPs allow their clients to run Perl scripts, and you also have to fiddle with UNIX file permissions to get the thing to run. You have to remember that the address of the CGI file, not the HTML file, is the correct URL for the page.

To go for the server-side option:

1. **Pop up the Site Preferences dialog box by choosing File⇨ Preferences⇨Site and check the box to enable CGI support, if you haven't already done that.**

2. **Set the SmartPage support dropdown list for server-side redirection, and close the dialog box by clicking OK.**

3. **Pop up the Production Publish Settings 4-tab dialog box by choosing Publish⇨Publish Settings from the main menu. If you're publishing to a remote site, you must first choose Production rather than Staging from the bottom section of the dropdown menu.**

4. **Make sure that the settings on the General tab are correct, and click the CGI tab to switch to it and set all five windows correctly for your server setup.**

   Unless you regularly use Perl scripting on your server, you have to ask your system administrator for help with this step. The Destination Directory is typically the cgi-bin directory of your web site. The Compiler Director is typically /usr/local/bin/perl. These settings may vary according to your server setup, however.

An update on CGI support settings is available as DrumNote No. #36 on the Drumbeat web site: `drumnotes.drumbeat.com`.

Creating browser-specific pages

Take a look at Figure 2-18, part of a page set up initially for Internet Explorer 4.0 and later. Each of the pieces of artwork has two dynamic features: pop-up caption text that's normally invisible and a zoom button. The two interaction types are

- **Enhanced UI:** `Show [text] when the mouse is over [image]`
- **Image:** `Zoom [image] when [zoomimage] is clicked`

Figure 2-18: This art page is designed for Internet Explorer 4.0 and later, with pop-up menu and zoomed images.

The zoom interaction has the effect of zooming in on the painting further in four clicks of the zoom button, after which the next click reverts it to normal size.

When you're making that page into a SmartPage, a couple of fix-ups are indicated. For the Any 4.0 Browser page, Drumbeat still considers both interactions valid. However, you may as well delete the zoom feature because it doesn't work in Netscape. In Internet Explorer, any image can be zoomed in and out as an option from the right-click pop-up menu. Figure 2-19 shows the dropdown list on the SmartPage toolbar showing that versions of this page now exist for all except generic browsers.

Figure 2-19:
Making the final SmartPage version!

As you create a "generic" page, you may be taken aback to see something like what's shown in Figure 2-20. Element positioning on generic pages is done only with tables, and neither layering nor dynamic effects are available.

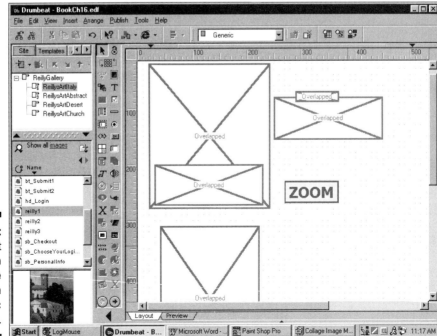

Figure 2-20:
Almost nothing on this page works for a generic version.

You may as well delete the interactions that pop up captions, and lay the page out differently, with permanently visible photo captions. It took just about a minute to make the fixed-up generic page shown in Figure 2-21. If the different placement of text boxes suggests a need for editing, no problem — you can make any text edits on this page without affecting the other pages.

After you've made a SmartPage set, you see that the pages are listed as separate in the Template Manager, as shown in Figure 2-22. By right-clicking one of these pages in the Template Manager and choosing Properties, therefore, you can set Publish options for one page version at a time. The Site Manager treats the set as one page; however, a little *s* suffix indicates the "smartness" of the page.

Reverting SmartPages

You can easily turn a set of SmartPages back into a single DumbPage: Simply right-click the page in the Site Manager and choose Revert Smart Page from the pop-up menu. The page reverts to the version suitable for the site's primary browser target.

Figure 2-21: A generic version fixed in a jiffy.

Figure 2-22:
SmartPage
sets are
shown as
separate
pages on
the
Template
tab.

The only conceivable difficulty Drumbeat may have is if the primary browser target for the site is one for which a SmartPage version is no longer available. (It's unlikely but possible.) In that case, Drumbeat reverts to the closest available page version, looking for "lower" versions first.

Chapter 3

Organizing Your Assets

. . . .

In This Chapter

▶ Off-the-shelf assets

▶ Tailor-made assets

▶ Conventional assets

▶ SmartElements

. . . .

*A*ll web sites have assets, even if they aren't called by that name. Joe Blow, making his first web site, doesn't think of his handmade button labeled Click Here to See My CD Collection as a site asset, but it is. Even a semiprofessional web designer using and reusing a style sheet may not think of the styles as assets, but they are.

To Drumbeat, assets include such obvious things as image and style libraries as well as less obvious assets, such as SQL queries and JavaScript fragments. Drumbeat provides a clever and practical way of both organizing all the assets used to create a site and keeping them at the user's fingertip — wherever they may be on your accessible network.

What Are Assets?

 The Drumbeat people may just as well have chosen the word *stuff* to describe what assets are because that's what they really mean. Assets are the *stuff* you need to make your pages, and they're organized in the Asset Center in the lower-left panel of the Drumbeat working screen. When you click the cute little Locate Assets button, you get to see the first in a series of cascading menus, showing the ten types of stuff that Drumbeat thinks of as assets. Think of this button as the Where's My Stuff? button. The list of asset types is shown in Figure 3-1.

Figure 3-1: A first-level list of asset types.

Hidden behind the pop-up menu shown in this figure is the rock-bottom-basic default list of media that Drumbeat supplies — the files are in the Media subfolder. *Media* is the most obvious asset category, and images are the most obvious type of media. As you click a GIF file on the list — Abracadabra! — the image appears in the little preview window (or *asset viewer*). You can drag any image you fancy to the current page from either the asset list or the viewer pane. Therein lies (much of) the genius of the Asset Center.

Media can be things other than images: Animations, audio files, video clips — even plain text. They all are under the heading of media. As a matter of fact, one of the default media objects is named LICENSE.TXT. When you drag it into a page (you can't preview text in the asset viewer, so you have to drag it from the media list), you see that it's a polite note saying that it's okay to use this stuff.

Formatted text, too, can be listed as a media asset. Just for fun, we decorated the license text in our word processor and saved it as LICENSE.RTF. It drops into a web page a treat, as shown in Figure 3-2; if you publish a page containing Rich Text formatting, you see that Drumbeat takes care of translating, as it were, from RTF to HTML. Amazing.

Figure 3-2: The newly fashioned RTF asset dragged into the layout area.

THIS DIRECTORY
contains media in various formats for your use. You are free to deploy this media on your internet web site or your intranet application. You may not sell this media. **This media** is the property of ESI Software Inc., **dba** Elemental Software, **and all rights to this media are reserved by Elemental Software.**

Adding Assets to Your Site

Rock-bottom basic media assets get old fairly quick, to be sure. Because pre-loaded images are mostly of the "built with Drumbeat" variety and extremely unhip, an early task — perhaps the *first* task — when you're generating a new web site is to go fetch more stuff.

Off-the-shelf media

You may be pleasantly surprised — we certainly were — when you dig a little further and browse the other off-the-shelf media Drumbeat offers. No fewer than ten complete kits of buttons, bars, tiles, and icons are provided in sub-folders one level down from the Media folder. Here are some examples:

- **Bridge:** A sober, businesslike collection.
- **Corporate Blue:** Many decorative ways of saying things, like Investor Info (you get the idea).
- **Playful:** Suitable for a personal site. (Hmmm, who are the generic couple in ply_man.jpg and ply_woman.jpg? Do they ever get involved in any hanky-panky?)

You can include one, some, or all these media folders, like this:

1. **Click the other button in the Asset Center, the Fetch Stuff button (technically, the Add Assets button).**
2. **Choose Media Folders from the pop-up menu, and you get to use the Select Media Folders dialog box.**
3. **Click the Add button and browse to the folder you want.**
4. **Finish by clicking the Done button, and all media files in your selected folder stream into the Asset Center. Magic!**

In the Add Media Folder dialog box, you get the option of adding media to only this web site *or* to all your sites forever until you say "stop."

Note that the Fetch Stuff button could also be called the Junk Stuff button because the same dialog box is used if you decide that you hate the Corporate Blue collection and never want to see those wretched icons again.

Also under the rubric of "off-the-shelf media," don't overlook any personal folders you may have hanging around — they may hold buttons and icons you've collected, thinking that they may come in handy one day. Importing them into Drumbeat is a breeze, and the "stuff viewer" makes browsing through them *so* easy. The one feature we wish we could add is a Delete This Trashy Icon button. The Delete button in the Select Media Folders dialog box simply removes media collections from the Asset Center; the files themselves remain on your system. The Drumbeat designers were probably right, though — there are better ways of cleaning house.

Custom media

As interesting as the Drumbeat-provided pix are, you would deserve to have your web designer's license yanked if you didn't add some of your own custom-made stuff — perhaps a navigation bar, a jokey divider, or some rollover buttons? Or you could throw in something in the corporate style if your boss is looking over your shoulder. You should collect these elements of your site's "look and feel" at an early stage and stick them in a special folder. It doesn't matter, though: If you love using the Add Assets button, you can use it to your heart's content. Just grab media files from all over and call them assets. When Drumbeat publishes your site, it rationalizes everything, normally collecting everything you've placed on a page into a single sub-folder that it names Media.

If you move media files to some other place on your system, they are no longer considered Your Stuff, and they disappear from the Asset Center. You can get them back by adding the new folder, but that's not enough in the case of media that have already been placed on the page. You need the extra step of updating the media path in a special dialog box you access by choosing Tools⇔Media File Paths, as shown in Figure 3-3.

Figure 3-3:
Update media file paths when media already placed have been moved.

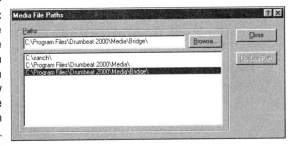

The Refresh button is there for an update of a different kind. If you add files to a folder that's already an asset source, they don't show up without a reload or refresh.

Types of assets

Any of the ten types of assets can be listed either unfiltered or filtered in various ways by using the Locate Assets button. The process of getting an asset listing is known as *querying* for assets.

Media: Media includes images, animations, audio, and video. There's not much more to say about images, except perhaps to note that a GIF file can be, of course, a pre-created animation. Drumbeat has a nifty built-in animation feature of its own, called a DynaImage. The individual frames of a DynaImage don't have to be in the media asset list. Drumbeat has, in fact, a better way of populating a DynaImage, as explained later in this chapter, in the section "Placing Assets on the Page." *Animations* are Autodesk animation files. (We have more to say about audio and video sources in the section "Using Assets on the Page," later in this chapter.)

SmartElements: SmartElements are the gizmos you drag to the page to make up the page elements. On the vertical SmartElements toolbar — the skinny toolbar down the middle of the screen — you see the standard SmartElements, but Drumbeat has heaps more. One way of inspecting them and using them is to display them in the Asset Center. A SmartElement with a line through it in the Asset Center is one that isn't available for the target browser of the site you're building.

Pages: Pages in your site are considered assets in the sense that they can be listed in useful ways and their properties revealed by right-clicking the list. Obviously, though, you can't drag-and-drop a page onto another page!

Interactions: Interactions are the hidden relationships you can set up between page elements — like making an image change when a user clicks a button. The Interactions Center is a far better place to manage them than the Asset Center, however. We deal with interactions, activations, and contracts (sometimes just different manifestations of the same thing) in Chapter 15.

Styles: Styles are ways of rendering text that can be used throughout your site. They end up in a style sheet rather than in the HTML file that describes the page. As with images, you can preview styles in the asset viewer and drag-and-drop them on some text in the layout area. Drumbeat provides, as it does with images, a set of styles for you to use if you can't think of anything better.

Content Tables: Content Tables are logical arrangements of sets of elements, which are often imported from a database or some other external file in tabular form. (Chapter 6 tells you all about them.) As you can with an image or a style, you can drag a Content Table from the asset list into the layout area, forming a ready-made table that Drumbeat calls an *AutoTable*. More often, the Content Table is exposed first in the Content Center, and stuff you put in specific table cells is available for use in layout.

Queries: Queries are logical statements that enable your site to communicate with an external database. (Chapter 10 is the bible on these things.)

Site elements: Site elements are almost all server-side SmartElements, such as recordsets and COM objects. You can use this filter to edit DataForms (revise, add, or delete database-driven pages) or use existing recordsets created from database queries.

Links: Links are simply the hyperlinks that originate on the page or the site. One reason you may want to query for these is that you can refine the query to get a list of *broken* links.

Contracts: Contracts are the actual code fragments that underlie activations and interactions. If you query for these elements in the Asset Center, you find them expressed in a more general way. We never list contracts in the Asset Center — we prefer to use the Contract Manager: Choose Tools⇨Contracts or click the Add Assets button and select Contracts.

Sorting and Ordering Assets

Those Drumbeat programmers really busted a gut trying to think of every possible way to sort and order asset lists. They came up with so many options, in fact, that the whole operation seems quite complicated at first. Don't worry, though: You quickly get used to it and can then appreciate its flexibility.

Sorting

The idea behind Drumbeat's asset sorting (it could also be called *filtering*) is to give you a full range of options for restricting the list to just what you need to see right now. We explain the procedure for sorting media — it's the asset you use most often and also the most complex sort procedure. (In other words, everything else in comparison seems like a piece of cake!) Fire up Drumbeat and follow along with us!

Figure 3-4 shows what you see when you click the Locate Assets button and choose Media. Notice that the second level of the cascading menu already offers four choices:

- ✔ Show all media
- ✔ Show all images
- ✔ Show all images larger than 10K
- ✔ Show all media in C:\Program Files\Drumbeat2000\Media

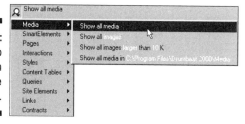

Figure 3-4:
Beginning to
drill down
into the
asset lists.

The underlined words on the menu are the basis for third-level options, as
you see if you click a word. Two of them filter the list of images, and one filters the list of all media.

When you choose Show All Images, you see the result. Notice that the word
images is blue and underlined in the query text to the right of the Get My
Stuff button. That's a signal that it's a third-level sort criterion. Click on the
word, and you get to change instantly from images to any of the other five
media categories (audio and video, for example).

Step back, query for media again, and this time select the third option, Show
All Images Larger Than 10K. Now you see that *both* the underlined words
have become third-level sort criteria. Larger can be switched to Smaller, and
10K changed to 5K, 25K, 50K, 100K, or 1000K. Similarly, if you select the last of
the second-level sorts, the media directory you sort for can become anything
that's on your current list of media folders. Figure 3-5 displays this hierarchy
of choices in a logical way, not as they appear on-screen.

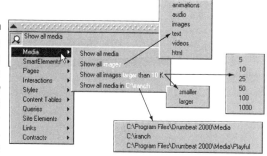

Figure 3-5:
Don't be
fooled: It's a
complete
set of media
asset pop-
up menus.

Whenever you filter assets beyond the top level, all the top-level sorted
assets remain on the list; those you nixed by further filtering are grayed out
and do not participate in any ordering of the list. For example, if you filter for

images smaller than 50K, the media that satisfy that filter move to the top of the list and can be ordered. All other images — and all other media — are grayed out but still active; you can still drag a grayed-out image into the layout area if you want.

Ordering

After you've filtered your list of stuff, you can order it in as many ways as you have columns of information, times two. Using the example of media assets, the list of media files has these columns: Name, Type, Dimensions, Size, and Location. (You have to expand the Asset Center pane to see all that property info.)

The list is always ordered somehow, and the label of the column that controls the sort order is shown in bold, with the other columns relatively gray. Just click a different column label to order by that property. Click the same one again, and the order switches from ascending to descending and then back again ad infinitum.

Another nice feature: When you expand the Asset Center to focus your attention on its contents, you see that all the column widths are variable. Grab one of the short, vertical dividing lines in the header with your mouse, and pull the line left or right.

This type of multisorting was not invented by Drumbeat, by the way. It's now fairly common in Windows applications and a terrific convenience.

Placing Assets on the Page

We note earlier in this chapter, in the list of asset types, that some of the stuff that's counted as assets is there just so that it can be sorted and listed. We ignore those assets in this section and concentrate on telling you how to use media and styles.

The simplest operation for deploying your assets is placing an image in Layout. This job couldn't be simpler: Scroll through the list, using the asset viewer to preview the image, and, when you find what you need, drag it to the page. Adjust the image position by using the mouse or the arrow keys (for pixel-by-pixel fine-tuning). Don't even bother with placing an image SmartElement first.

The next few paragraphs show the more complex ways of using assets:

To place a pair of images as a rollover: You *must* first place an image button SmartElement on the page. Then you have some choices: Either stash the image pair in a content table cell, drag both versions of the image to the button (mouseover version first), or edit the image button's Attributes Sheet to list the images. Which choice you take depends on what kind of mood you're in (and which bits of this book you remember). You can drag images from the Asset Center and drop them directly into a Content Table cell (make sure to assign the Content Table column as Multiple Content Allowed. You do that by right-clicking the column header and choosing Properties and then choosing Allow Multiple Content). The procedure for assigning an image list to the image button's Attributes Sheet is totally different. Select File List as the content type — it leads you to a standard Windows dialog box to select the file and is not really connected to your asset list. (Content Tables are fully explained in Chapter 6.)

 To make a DynaImage: First, place the SmartElement on the page; the same options then apply. In this case, we prefer to edit the Attributes Sheet because the file select dialog box enables us to Shift+select the whole set of animation frames in one swoop. Drumbeat takes care of the animation.

 To place audio: You have several choices. Get Plain Jane audio quality by dragging an audio SmartElement into the page basement and then dragging an audio file from the Asset List and dropping it on top of the audio icon.

This technique produces a standard HTML <EMBED> tag, suitable for only low-quality .au, .midi, and .wav files. To make matters worse, Drumbeat allows you to control only the LOOP attribute and doesn't allow you to specify AUTOSTART or HIDDEN. (Drumbeat treats both as always true.) In other words, use this technique only if you want poor-quality audio that starts when the page loads, with no way for the user to stop it.

If you want to be more sophisticated and have better control over your audio and video media, you can use the SmartElements representing the Windows Media Player. Both ActiveX (for Internet Explorer) and plug-in (for Netscape) versions are available as part of the standard Element Library. They aren't on your SmartElements toolbar by default, however — you have to go fetch them, as explained a little later in this chapter, in the section "What Are SmartElements?"

 If you see that media assets are not being published correctly along with your pages, check to ensure that you have selected the Copy Media option in your publishing settings. When you use the Publish Settings Wizard to set up your site, this option is checked by default. Verify it by choosing Publish⇨Publish Settings. The check box you need is in the lower-right corner of the Media tab.

Assets You Already Have: SmartElements and Interactions

As we mention in the section "Types of assets," earlier in this chapter, you can list, sort, and manage certain assets in places other than in the Asset Center. SmartElements, pages, interactions, Content Tables, and contracts all have their own management areas.

Although pages and Content Tables are assets you absolutely have to create for yourself, SmartElements and interactions (and the contracts that underlie the interactions) are built in to Drumbeat as part of its feature set. You can import and register new SmartElements, and you can create new contracts and interactions (we go on about this subject at length in Chapter 15), but for now we assume that, like most Drumbeat users, you work most of the time with what Drumbeat provides.

What are SmartElements?

Almost anything you can think of that can be part of a web page is represented in Drumbeat by a SmartElement. Obviously, the complexity of SmartElements varies all the way from a horizontal rule, which simply creates the <HR> markup tag, to a plug-in that lets you embed a virtual reality tour of Paris. Deploy any SmartElement you fancy by dragging or click-move-clicking from the SmartElements toolbar into layout. SmartElements that have no visual representation on the page are automatically sent to the area known as the basement. When you install Drumbeat, a couple of dozen SmartElements are scattered on the toolbar by default — although you can customize the list using more than 100 objects in the *Element Library*. A more useful division of SmartElements occurs between the *standard* SmartElements that cannot be imported, exported, edited, or deleted; and *registered* SmartElements that can be imported, exported, edited or deleted and do not display their content until the page is published.

You *select* a SmartElement by simply clicking it with the mouse. Its icon adopts a "depressed" rendition (no, that doesn't mean that it changes to a sad smiley face ☹). Your next click places the SmartElement in the layout area, and you can then adjust its exact position.

 A *SmartElement locking* feature enables you to place a whole set of SmartElements of the same type by repetitively clicking in the layout area. You set the lock either by clicking the Lock Tool or by double-clicking the SmartElement you're interested in.

If you need a set of 20 radio buttons, for example, select the SmartElement radio button, set the lock, and then strew your buttons on the page with 20 clicks. Unlock by clicking the lock icon again.

If a SmartElement icon is grayed out on the toolbar, it's because the icon is specific to a certain browser level and your site has not been rated for that browser.

Standard SmartElements

Most of the SmartElements already sitting on your toolbar are the relatively simple page elements that all web designers use repeatedly. Eight of them are form elements. Three or 4 belong in the basement. Table 3-1 describes all 32 standard SmartElements, not all of which are on the toolbar by default.

Table 3-1		Standard SmartElements on Your Toolbar (Whether You Like It Or Not)
Icon	*SmartElement*	*What It Does*
	Animation	Supports Autodesk animations. Can also be populated with a set of individual GIF files, just like a DynaImage. If you use this technique, however, you can't control the resulting animation nearly as well as if you use a DynaImage. *A GIF file that's already animated does not count as an animation.*
	Audio	Goes in the basement as a container for .au, .midi, and .wav audio files. The only attribute that can be controlled is LOOP.
	Auto table	Displays a Content Table on the page in tabular form, with many controls on formatting and style.
	Channel button	*Just in case* anyone is still remotely interested in push technology, Drumbeat supports Internet Explorer channels. The Channel button links to the CDF file. The site must be rated for Internet Explorer 4 and later and have ASP or JSP support.
	Check box	Binary form element.
	Command	Belongs in the basement and is needed when a database includes a stored procedure that returns values that have to be read back. Okay for only ASP- or JSP-supported sites.
	Cookie	Container for persistent information that is written to and read back from the user's computer (unless it's blocked). Not available for sites rated Generic.

(continued)

Table 3-1 *(continued)*

Icon	SmartElement	What It Does
	Data binding	Unique to Internet Explorer; allows for dynamic data tables linked to small databases that download to the user's computer with the page.
	Dropdown List	Form element. Can be populated manually or from a Content Table.
	DynaImage	Supports Drumbeat's own animation format, made up of individual GIF frames. Can be activated to play when a button is pressed or stepped through one frame at a time. Controlled by timer in the basement.
	Edit Box	Standard text-input form element. However, you can cunningly convert it into a TEXTAREA form element by checking Multiline on its Attributes Sheet.
	Form Button	Form element that can be given the status of Submit, Reset, or plain old Button.
	Hidden Form Field	Appears in the basement, and its text is set and read by means of interactions with other SmartElements.
	Horizontal Rule	The standard HTML rule.
	HTML Passthrough	Drumbeat claims to be capable of creating any HTML you may ever need by its own visual, "intuitive" methods. However, it hedges its bets by enabling you to include HTML markup that you've created by other means. Add them as assets, and drag-and-drop them on this SmartElement.
	Image	Container for an image. This SmartElement is almost redundant because you can drag an image into the layout area from the Asset Center regardless of whether you have first placed a SmartElement.
	Image Button	Container for a multiple image, or rollover button. Not available for sites rated Generic.
	Image Check box	Drumbeat's own invention: a container for a set of three images that behave as a check box form element. Image 1 is the unchecked state; Image 2, mouseover; Image 3, checked. Not available for sites rated Generic.
	Image Map	Container for an image you intend to use as the basis for client-side image mapping.

(continued)

Icon	SmartElement	What It Does
	Image Radio Button	Another of Drumbeat's inventions: a container for a set of three images that behave as a radio button form element. Not available for sites rated Generic.
	List Box	Form element. Like a dropdown list but with drag "handles" for you to expand it to show as many list items as you want. Also allows multiselect.
	Looper	Container for a data loop, enabling multiple records from a database to be displayed on the page without being specified individually. Okay for only ASP- or JSP-supported sites.
	Radio Button	Standard radio button type form element. Meaningful only if it's part of a set, because only one button in a group can be selected.
	Recordset	Represents the result of a database query and lives in the basement. Okay only for ASP- or JSP-supported sites. In the JSP version, it's a BeanRecord set.
	Scrolling Image	Container for an image that scrolls repeatedly. You can set its scroll direction but, alas, not its speed or number of repeats.
	Scrolling Text	Container for text that scrolls up. Curiously, you can't drag a preexisting text file from the Asset Center to this SmartElement, as you can for a normal text SmartElement. Instead, you enter text by hand into a composition box or paste text from the Windows Clipboard.
	Slide Show	Container for a set of images displayed in "slide show" style, using dynamic HTML effects.
	Smart Spacer	Element that's invisible on the published page but acts to space visible page elements appropriately when they are populated with content that can vary in height.
	Text	Standard text container.
	Ticker Tape	Container for text that scrolls from right to left. Like the scrolling text SmartElement, doesn't allow a text file to be dropped in.
	Timer	Places a timer element in the basement, as a vehicle for constructing JavaScript functions that are time-dependent. Not available for sites rated Generic.
	Video	Container for embedded video.

No SmartElement represents a form, as such. Whenever you slap a form element (such as an edit box) down on a page, it automatically creates a form, and a Form Element icon appears in the basement, to which you can attach the form's own attributes. All form elements (radio buttons and check boxes, for example) become part of the same form on the page. *Drumbeat does not allow you to put more than one form on a page.*

The Element Library

You can inspect and manage the complete set of SmartElements in the Element Library, by choosing Tools⊅Element Library or by clicking the icon at the top of the SmartElements toolbar. The standard SmartElements are all contained on one of 11 tabs, as shown in Figure 3-6.

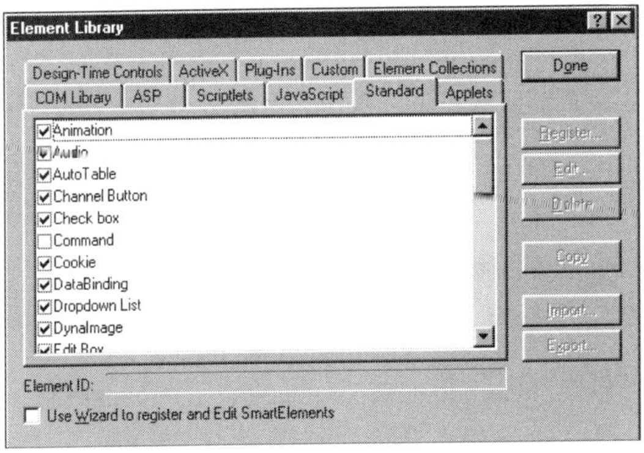

Figure 3-6:
Part of the
list of
standard
SmartEle-
ments in the
library.

Notice in the figure that not all the standard SmartElements have check marks next to them. Those that are checked appear on the toolbar, so that's obviously exactly how you control the content of that toolbar — including and excluding SmartElements by clicking the check boxes. SmartElements cannot be placed in the layout area directly from the library; you have to drag them from either the toolbar or the Asset Center.

The other ten tabs in the library are for different technology types that Drumbeat lets you use under license. Figure 3-7 shows a selection of SmartElements available as *applets*. Because these elements are registered SmartElements, the visual representation in the layout area is incomplete in some way but occupies the correct amount of space so that you can design around it effectively. The pocket calculator applet, for example, looks about right but does not work until you publish the page.

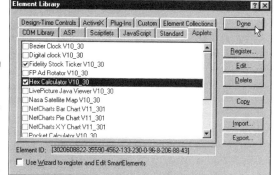

Figure 3-7:
Part of the
list of
applets in
the Element
Library.

Poke around in your Program Files\Drumbeat 2000\SmartElements folder,
and you should find SmartElements.doc, a useful guide to the SmartElements
menagerie.

Whenever you're using Drumbeat, especially when you're confused or working with an unfamiliar SmartElement, remember that *everything has attributes*.
Attributes hope and pray that you'll want to change them — hopefully, to
make a recalcitrant SmartElement behave as you want it to. Attributes Sheets
for registered SmartElements can be quite complex.

Display the Attributes Sheet for any SmartElement by first selecting the
SmartElement and then either right-clicking and choosing Attributes from the
pop-up menu or clicking the Attributes tab in the Site Management Center
(the upper-left part of the screen).

Part II
Adding Design and Style

The 5th Wave   By Rich Tennant

"Maybe it would help our Web site if we showed our products in action."

In this part . . .

Discover in this part all the tools Drumbeat provides for designing and styling web sites quickly and easily. We reveal the inside tricks for efficient design that usually only experienced Drumbeat users know. We even include a special chapter devoted to tips and tricks for cutting your design time in half or more.

Chapter 4

Designing with Templates

- -

- -

*J*ust as most computer programmers keep a "petting zoo" of frequently used subroutines, most Web designers have an equivalent collection. Particularly on large sites with a strong visual identity, common design elements are usually kept in some sort of skeleton file used as the starting point for each new page.

It's a *template*, whether or not it's called by that name, and Web design aids such as Drumbeat have made template management an important labor-saving aspect of site design. When you use the Drumbeat templating features to make a change to a design element that's common to a group of pages, the change ripples throughout the whole group of elements. A change to the master template is implemented immediately throughout the site.

You're probably familiar with templates. If you're not, just hold on to this thought: A template is *not* a page. Visitors to your site never see the template as such.

Making Design Templates

Even if you're not convinced of the usefulness of templates, you can't avoid having at least one: the master template. It arrives as a part of any Drumbeat site you create, showing only the home page as shown in Figure 4-1, and you have no way to delete it — or even rename it. No one can force you to *use* it, of course, although the idea is that anything you slap on the master template appears on every single page in thc site.

Figure 4-1:
A brand-
new site.

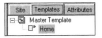

So what sort of things belong on the master template? The answer is almost anything you could put on a page. Candidates for Most Irritating Web Site may include sites whose master template contains these elements:

✔ An endlessly looping .wav file of the Republican Ladies of Arkansas singing "Happy Days Are Here Again" (unaccompanied)

✔ An endlessly looping animation of Beavis and Butt-head eating fast food

✔ A large JPG image of Barney the Dinosaur moving across the page very slowly and obscuring the text

✔ An image link to an Internet advertising service promoting the Ukrainian machine-tool industry

You could put all these massively annoying SmartElements on the master template and guarantee that they'll be seen (or heard) on every page in the entire godforsaken site. Most web designers, however, don't set out to annoy their site visitors. Here are the sorts of things you may, more typically, want to put on a master template:

✔ Link colors

✔ Guides for placing elements

✔ Navigation bar

✔ Corporate logo

✔ Background GIF image

✔ Disclaimer text ("Void where prohibited" or some similar nonsense)

✔ (Ugh) Rotating banner ads — hopefully featuring something more interesting than machine tools

Figure 4-2 shows the master template of an auction site shown in the process of construction in this chapter. Online auctions are all the rage now, and we don't see why we should be left out. The main sections of the Drumbeat Action Auction Web site are Buyers, Sellers, and How To. The site's backgrounds differ from section to section, its graphics images change, and its banner ads are . . . banned. The two elements that are a constant throughout the site are a main title and a navigation bar that enables users to click around the site hassle-free. Because the navigation bar is an active image, with hot spots in the obvious places linked to the main site sections, those are the only two components of the master template. Every page in the site inherits these elements and is known as a *child* of the master template.

Figure 4-2:
The master template of the (imaginary) Drumbeat Action Auction site.

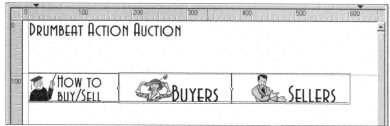

Because the figure shows the template, the artwork appears clean. On any page that's the child of a template, the artwork appears with a fairly heavy dot pattern over it, as a reminder that it doesn't belong to the page and that you therefore cannot edit it on the page. If you want to change it, you must edit it on the template.

Snapping to it with grids and guides

Another common feature of the master template is a set of guides, or *guidelines*. When we first heard the term "snap-to guides," it brought to mind a party of weary hikers being told that they had another five miles to go before lunch. Now, of course, we realize that it's jargon from the computer-aided design fraternity. If you have "snap-to guides" enabled and drag a page element (such as an image) within "snap range" of a guideline (5 pixels, by default) and drop it, the element automatically aligns its edge exactly to the guide.

You can create guidelines in a couple of ways. One is to click either of the rulers — the horizontal ruler to create a vertical guide, or the vertical ruler to create a horizontal guide. You can then adjust ruler positions by hovering the mouse pointer over them and dragging when the mouse cursor looks as though it wants to drag something.

In this case, you use the other way, which is to select the navigation bar image, right-click, and choose Make Guides for Current Selection⇨Left followed by Make Guides for Current Selection⇨Top. The left guide creates a margin position for every page in the site, and the top guide makes aligning page-by-page additions to the global navigation bar easy. The guidelines appear in solid red on the template and as broken lines on each page that inherits this template, as a reminder that you can't move them without returning to the template. By the way, you can't tell by looking at Figure 4-2, but you can pick any color you want for the guidelines.

While we're on the subject of snapping, you've probably noticed that elements tend to snap to the 10 x 10 pixel dot grid that's all over the layout area. The grid is another form of guide you can snap to if you choose. The dialog boxes shown in Figures 4-3 and 4-4 (you open them by choosing View⇨Ruler⇨ Settings or View⇨Grid⇨Settings) give you more control over the grid and guide functions than you're ever likely to need. You can, for example, inhibit snapping (making the layout area more polite, perhaps?) and change the snap range. Using the little grid window in Figure 4-3, you can have hours of endless fun dragging the grid pattern around (*minutes* of fun, anyway).

The guide and grid settings aren't really a property of any template — they're a global preference you can set and reset at any time.

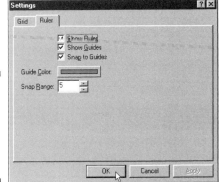

Figure 4-3:
Manage the ruler and guideline options here.

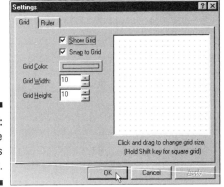

Figure 4-4:
Manage the grid options here.

Setting link styles on the master template

We have to tell you about one other important attribute of a master template, although you can't see it even if it's staring you in the face. Take a look at the Attributes Sheet of the master template — four of the things you can fiddle with are for setting link colors. That's a good idea because if you set them up here, you never have to worry about them again for this site. Link colors are not elements you normally want to vary from page to page in a site, although you can, of course.

We tell you how to set link styles in the section "Setting background and link colors with templates," in Chapter 1, but here's the process again, just to stop you from getting the book all dog-eared trying to find the right page: Click the Locate Assets button in the Asset Center and choose Styles⇨Show All Styles. As you scroll through the styles, you should come across four Drumbeat-supplied styles named LinkColor, VLinkColor, ALinkColor, and HLinkColor. These special global styles apply to all your web sites and set *only* text colors, without specifying font, size, weight, background, and all the other things styles can do.

The following set of steps shows you how to set a link style for only this site. The other three link styles are for visited links, active links, and hover links (Internet Explorer only). They're the same, only different:

1. **In the Asset Center, double-click the LinkColor style. This step opens the Styles dialog box, with the LinkColor style selected.**

2. **Click the New button.**

   You should see the Style Properties three-tab dialog box. The only thing you should mess with here is the color picker.

3. **Select whatever color you want for your links. Select a color from the Windows palette or choose Define Custom Colors and select a color from the Color picker.**

   You can specify the color by using RGB settings in this dialog box, if you want.

4. **Click OK to approve everything.**

5. **In the final dialog box (Save As), give your style a name (AuctionLink, for example) and click OK.**

   If you want to reuse this style in other sites you build, you can make it a global style by clicking the radio button for the option Make This Style Available to All Sites. If you're using it in only this site, leave it alone.

6. **Return to the Attributes Sheet of the master template, yank down the Link Style dropdown list, and scroll the style list to AuctionLink.**

   If you've already made any links on child pages of this template, their style now changes.

If you want to modify the LinkColor style (rather than create a new one), a "Remember to republish" warning box pops up. Take this warning seriously! It's not just some disclaimer that the Drumbeat attorneys stuck in there. Because LinkColor is a global style, a change affects every site you build with Drumbeat.

Toying with Templates within Templates

The title and the navigation bar and its associated guides are all there is to the master template. However, you need at least three additional child templates — for the three main sections of this site (Buyers, Sellers, and How To). Each inherits the components of the master template and superimposes components of its own, which are then inherited by all child pages of the template.

The Action Auction site will have about 30 pages. You could go about constructing it in one of many ways in the Drumbeat Site Manager, including the extreme right-brained approach of not actually constructing it, but rather focusing on the graphics and making pretty pages and then figuring out later that you could have saved a great deal of work by using sensible template management. We describe the opposite approach, which is to set up the template structure and site tree in as much detail as you feel comfortable with, without worrying much about content. Drumbeat does a good job of making sure that anything you can do, you can also undo.

As we mention in Chapter 1, the Template structure and the Site structure are totally different views of the site.

Template view

Whenever you click the Template tab in the Site Management Center (assuming that the tree is expanded), you see a family tree of your site's pages, arranged purely to show how each page inherits content elements from the templates. It's a "designer's-eye view." Sometimes, it looks similar to the logical "users'-eye view" of the site in the Site Manager. In theory, however — and sometimes in practice — the two views may be totally different.

In this section, we show you how to create the three main templates as children of the master template. Figure 4-5 shows the master template being selected by right-clicking and choosing Insert⇨Template. (The alternative is to use the same option from the main menu or its keyboard equivalent, Alt+I, T).

Figure 4-5:
Creating
and naming
subtem-
plates.

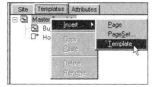

Select each child template in turn and rename it by using the F2 key shortcut
(or right-click and choose Rename from the pop-up menu). The primary template structure is done in a jiffy, as shown in Figure 4-6.

Figure 4-6:
The tem-
plate
structure's
all done (for
now).

Site view

Where's that cocktail napkin we doodled last night as we were planning this
enterprise over a beer in the Cat & Fiddle? It's time to turn a cocktail napkin into
a structure in the Drumbeat Site Manager — and this part's really, really, easy.

Click the Site tab in the Site Manager, and then repeatedly select a page and
click the Insert Page button. Select each new page and rename it by pressing
F2, and then move on to the next page on the list. Figure 4-7 shows the process
halfway done. As long as the Insert Page button is set to insert single pages,
you may find that using your Insert key is even quicker for creating pages subordinate to the page that's selected.

Figure 4-7:
Create the
site tree by
clicking the
Insert Page
icon and
pressing F2
to rename.

Back to the Template tree

On the Templates tab, you see that all the pages have been assigned to the master template and that nothing seems to belong to the other three. Drumbeat doesn't know, of course, what belongs to what until you tell it. It's just a matter of dragging pages to the appropriate templates, and you're soon done, as shown in Figure 4-8. Note that, in this view, pages are stacked under their templates in alphabetical order.

Figure 4-8:
These templates now have pages assigned to them.

You could even use the trick with the Insert key to create your site in Templates view. Simply select a template and press Insert, Insert, Insert. Just don't forget that the Insert Page button (in the Site Manager) has to be set for single pages. In this mode, however, you cannot make pages children of other pages. For that task, you have to be in the Site Manager.

Layout with Inheritance

The master plan of the imaginary auction site is that a database of auction items is lurking in the background. It's a cookie site, so after a visitor has interacted with it in some way, it knows their identity and history.

The Buyers section of the site offers two ways to find stuff: Browse and Search. There are 15 browse categories (for example, antiques, autos, and books). From each category listing, buyers can follow a hyperlink to a page for entering a bid. A Going, Going, GONE page features an item whose auction period is closing right now.

The Sellers area has a form for filling in details of what you have to sell, a preview of what the listing will look like, and a Thank You page that appears when you confirm (maybe it says "That'll cost you $20" too). Also, making full use of the cookie system, there's a page where sellers can check in to get info about the status of their ongoing auctions.

The How To area is three pages of general info. If Figure 4-8 seems incomprehensible, the info area should help.

Time for some subtemplates

The following paragraph tells you how we would proceed with the design of this site if we were as well-organized as we tell other people to be.

First, we would design all three subtemplates. Figure 4-9 shows the Buyers' design, with artwork superimposed on the master template and the Browse and Search features added from the Buyers template. The other art has been placed on the page itself.

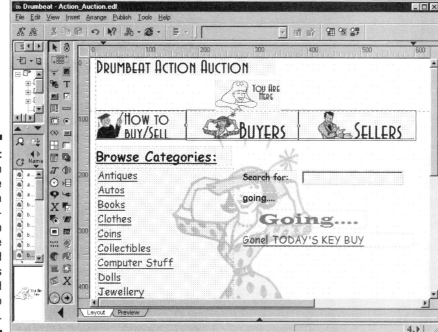

Figure 4-9: The main page of the buyers' area shows components on the page itself and others inherited from two templates.

Subtracting inheritance

Suppose that you get all the way to your final page design and decide (or, more likely, your client decides) that you don't like the inherited elements? You have several options:

- ✔ On the Templates tab, drag the page to the master template (to remove all inherited design except what's on the master template).
- ✔ Create a different subtemplate and redesign it, and then drag the page to it.
- ✔ Create a different template as a child of the original subtemplate, and *subtract* some inherited elements.

That last option may need a bit more explanation. Suppose that you get to the page in the Action Auction site where your users enter a bid, and it looks too cluttered. You decide that the reason is that the inherited elements from the buyers template, when they're added to elements on the master template, are simply too much. On the Templates tab, just right-click the buyers template, and choose Insert⇨Template from the pop-up menus.

We realize that we said earlier in this chapter that child templates inherit everything from their parent templates, but we lied. On the Templates tab, select the child template you need to change, and then switch to the Attributes tab and click the little button that looks like a crop circle (you can see it in the margin). The dialog box shown in Figure 4-10 is displayed and tells you which attributes of the parent template you have the option of "disinheriting." If you're an HTML buff, you should recognize this list as the attributes of the <BODY> tag.

Figure 4-10:
Use this
dialog box
to subtract
certain
inherited
elements
from a tem-
plate.

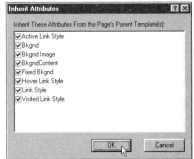

After you uncheck Bkgnd and Bkgnd Image, you're free to reassign something less cluttered for the detail pages.

Because of some quirk in Drumbeat, you can override an inherited background image on any page by simply Shift+dragging a new image to the layout area. Logically, this shouldn't happen, but it does. What can we tell ya?

The only remaining task is to assign the bid page to its special template. It's simplicity itself: Still on the Templates tab, simply drag the page to its template. Figure 4-11 shows a part of the new tree; we placed the GoingGoingGONE page under that template, too, so that only the Buyers Front Page and the 15 auction category pages are now children of the Buyers template.

Figure 4-11:
Two pages
have
switched
parents.

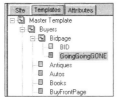

Template Tricks and Tips

Guidelines placed on templates (see the section "Snapping to it with grids and guides," earlier in this chapter) are a terrifically good way to get images placed on pages with pixel-precision. If you have an image that changes in content but not in position as your users click through your site, use guidelines to guarantee that the image doesn't "jink" (show a noticeable shift) as the page changes.

If the guidelines are cluttering up your layout area, delete them after they've done their job. Hover the mouse pointer over any part of the guideline so that the pointer changes to "move guide" shape. Hold the left mouse button down (the guideline's appearance changes) and press the Delete key. Alternatively, right-click and choose Remove This Guide from the pop-up menu. To clear all guides, right-click any vacant spot in the layout area and choose Remove All Guides from the pop-up menu. To temporarily turn off guideline display, use the menu option View⇨Ruler⇨Settings and uncheck the Show Guides option.

You can also position elements in the layout area by using the upper-left coordinates in pixels. Just insert the coordinates on the element's attributes sheet. The measurements are in pixels, which specify the distance from the upper-left corner of the layout area to the upper-left corner of the element.

Drumbeat provides an option to turn a page into an instant template: Go to the Templates tab, right-click the page, and choose Create Template from Page. The template appears immediately above the page, and the page itself is still there, shown as a child of the new template. You probably will have to delete some elements from either the new template or the page. Use this feature after that midnight decision to have a whole series of pages using the same design as one you've already spent hours working on.

Chapter 5

Using Styles

. . . .

. . . .

*W*eb style can mean a number of things: flashy, dynamic effects; killer sounds; zooming VRML. All these things have made the Web into a veritable playground for daring digital designers. If you're looking for that type of stuff here, though, 'fraid you have the wrong idea. What we talk about in this chapter are the styles that apply principally to text on your Web pages and also to many other elements. The Drumbeat Style Builder is a whole new sandbox you can play in to create a custom look for your Web sites.

Call In the Style Police!

HTML was originally designed to be merely a way to share documents across the Internet, not as a medium for mass marketing. Besides, the documents people wanted to share in the late 1980s and early 1990s were boring scientific tomes, and those folks didn't give a whit what the documents looked like, as long as they were readable and could be transferred easily and quickly from one system to another.

Gone are the days of substance over style. And we don't see many people weeping about it, either. Style now rules on the Web. If you don't got style, you don't got nuttin', and nobody will come take a gander at your site.

The world of Web style got so cluttered so quickly with different approaches to adding style to HTML that somebody finally had to call in the style police, and the approach they came up with for controlling the riots was Cascading Style Sheets (CSS).

CSS has quickly emerged as the standard to which the Web of the future aspires. The basis for all the text styles and positioning on pages in Drumbeat, if you choose the Any 4.0 option for your page (which includes Netscape Communicator and Internet Explorer 4.0 and higher), is CSS styles. Whenever you design pages for Navigator 3 or generic browsers, the styles are interpreted to the nearest equivalent, and Drumbeat does its best to make them look the way you want with conventional HTML (until everybody gets rid of those unstylish, outmoded browsers).

Every text element and quite a few other elements, such as images and image buttons, accept styles. Although an element doesn't always use the full range of style properties, it uses the style properties that apply to it:

- **Text element:** Shows any font style, size, color, background, border, or box properties applied to it
- **Image:** Shows border colors and styles, if those elements are chosen
- **Form button:** Shows font colors, background colors, and borders

Browsing styles

Drumbeat comes preloaded with a number of predefined styles. The purpose of these prefab styles is just to give you the idea and get you started. You can use these styles, change them however you want, or decide that you hate them so much that you delete them all and start over with your own styles. We don't recommend that last option — at least until you get your own collection together — for reasons we explain in the Warning paragraph at the end of this section.

The best way to see what you have is to browse the available styles in the Asset Center:

1. **Click the Locate Assets button and choose Styles⇨Show All Styles.**

2. **Click any style on the list to see a preview of it in the asset viewer. Then press the arrow keys to scroll up or down through the styles, as shown in Figure 5-1.**

From the Asset Center, you can

- Drag a style directly to a text element (or several at a time).
- Double-click a style to edit it in the Style Builder.

You can get to the Style Builder in a couple of other ways, too.

 To open the Style Builder, click the Add Assets button and choose Styles *or* choose Tools⇨Styles.

Figure 5-1:
Preview
styles in the
Asset
Center.

In the Style Builder, all the available styles are listed, as shown in Figure 5-2. You can preview a style by clicking it on the list. Press the arrow keys to scroll through the list and create your own font-astic fashion show.

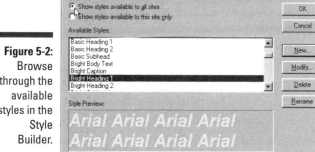

Figure 5-2:
Browse
through the
available
styles in the
Style
Builder.

All the default styles you see when you first start Drumbeat are *global* styles, which means that they're available in all the sites you build. If you don't like them or don't need them or they get in your way, you can delete them. *Beware if you do!* If you've used a style in another site, the style is gone forever, and any elements to which you've assigned the style are assigned the style None. That means zip. Nada. It's plain-Jane browser defaults for you, buddy.

Creating new styles

Any Web designer worth her vintage programmer's T-shirt knows the next obvious step after seeing the styles available to you in Drumbeat by default: You want to create your own styles. No copycat fashion victims here. You can create a whole suite of styles to easily display your own Web fashion sense. To create a new style:

1. **Open the Style Builder. (Click the Add Assets button and select Styles or choose Tools⇨Styles).**

2a. **Click New to create a new style or click Edit to change an existing style.**

2b. **Here's a better method: Whenever you're creating a new style, first select a style similar to what you want, and then click New.**

    If you don't select a style first, the Normal style is the default selection on which your new style will be based.

 If you want to edit an existing style (rather than create a new one), you can get straight to the job by double-clicking a style in the Asset Center (first, click the Locate Assets button and then choose Show All Styles). Or select any element that has a style applied and click the ellipsis button next to the Style box on the Attributes Sheet.

The Style Properties dialog box has three tabs, showing the three categories of style properties: Text, Background, and Box. The most common properties for text styles are on the Text tab, as shown in Figure 5-3, although you can get fancy with some of the properties on the Background and Box tabs.

To customize a style:

1. **Select a font from the font dropdown list.**

    The dropdown list shows all the fonts installed on your computer. (Just because it's available to you doesn't mean that it's available to your site visitors, so it's wise to be conservative in your choice.)

2. **Select a font size in points (10 or 12 is average text size, depending on the font).**

3. **If you want the text to be bold, select 700 from the Weight dropdown list.**

    (Anything over 600 has about the same effect on most fonts). If you *just happen* to have a font with finer weight distinctions, you can select anything from 100 (lightest) to 900 (heaviest).

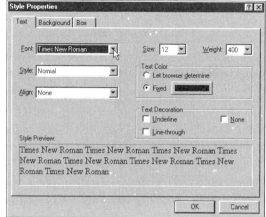

Figure 5-3:
The main
text style
properties
are shown
here.

4. **Select a color for the font by clicking the color bar and selecting a color from the Windows color palette.**

   You can expand the palette to select a custom color or designate a color by entering RGB values (read more about this subject in the section "Applying link styles," later in this chapter). If you want to leave color choices up to the browser (or user preferences specified in the browsers), you can click the Let Browser Determine option.

5. **If you want text decoration, such as underlining or line-through, you can click a box (or two) in the Text Decoration area.**

   Because the default is None, you don't have to select it. Selecting None for a link style, however, has the effect of turning off underlining for links — something many designers hanker after.

6. **When you've selected all the style properties you want, click OK. In the Save As dialog box, give your style a name, as shown in Figure 5-4.**

   Make the style global if you want your style to have a life outside this site. Just click the Make Style Available Throughout All Sites option. Otherwise, the style is local and has a life in only this site.

7. **Click OK.**

After you save a style as *local,* you have no way to go back and change it to *global* instead. You have to either remove the style (select it and click Delete) and start over or create a new style based on the selected style and save it under a new name — and, this time, try to remember to click that button in the save dialog box!

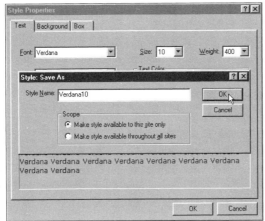

Figure 5-4:
Name and
save a style
as either
local or
global.

When you're done creating a new style, it should appear on the style list when you return to the Style Builder. You can create another style or get back to work by clicking OK again.

All the style properties available in the Style Builder are explained in Table 5-1. Examples of background and box properties are shown later in this chapter, in the section "Using background and box properties."

Table 5-1	Style Properties in the Style Builder
Style Property	*Description*
Font	The list of fonts you see on the Font dropdown list are the ones installed on your machine. You can use any font on your computer. Remember, however, that in order for visitors to your Web site to be able to see the font, it must also be on their computers.
Font size	Font sizes are specified in point size. The browser is responsible for turning that measurement into screen equivalents. On pages targeting generic and Navigator Version 3 browsers, point sizes are translated into relative font sizes instead.
Font styles	Font styles cover Normal, Italic or Oblique. *Oblique* is just another term for *italics* in sans serif fonts. Serif fonts, such as Times New Roman, have curlicues on the ends of their letters; sans serif fonts, such as the Web-popular Arial font, don't.
Font weight	The normal font weight is 400; **boldface** is 700. Some fonts have varying weights, from light to extra bold, which is why you can designate anything between 100 and 900. You generally don't use anything other than normal (400) and bold (700), however.

Style Property	Description
Text color	The color for the font display is also known as the *foreground* color in some applications. You can select a color from the default Windows colors palette or a custom color from the color spectrum. On the Custom Colors palette, you can designate a color by RGB value.
Text decoration	Your decoration options are Underline, Line-through (the strikethrough text popular with lawyers) or None. Text-decoration choices are respected only by browser versions 4.0 and later. (However, you can make text underlined by using the Text Formatting toolbar, a method that works for all browsers.)
Align	Align the text in a text block by choosing the Left (the default), Center, Right or None options from the dropdown list. If you leave the Align option set to None, the default is Left, unless another style with an align attribute is combined with this one.
Background	A background color or image can also be part of a style. A background color works only in Version 4.0 browsers and later (Netscape or Internet Explorer). A background image works (at the time this chapter was written) only in Internet Explorer 4 and later.
Box properties	Box properties are applied to the box (or container) for the element. They include Margin and Border options, which are designated in pixel widths, Box Color (or border color), and border Style. Border styles and color apply to only 4.0 browsers and later. If you select a box color, you must also select a border width and a style other than None in order for the style to take effect. Because the Netscape and Microsoft browsers display background colors and images differently, be careful how you use box properties, and don't forget your cross-browser tests!

Using Text Styles

The most obvious use for styles is in creating the styles you want for text on a page. You want header fonts and plain-text fonts and link colors and maybe some other special fonts in different sizes, shapes, and colors.

A single section of text element may have more than one style applied to it in different ways. You can, in fact, assign styles in one of three different ways (in order of precedence):

✔ **Link:** Apply link styles to a page or template from the Attributes Sheet. Link styles always overrule other styles applied to an element.

✔ **Inline:** Apply inline styles from the Text Formatting toolbar. You cannot use named styles with inline editing. In addition, inline styles are limited to the options on the toolbar, which are not as extensive as those in the Style dialog box. Inline styles always overrule container-level styles, but are superseded by link styles when the text is a link.

✔ **Container-level:** Apply container-level styles to the "container" or text element. A container style applies to all the text within that container. Inline styles can overrule individual properties of the container style.

You can apply the styles listed in the Asset Center and the Style Builder at only the container level — that is, you assign them to the whole text element. If you want a section of text within that text element to be formatted differently, you can do it in text editing mode by using the Text Formatting toolbar.

You can apply a style to one text element at a time or to a whole group of text elements at a time. To apply a style to a group of text elements:

1. **Marquee-select all the text elements in the layout area to which you want to apply a style.**

2. **Drag a style from the Asset Center to one of the boxes *or* click the Attributes tab and select a style from the Style dropdown list.**

Using inline styles

Inline styles are those you apply by using the Text Formatting toolbar. You may be inclined at first to select all the text within a text element and apply font types and sizes with the Text Formatting toolbar. If this were the only way you could apply styles, however, that task would quickly get tedious. You can use a far more efficient method by applying a style to a text element with the Style selector on the Attributes Sheet.

Inline styles are useful for applying formatting to words, sentences, or sections of text within a text element. For example, you can apply a named style that's defined as 10-pt. Arial black to a text element. Then you can select a word or a sentence within the text element and make it italic or bold by clicking the Italic or Bold button on the Text Formatting toolbar. Or, you may want to select a text string that's a line of code and apply a monospaced font, such as Courier, to set it off as code.

Figure 5-5 shows text styles applied in four different ways in one text box.

Inline style (italics) ⎯⎤   ⎡⎯ Container style (10 pt. Arial)

Link style (blue, underlined) ⎯⎤   Inline style (Courier)

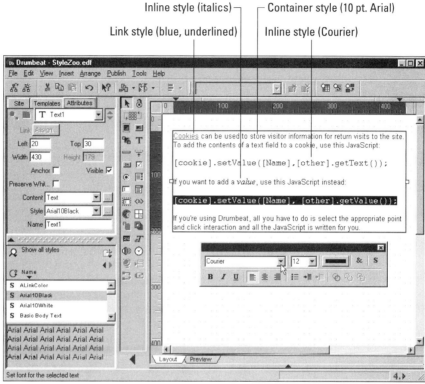

Figure 5-5:
This text
block
includes a
container
style, two
inline styles,
and a link
style. Can't
ask for
much more
than that.

Although it's fairly obvious how to apply an inline style, it's not so readily apparent how to *remove* an inline style after you've applied it. To remove an inline style:

1. **Select the text you want to "unformat."**

2. **Click the Style (S) button on the Text Formatting toolbar, as shown in Figure 5-6.**

Figure 5-6:
Removiing
an inline
style.

You can remove all inline styles applied to a text block by selecting the entire block of text inside the text box (pressing Ctrl+A does the job) and then clicking the Style button. Don't select any link text, however, because you can't remove link styles this way. The only way to remove a link style is to unlink the text first (select the link text and click the Undo Link button on the Text Formatting toolbar).

If you copy and paste text from a .rtf or a Word .doc file into a text element in Drumbeat, you can use the Style button to remove any styles that come trailing along with it.

Applying link styles

Link styles are part of the properties of a page, just as they are in HTML. If you create your own HTML code, you're familiar with how to set link colors with LINK, VLINK, and ALINK attributes in the BODY tag of the page.

In Drumbeat, you use styles for links instead. Using styles for links means that you can also assign other properties than just color. You can make all your links the same font (or not) and decide whether you want them underlined. Link styles can be applied to only a template or to a page. If you apply a link style to the master template, the style applies to the whole site (unless you later disinherit these properties on a subsequent template or page). If you apply a link style to any template, the style is inherited by all pages under that template — again, unless you disinherit these properties for a page.

Whenever you open a new site, the master template, by default, controls all link styles and those styles are set to None. This setting means that because the pages you create have no link color or style specified on the page, the page merely uses the browser defaults when the pages are viewed. Users, in turn, can control the browser defaults with their preference settings in the browser, although lots of users aren't even aware that they can change these settings themselves. To avoid having your pages viewed with somebody else's awful sense of color or the plain colors the browser defaults to, you have to choose link styles.

To apply a link style to be used throughout a site:

1. **Select the master template on the Templates tab and then click the Attributes tab.**

2. **Click the dropdown arrow next to the Link Style edit box and scroll to find and select a style, as shown in Figure 5-7.**

Figure 5-7:
Set a link
style on
the master
template.

To apply a link style to a page or a template other than the master template, first select the page or template and then click the Attributes tab. Click the Inherit button in the upper-left corner. Click to remove the check from all the Link Style boxes, as shown in Figure 5-8. Then you can set the link styles on the attributes sheet for that page or template. You can set these four types of link styles:

- **Link Style:** Applies to unvisited links

- **Visited Link Style:** Applies to visited links (links that have already been followed)

- **Active Link Style:** Applies when the link is clicked, creating a momentary "flash" effect

- **Hover Link Style:** Applies when the mouse is over a link, creating a "light up" effect (works only in Internet Explorer 4 or later)

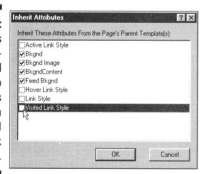

Figure 5-8:
This page is
being disin-
herited. It'll
have to
make its
own way in
the world
with link
styles.

If you have link text embedded in text blocks with different fonts and sizes, you will most likely want the links to have the same font as the surrounding text and differ only in their color, You don't want the link style to be controlling the font choice or size. That's where style inheritance comes in.

The smart way to designate link styles is to use a style that specifies only a color and leaves the font choices blank. Then the font face and size can be inherited from another style applied to the element or text string.

To make things easy, Drumbeat has supplied four default link styles that set only the color property:

- **LinkColor:** Blue
- **VLinkColor:** Red
- **ALinkColor:** Green
- **HLinkColor:** Orange

When you check out these styles in the Style Builder, you see only two properties defined. The principal one is color. You may easily overlook that the second style property, Text Decoration, is set to None. It means that links are not underlined (in 4.0 browsers and later). Drumbeat has followed recent Web convention in using this setting. The rest of the options are blank, as shown in Figure 5-9.

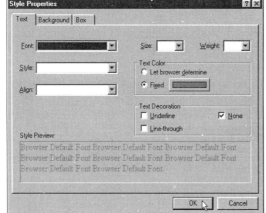

Figure 5-9:
This poor link style contains only a color definition.

The default styles LinkColor, VLinkColor, ALinkColor, and HLinkColor, like all the initial styles in Drumbeat, are *global* styles, which means that they're the same for all sites on which you use them. So, rather than change these default colors, create a new style based on the selected link style and save it under a new name. To create a new link style for only link colors:

1. **In the Style dialog box, select any of the default link styles (ALinkColor, for example, because it's at the top of the alphabetical order) and click New.**

2. **In the Style Properties dialog box, click the color bar.**

3. **Select a color swatch from the Windows color palette and click OK.**

   If you don't see a color you like, you can click Define Custom Colors and select a color from the color spectrum. If you know the RGB values of the color you want, you can enter them in the Red, Green, and Blue boxes, as shown in Figure 5-10.

   If you want to use this color again on your site, you may want to add it to your list of custom colors. Click one of the blank color boxes first, and then click Add to Custom Colors.

4. **Click OK to apply the color.**

5. **If you like your links underlined, uncheck the None option in the Text Decoration area. If you prefer your links plain, leave the None box checked.**

6. **Click OK when you're ready to save your style. In the Save As dialog box, enter a name for your new style. Don't forget to decide whether you want to save the style as local or global before clicking OK.**

Figure 5-10:
Select the
RGB values
for a color
in the
expanded
Color dialog
box. You
have an
endless
number of
choices.

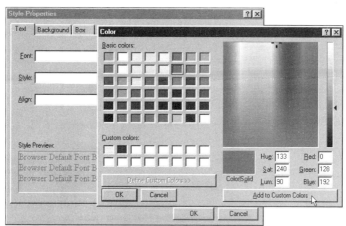

Using background and box properties

You probably won't use the Background and Box tabs in the Style Builder much. They do come in handy occasionally, though. Their most common uses are probably for putting a border around an image and for creating a background color for a text block.

To put a border on an image, you can simply designate a border width on the Attributes Sheet for the image. The default is 0; change it to a number for pixel width. The default color for the border is black if the image isn't linked. If it is linked, the image border takes the link color.

You can add a colored border of your own choice if you apply a style with border properties defined. (This style even overrules the link colors, which would otherwise be used for the border on a linked image.) To create a border style:

1. **In the Style dialog box, click New to create a new style, and then click the Box tab.**

2. **Click the Box Color, Fixed option, and then click the color bar and select a color.**

3. **On the Box tab again, select a Style for the border.**

   Solid is the only choice that works across browsers.

4. **In the Border box, enter a number for pixel width.**

5. **Save the style and apply it to an image by selecting the style from the Style dropdown list on its Attribute Sheet.**

Figure 5-11 shows a style named Border being applied to an image of a diver.

Figure 5-11:
The diver gets a deep blue border with a style that has border properties applied to the image.

You can combine the background and box properties for styles to put a background color on a text block.

To define a text style with a color background:

1. **In the Style dialog box, click New to create a new style.**

2. **On the Text tab, select your font styles.**

3. **On the Background tab, select Fixed for the Background Color option. Then click the color bar and select a color.**

4. **On the Box tab, define the properties for the box:**

   - In the Box Color area, select Fixed and select the same color as you chose for the background color. This step makes the whole box, not just the text background, fill with the color and works better in different browsers.

   - Enter a number in pixels for the margin width, to offset the text from the inside edge of the border, and a number for the border width.

   - For Style, select Solid. Figure 5-12 shows an example.

5. **Save the style. Then apply it to a block of text to see its effect.**

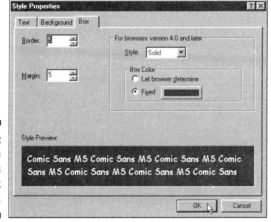

Figure 5-12:
Select style
properties
on the Box
tab.

Because this kind of style looks slightly different in Netscape and Internet Explorer, make sure that you check it in both and tweak as necessary.

If the border width is 0, the Fixed option in the Box Color area is ignored and you don't get a border. Likewise, if the Style of the border is set to None, you don't get a border, even if you've set a width and chosen a color for it.

Another useful thing you can do with the Background properties for styles is create a style to use for standard form buttons. If you select a background color for a style on the Background tab, the form button takes that color. The button label takes the font style you chose on the Text tab. (This technique is illustrated in Chapter 13, in the section about DataForms in disguise.)

We do something slightly more fun here, though, and create a button with a background image that can be found on any Windows system:

1. **In the Style dialog box, click New to create a new style.**

2. **On the Text tab, select a text style.**

   We chose Arial, 10 pt, 700 weight.

3. **On the Background tab, click Browse and navigate to the C:\Windows directory. Find the group of .bmp files in that directory and select one.**

   We chose Pinstripe.bmp. The pinstripe buttons are shown in Figure 5-13.

4. **Save the style and call it something like** ButtonBkgnd.

5. **Drag the Form Button element from the SmartElements toolbar to the page. On the attributes sheet for the button, assign the style by using the Style dropdown list.**

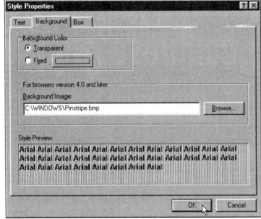

Figure 5-13:
Using a Windows system .bmp file to make a pinstripe button background. Snazzy, huh?

Voilà! You have a custom form button that works like an ordinary form button and looks like a designer's showcase, as shown in Figure 5-14. (This trick is a little gamey; because the button may look different on different browsers, be careful to check it out.)

Positioning with Styles

The position of an element in Layout is also a property that gets written to the style sheet Drumbeat generates for you if you target Version 4.0 browsers or higher. Every element you place in the layout area in Drumbeat has positioning properties, as they're known in CSS (Cascading Style Sheet) lingo.

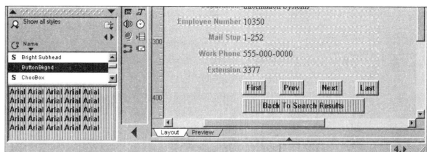

Figure 5-14: Custom-tailored form buttons with a background file.

The positioning properties are shown on the attributes sheet as the Top and Left properties. Width and Height properties for some elements may also be written to the style sheet.

CSS positioning is used in all pages targeting 4.0 browsers and later. For pages targeting generic browsers and Navigator 3.0, Drumbeat generates HTML tables to position elements as accurately as possible according to their placement in the layout area.

You generally don't have to worry about positioning because it's all done for you in WYSIWYG fashion in the layout area. You should be aware, however, that Drumbeat uses *absolute positioning.* The kind of positioning you may be used to doing with the CENTER tag in HTML, therefore, does not work.

The table conundrum

Drumbeat does not let you get at the code level for HTML tables (alas) and you cannot construct your own HTML tables in Drumbeat (alack). Web authors who are used to designing their own tables for positioning have to rethink their approach. After you get used to the situation, however, you discover that most things you're accustomed to doing with tables can be done with styles just as well, with the added benefit of the extra features that styles give you.

For the times you really need to use a table, however, here are some different ways you can use tables in Drumbeat:

✔ If you want just a simple table, you can put the contents in a manual Content Table and then use an AutoTable to display the contents. AutoTables don't let you control specific cell properties, however, and are probably not what you want if you're looking for design control. (See the section about AutoTables in Chapter 6 to find out how to use one.)

✔ Select Navigator 3.0 support for your site or make a Navigator 3.0 browser-specific page. (See Chapter 15 to find out all about SmartPages.) Then position elements in the layout area as you normally do. The output is an HTML table. (Use the `CENTER` tag in the Meta Tag information of the page if you want to center the table.)

✔ Bring into your Drumbeat site as an external page a page you've designed with tables the way you want them. (See the section in Chapter 2 about using external pages to keep your code intact.) Drumbeat doesn't alter the code and you cannot edit it in Drumbeat, although Drumbeat will publish it for you if you want.

✔ Use the HTML Passthrough element on the page. (It's on the SmartElements toolbar. See the section in Chapter 3 about standard SmartElements for a little more info about this SmartElement.) Set its content to an HTML file in which you've created your table code.

The Lazy Designer's Guide to Using Styles

Got a bunch of similar sites you need to set up or a bunch of connected sites that all use the same basic setup? Here's a plan for you:

1. **Set up a new site and call it** SiteTemplate **or something similar.**

2. **Define the link styles for the site. Then define the styles for the text and headings you want to use. Save them as local styles for the site.**

   In the Style dialog box, you can click the Show Styles Available to This Site Only filter option to reveal all the custom styles set up for the site.

3. **Add to the site the media folders you want to use.**

4. **Set up templates that contain guides for text and image placement.**

5. **Choose File⇨Snapshot (or press Ctrl+S). Navigate to the Drumbeat program files directory and select the Starting Points folder (C:\Program Files\Drumbeat 2000\Starting Points, by default). Save the file in this folder with your template name.**

The next time you want to start a site with all these features in it, just select Based on Starting Point in the New Site dialog box and select your site template. Everything will be in place, waiting for your design input. The file just saved is now available by name on the Starting Points dropdown list.

If you choose a Starting Point in the New Site dialog box, you're making a copy of the Starting Point for your new site. You are *not* changing the original Starting Point, which remains intact for future multiple use.

Chapter 6

Making Quick Work of Content Tables

*U*nlike the attic in most houses we've ever lived in, Drumbeat has an attic that's *not* cluttered with junk, like model aircraft that never flew, heirlooms we all secretly hate, old magazines ("Wow! The Nixon-resignation special issue! Think that's worth something at e-Bay?") and an applebox full of our 5th grade assignments we seem to remember being proud of at the time. The Drumbeat attic has *useful* stuff in it.

In fact, it's a convertible space — housing either the Interactions Center, the Script Center, or the Content Center. This chapter is about the goodies you can put in the Content Center and how you can put them to work in making interesting Web pages.

Another Way to Organize Assets

Think of a Content Table as just a way of organizing site assets that you know (or suspect or hope) you will need — very likely more than once. Lists of assets in the Asset Center can get fairly long and can display only one type of asset at a time. Content tables can hold a mixture of text and these media types:

✔ Animations

✔ Audios

✔ Documents

✔ Executables

✔ HTML files

✔ Images

✔ Metafiles

✔ Videos

If you set up the Content Table cells correctly, they can contain more than one element — for example, you can stick a double image for a rollover effect up there and forever after treat it as though it were just one image.

Another way Content Tables can make your life sweeter is by enabling you to use placeholders for content that hasn't yet been finalized. If your client hasn't decided on a logo or a formatted mission statement or the icon designer has gone to Atlantic City, leaving you without a Back button, just put in something representative until they catch up with you.

Objects you place in a Content Table don't disappear from the Asset Center (if that's where they came from) — they're still available both ways.

Any object that gets on the page from a Content Table knows that that's how it got there. If you check its attributes on the Attributes Sheet, its content is listed as the content of Row X, Column Y of Content Table A, not as the file at C:\Program Files\Drumbeat2000\Mysites\TheMadHatter\Images\dormouse.gif.

Technically, Drumbeat calls it *static content*.

"So what?" *Here's* what. Suppose that you built a nice nonprofit site a year ago and a condition of the contract was that you had to sprinkle the following acknowledgment text in about a hundred places:

```
This foundation is supported by a generous endowment from
            Maude Blenkinsop in memory of the late Col.
            Erasmus Blenkinsop.
```

Brrrringgg!!!! There's the phone, with your client on the line. Uh-oh — Maude had a hissy-fit and the endowment contract is in shreds on the floor of her Pasadena mansion. Fortunately, they've found another vict — er, generous donor. Could you change all the Blenkinsops to McCrearys immediately?

If it came from a Content Table — sure, you make one change.

If not — you're up all night.

Creating a New Content Table

Figure 6-1 is a reminder of the button you click to display the Content Center. If the attic isn't open at the time, it opens automatically. Figure 6-2 shows the toolbar you get to play with now, with the Add Row/Column button expanded to show that you get two buttons for the price of one.

Figure 6-1:
Click to open
the Content
Center.

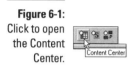

Edit ⌐ Delete

Drop-down list of Content Tables ⌐ New

Figure 6-2:
The Content
Center
toolbar.

Until you've created a Content Table, you obviously don't have the option of adding a row or column — the button is grayed out.

Decisions, decisions

Click that New Content Table button and you're one more click away from creating a fresh Content Table. A *minimum* of one more click. Like all good modern computer software, Drumbeat gives you lots of flexibility to create whatever makes you happy, although that entails a fair number of decisions. The good news is that you can tiptoe into the Content Table business rather than plan everything perfectly right away.

What you must decide right away

Figure 6-3 shows the dialog box that pops up to prompt you to make up your mind about what you want. It's trying to tell you to christen it by providing a name. Not a bad idea — but you can postpone that decision if you want. The one thing you absolutely *must* decide now is what type of Content Table you need.

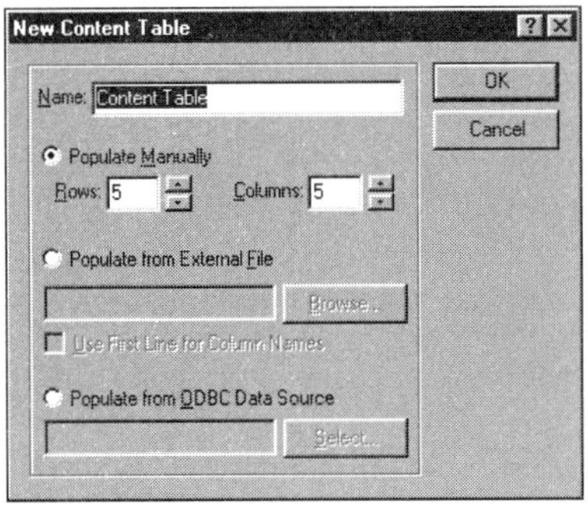

Figure 6-3:
Create a
new Content
Table here.

Table 6-1 is a content table that explains Content Table types (is this a meta-table?)

Table 6-1	Content Table Types and What They Mean
Type	**Implication for You**
Manual	Completely free-form. Stuff anything in you want, and edit everything later.
External	Initially gets its content from a text file you already have available, in Comma-Separated Values (CSV) format. You can mess around with it later, however, even adding or deleting rows and columns. After a CSV Content Table is imported, it behaves no differently from a manual table.
ODBC	Gets its content from a proper database, imported via the Drumbeat Query Manager. The query dictates the content, and the only things you can edit later are the names of rows and columns and the name of the Content Table.
CSV updateable	A hybrid of the preceding two types. The source of this type is a CSV file, although it arrives via an ODBC link and therefore can be updated. Manual editing is restricted just as for the ODBC type. Details of this hybrid are in Chapter 9, in the section about the updateable CSV-derived pageset.

What you can put off until later

Assume that you're dealing with a manually populated Content Table for now — it's the default type, and we get to the other types later in this chapter.

The other two properties that the dialog box shows in the preceding section, in Figure 6-3, encourages you to decide are the dimensions of your table. The number of rows and columns, in other words. If you happen to know how much table-space you need, fine — put it in. If not, that's fine, too — you have at least three ways of adjusting these properties later.

What you can do only after you've created your Content Table

Figure 6-4 shows a virgin Content Table, accepting the defaults of 5 rows and 5 columns, populated manually. We've inventively named it `Manually-entered stuff`.

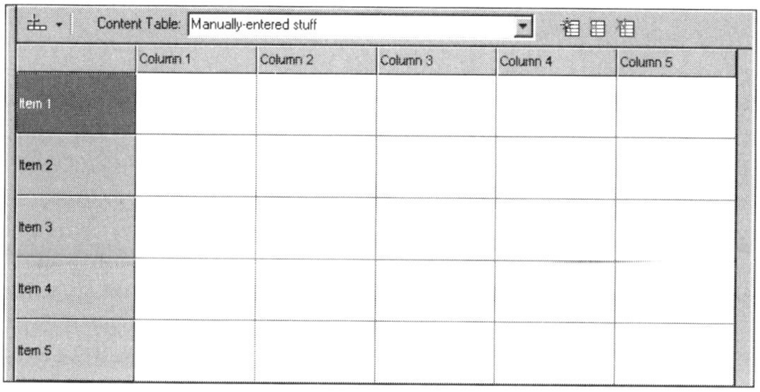

Figure 6-4:
A virgin
Content
Table,
5 rows by
5 columns,
awaits some
content.

	Column 1	Column 2	Column 3	Column 4	Column 5
Content Table: Manually-entered stuff					
Item 1					
Item 2					
Item 3					
Item 4					
Item 5					

Notice how boring the labeling is. Item 1, Item 2, Column 1, Column 2. (Yawn.) You really ought to make those labels a bit more informative, for the columns, at least — because at the same time as you label columns, you need to define what kind of stuff they're expected to contain.

Drumbeat expects you to declare what you're storing in a Content Table on a column-by-column basis. You can mix text, audio, plug-ins, whatever, in the table although each column must be devoted to only one content type.

Labeling columns and designating their content

Either double-click a column header, or right-click and choose Properties from the pop-up menu. You see that the column name is something generic, like Column 1, and its Type option is Unspecified.

Renaming a column is easy. Designating its content type is easy too, really — you just need to be aware of what the choices mean.

If you select Text, you get to choose between formatted and unformatted text, on the third dropdown list. In most circumstances, you need Formatted. (The following Technical Stuff paragraph lists some exceptions.) If you select Media File, you should use the third dropdown list to specify which of the eight media types you have in mind, as shown in Figure 6-5.

Figure 6-5:
Select the
media type
for a
Content
Table
column.

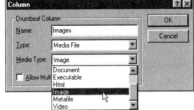

Sometimes Content Table columns need to contain URLs or file paths as "pointers" to other content. You may, for example, want to include an image on a different machine that somebody else is responsible for updating — a weather map, maybe. A good way to do that is to include the path in a Content Table and impose it on an image SmartElement as static content. For that type of text, Unformatted is recommended, although your pointers don't stop working if they're in columns designated for formatted text. The only circumstance in which you *must* use unformatted text is if you want to embed HTML in the text and have it interpreted inside an AutoTable (described in the "AutoTables" section, later in this chapter) that's populated from the Content Table.

Labeling rows

To label a row, just double-click the row label cell. A mini-dialog box pops up, enabling you to choose a name other than the default. The length of your label seems to have no limit, and we've even managed to enter foreign stuff, like *Déjà vu,* using our Alt key. Figure 6-6 shows a Content Table labeled, with Column 1 reserved for the disclaimers our attorneys are sure to tell us to use one day.

Storing Things in Content Tables

If you're reading this chapter from start to finish, you'll notice that we got a little ahead of ourselves in the preceding section. Had the nerve to stick some text in that Content Table before we had explained how. Well, never mind. (If you've just opened the book to this page, just jump right on in and pretend that nothing has happened.) Double-click any cell in a Content Table and one of four things happens, depending what you've already done to the column the cell belongs to.

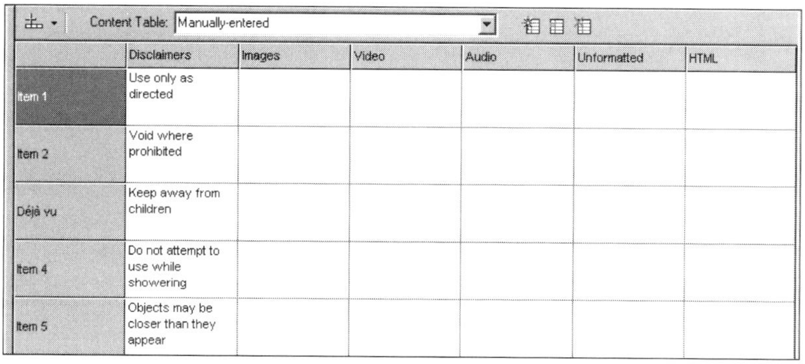

Figure 6-6:
This
manually
populated
Content
Table has
columns
designated
for an
assortment
of media
types.

	Disclaimers	Images	Video	Audio	Unformatted	HTML
Item 1	Use only as directed					
Item 2	Void where prohibited					
Déjà vu	Keep away from children					
Item 4	Do not attempt to use while showering					
Item 5	Objects may be closer than they appear					

Content Table: Manually-entered

If you've designated the column as formatted text: A Text Editor dialog box pops up, hoping that you'll write something in it.

If you've designated the column as unformatted text: A text editor without a formatting toolbar pops up, hoping that you'll write something really texty in it. _If you've designated the column as media:_ A Media Properties window pops up, enabling you to browse to find the path to the media file you need.

If you've forgotten to designate the column as anything: Drumbeat goes into a sulk and trashes your entire Asset Center. Just kidding — it merely forces you to make a decision by looping you back to the same dialog box you may have seen earlier.

Do not check Use First Line for Column Names.

To place media in Content Table cells, it's likely to be easier to drag the files in from the Asset Center. That's particularly true for images, which you get to preview so that you don't get a shock when they pop up in the Content Table. _Be patient!_ If an image file is anything bigger than a tiny bug, it takes a little time for the transfer to happen, and, while it's happening, it looks as though the operation is being prohibited. You can release the mouse button without waiting for the "prohibit" sign to vanish.

Thumbnail versions of images do appear in Content Table cells — see Figure 6-7.

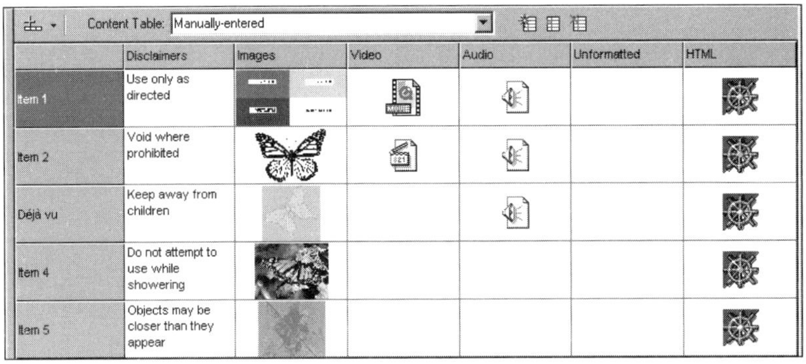

Figure 6-7:
This
manually
populated
Content
Table holds
an assort-
ment of
media types.

Importing Content from a CSV File

The Content Table shown in Figure 6-7 was intended as just a few practice swings before facing the opening pitch. We're definitely not the type of people who put legal disclaimers all over our Web pages.

We have been known to get attacks of organization mania, though — particularly when it comes to using sets of buttons, icons, bars, and such. The kits Drumbeat provides in the folders named Bridge, Goth, Kids, and so on are quite useful — although their labeling is somewhat cryptic. The system obviously has some logic to it (ar2_button_up1.gif, ar2_button_up2.gif, ar2_button_up3.gif) — it just isn't obvious.

Cracking the code

The image-naming code can be cracked quite easily, in fact — and not many Drumbeat users know about it. Each of the media subfolders contains, as well as the media files themselves, a CSV file as a guide to their logical relationships. How can you make use of a CSV file in Drumbeat? By using it to make a Content Table, of course. It's as simple as following these steps, using the Greek Ruins folder, one of the folders of free clip art included in Drumbeat. If you've installed to the default location, you'll find the folder at C:\Program Files\Drumbeat2000\Media\Greek Ruins:

1. **Click the New Content Table button.**

2. **Click the Populate from External File option button and browse to C:\Program Files\Drumbeat 2000\Media\Greek Ruins\Greek Ruins.csv.**

3. **Click OK.**

You now see the 4-column x 15-row Content Table that's partly shown (renamed) in Figure 6-8. All columns are designated as formatted text by default.

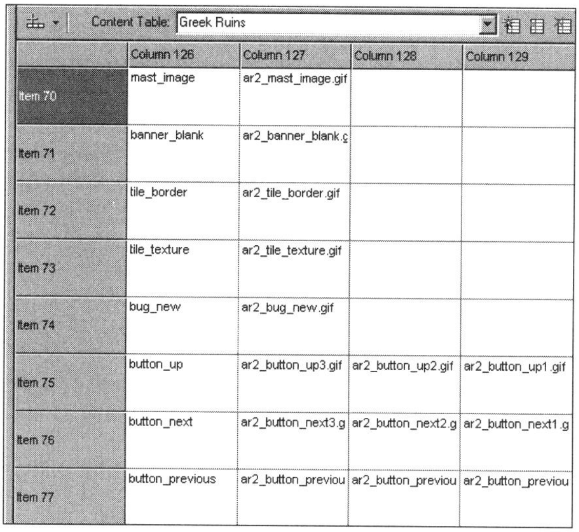

	Column 126	Column 127	Column 128	Column 129
Item 70	mast_image	ar2_mast_image.gif		
Item 71	banner_blank	ar2_banner_blank.g		
Item 72	tile_border	ar2_tile_border.gif		
Item 73	tile_texture	ar2_tile_texture.gif		
Item 74	bug_new	ar2_bug_new.gif		
Item 75	button_up	ar2_button_up3.gif	ar2_button_up2.gif	ar2_button_up1.gif
Item 76	button_next	ar2_button_next3.g	ar2_button_next2.g	ar2_button_next1.g
Item 77	button_previous	ar2_button_previou	ar2_button_previou	ar2_button_previou

Content Table: Greek Ruins

Figure 6-8:
This Content
Table was
populated in
one fell
swoop from
a CSV file.

An incredibly well-organized image archive

The leftmost column is the same for all the Drumbeat image sets, and it's supposed to express the type of image that's in each row: Masthead, Banner, and Tiled background, for example. Although Drumbeat has an option to use the first line of the file for column names, you have no similar option to use the first *value* of each line for *row* names. That's a pity because that would be very convenient here.

However, it's not a great deal of trouble to just name each row appropriately.

To name a Content Table row: Double-click the row label cell and enter the name.

Do that 15 times. Then delete column 1 entirely because it's no longer needed.

To delete a Content Table column: Right-click the column label cell and select Delete from the pop-up menu.

After you've created a Content Table in this simple fashion, it's no longer associated with its CSV file. You're free to edit the content just as though it were a manually created table, and the implication of that is that you have no way to update the table if the underlying data file changes. For an advanced technique that does stay linked to the data, see the section in Chapter 9 about the updateable CSV-derived PageSet.

Image columns

After you delete the image type information, the table is reduced to three columns, representing the fact that each type of image can have as many as three different renderings. Buttons, for example, have a normal and a mouseover rendering. Some even have an "off" rendering — Image Radio Button SmartElements and Image Check Box SmartElements require three image versions in order to work correctly.

Your task now is to insert new columns to take the actual images rather than their names. It would be nice if you could just substitute each name with its image equivalent, but that wouldn't work. Can you guess why?

Correct. Because every column in this table is designated for formatted text, an image doesn't drop into a cell. If you changed the column to accept media, you would lose the text.

To insert a new column: Click the column header to the *right* of the intended insert point. A slim, cross-hatched border should appear around the header cell to indicate that the cell is selected. Either click the Add a New Column button (refer to Figure 6-2) or right-click and choose Insert from the pop-up menu, or choose Insert ⇨ Column from the main menu bar.

Figure 6-9 shows a new column inserted beside the original column 1, designated for images, and used to contain the set of "Normal rendered" images, dragged in from the Asset Center. The column has been renamed `Normal images`.

Now you can delete the original CSV column because you don't (or at least you shouldn't) care any longer what these images are called.

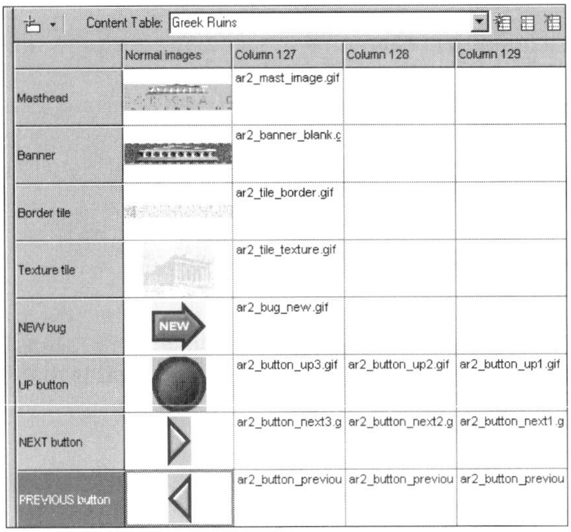

Figure 6-9:
The first column of images is inserted.

A special column for mouseovers

The task of organizing your image archive will be complete if you make one more column. You want the new column to appear on the right end, and because inserted columns arrive to the left of the insertion point, you have a problem. No, you don't.

 Click the Edit Content Table button on the Content Center toolbar. Up pops a dialog box, telling you that this Content Table has 15 rows and 3 columns. Change the 3 to a **4**. Click OK and ignore the warning message.

Double-click the header of the new column, designate it for images, and call it **Mouseover combos**. Make sure to check the Allow Multiple Content option because it's the column where you preset dynamic mouseover versions of the buttons that have two or more renderings, as shown in Figure 6-10.

Figure 6-10:
The mouseover combos column is designated for multiple content.

Check this box to allow more than one image

Follow these steps to create the double-image combo you need for mouseover effects:

1. **Pick the image that you think is right for when the mouse is located over the button.**

2. **Place that image in the appropriate cell by either dragging-and-dropping from the Asset Center or by Ctrl+dragging from the same row of the Content Table.**

3. **Pick the "normal" rendering and drop that *on top of* the image that's already there.**

 Dragging images around Content Tables is a bit like the Word 97 selected-text-move options: If you simply drag the images, they move from cell to cell. Ctrl+dragging places a *copy* of the image in the destination cell.

Now, of course, you no longer see the Mouseover rendering of this button because it's hidden by the Normal version — just as it will be on the page. However, the little red diagonal in the upper-right corner of the cell is a giveaway that more than one image is there, and the pop-up menu you see after right-clicking the cell includes two new options: Show Content Order and Show Next Media.

The Show Next Media option cycles to the image underneath, and the Show Content Order option pops up the dialog box shown in Figure 6-11. The dialog box is a useful one, enabling you to preview all versions of the image and change the content order if you put the wrong image in first by mistake (or just for the fun of it).

Figure 6-11:
Inspect and
manipulate
all layers of
a multiple
content cell
here.

Putting Things on the Page from Content Tables

After you have some stuff organized in a Content Table, dragging it to the page is a piece of cake — that's the whole point, really. The only thing you have to watch for is that you drag appropriate content to a SmartElement. Drumbeat keeps you honest by and large by prohibiting mismatches, with at least one important exception.

The only downer about Content Table management is that, having gone to all the effort of assembling the stuff in good order, you have no way to export the table to other sites. We hear that we're not the only users to have had a tantrum about this situation, so Content Table export may become a Drumbeat feature — or perhaps already is.

Working with single-cell content

Most SmartElements can accept content of the correct type from a Content Table cell. In fact, whenever you see that the Static Content option on the dropdown Content list on an element's Attributes Sheet, it means that it's okay to feed that element from a Content Table cell, although it may not necessarily make sense.

You can drop text on a text box — obviously. You can also drop text on an edit box form element (you don't see it until you publish — it becomes the element's VALUE attribute). That can make sense, for defaulting form input fields. You can also drop text on check boxes and radio buttons, although that doesn't seem to make much sense.

You can drag an image to an image SmartElement — or to an image map, an image button, or a scrolling image. Drag any kind of media, including text, into empty space on the page, and the media appears. Drag media other than text into a text box, and the path to the media file appears.

Video and audio content can, obviously, be dropped on the equivalent SmartElements. HTML files need an HTML Passthrough SmartElement. You can perform all these operations also from the Attributes Sheet of a SmartElement, although less conveniently. Media types primarily take care of themselves.

The one great trap is the mouseover image pair. If you drop a mouseover pair into empty space or on a standard image SmartElement, it looks okay at first, although you soon will have write 50 times on the school blackboard: "I must place an image button SmartElement on my pages, or else my mouseovers will not work."

Image check boxes and radio buttons, as mentioned, don't work correctly unless you supply them with three images — CHECKED, UNCHECKED, and MOUSEOVER.

We have to advise you to leave a couple of media types alone. *Metafiles* are images in a Microsoft format that do not publish to the Web. If you try dropping a metafile onto an image SmartElement, you'll fail. You can, however, drop one into empty page space, and if you do, it becomes impossible to delete. *Executables* are .exe files that can theoretically be embedded in Web pages, although none of the standard SmartElements supports them.

Using an entire column

For at least one reason, you may well have to use an entire column of a Content Table to populate a SmartElement: whenever you're creating a list box or a dropdown list. Drumbeat has a fairly nifty dialog box for this task built into the Attributes Sheets of these elements, although under some circumstances a Content Table may work just as well and be much easier to edit later. Figure 6-12 shows a Content Table of month names made for a trilingual site. The *content* of each of the page versions is the appropriate column, but because the *values* are the same numerals in every case, the same information is passed when the form is submitted, regardless of which language the user is working in. Again, selecting Static Content on the Attributes Sheet is the cue to Drumbeat that a Content Table will be linked to this element.

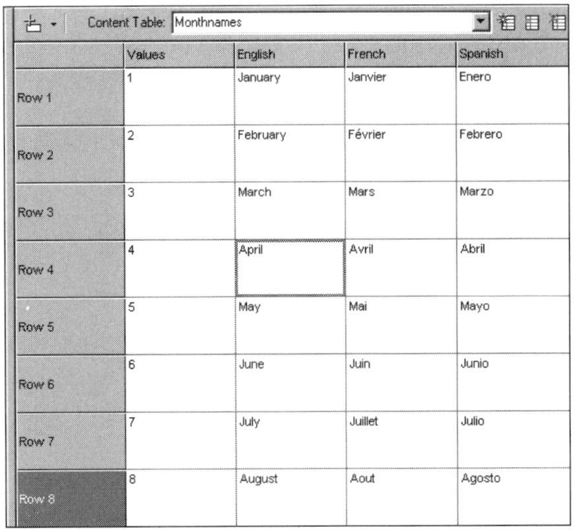

Content Table: Monthnames

	Values	English	French	Spanish
Row 1	1	January	Janvier	Enero
Row 2	2	February	Février	Febrero
Row 3	3	March	Mars	Marzo
Row 4	4	April	Avril	Abril
Row 5	5	May	Mai	Mayo
Row 6	6	June	Juin	Junio
Row 7	7	July	Juillet	Julio
Row 8	8	August	Aout	Agosto

Figure 6-12: This Content Table is designed to populate a multilingual list box.

Using the whole Content Table

Nothing, perhaps, makes a Content Table feel that it has fulfilled its destiny as much as being used in its entirety. At least two Drumbeat-approved operations fulfill this destiny: AutoTables and PageSets.

Drumbeat doesn't let you create your own HTML tables, preferring to place things on pages by using more advanced techniques. (If your site is targeted at generic browsers or Navigator 3.0, however, Drumbeat uses table positioning behind the scenes.)

The *only* way of populating the SmartElement named AutoTable is by dumping the entire contents of a Content Table into it. Figure 6-13 shows a Content Table made up for part of a garden seed supplier's page. This example is interesting because it uses a range of techniques to achieve its effect. We named the AutoTable Veg-E-Table — sorry about that.

Column 1 is designated for images. Columns 2 and 3 are designated for normal formatted text. Columns 4 and 5 provide, between them, hyperlinks to other pages of interest. Column 5 is designated for unformatted text because it contains the URLs that are the hyperlink destinations. Column 6 is supposed to contain lists of the available varieties, but because the length of some of those lists is variable, we made use of the fact that Drumbeat enables us to place HTML in unformatted text cells and made a little drop-down item out of each list. Figure 6-14 shows the actual content of the hot peppers list cell.

Special treatment for this header   Hot column   URL Column

Figure 6-13:
Don't forget
your vegeta-
bles! You
can find
some on this
part of a
garden seed
catalog
page.

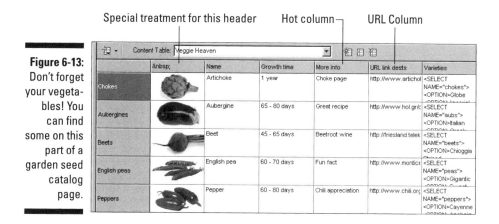

Figure 6-14:
Creating a
dropdown
list in an
unformatted
text cell.

Note one little prank we had to get up to, in the upper-left corner of Figure 6-16. When we dump this Content Table into an AutoTable, the column labels end up as the header row of the table, as shown on the page. We didn't want any content in the extreme upper-left cell, and Drumbeat doesn't allow blank column labels, so we artfully slipped in a nonbreaking space entity.

Figure 6-15 shows the two dialog boxes we navigated to get the Veg-E-Table published. Note that we removed the URL column in the Content dialog box because we didn't want the column showing on-screen; we set up Column 4 as the "hot column" and Column 5 as the URL Column in the Column Content Link dialog box. You can easily display both these dialog boxes from the AutoTable's Attributes Sheet, and you can display them again later with equal ease for editing. Figure 6-16 shows the final appearance of the page, after some extra cosmetics.

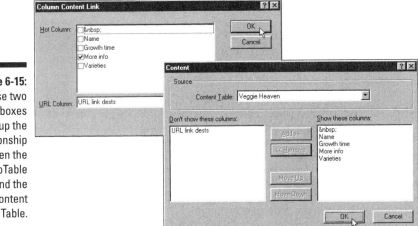

Figure 6-15:
These two dialog boxes set up the relationship between the AutoTable and the Content Table.

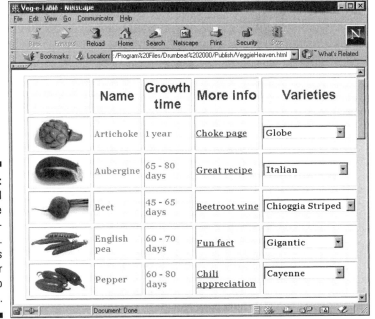

Figure 6-16:
The final appearance of the Veg-E-Table. Vegetables have never looked so good.

Editing Content Tables

We don't have much to say, really, about deleting a table — a box pops up to warn you that any content you've already used in a SmartElement will disappear too (and they mean that), and that if you go for it — poof! — it's gone. Hit that Edit button, and you see a dialog box that's the same as the top half of the dialog box you created the table with in the first place — use it to rename the table and add or subtract rows and columns.

To edit the content of a Content Table cell: Double-click the cell, or right-click and choose Open from the pop-up menu. The appropriate dialog box pops up — an edit window if it's a text cell, and Media Properties if it's a media cell. Note that the right-click pop-up menu includes Cut, Copy, and Paste options for handling cell content. Remember that you can also drag content around with your mouse — and drag a *copy* if you hold down the Ctrl key.

With images in Content Table cells, an important difference exists between double-click and right-click or Open actions. Double-clicking works as described here, but right-click or Open brings the image into your default image editor for editing.

To rename and redesignate columns or to rename rows: Double-click the row or column header, or right-click and choose Properties from the pop-up menu. You cannot redesignate column content type without some thought, of course. If you redesignate a column for audio media, for example, any audio already present in the column simply disappears. You cannot drag rows and columns around with the mouse, but, by using the same pop-up menu, you can cut, copy, or paste them. Pasted columns are placed to the left of the selected column; pasted rows are inserted above the selected row.

To insert rows or columns: Select the row below the intended row insert point or the column to the right of the intended column insert point. Use either the two-in-one button on the left end of the Content Center toolbar or the pop-up menu you see by right-clicking.

It's perfectly permissible to move a column from one Content Table to another, by cutting-and-pasting or copying-and-pasting, using the pop-up menu shown in Figure 6-10.

To delete rows or columns: Select the row or column, right-click, and choose Delete from the pop-up menu or use your Delete key.

Thumbnail image options: Choose File⇨Preferences⇨Drumbeat from the menu bar and then click the Content tab in the Preferences dialog box. Notice that you have options to have or not have thumbnail images displayed in Content Tables and to force them (or not) to fit the cell.

Chapter 7

Using Frames

. . . .

. . . .

Creating framesets used to be one of the biggest headaches in Web page authoring. If you weren't careful, you could find yourself wandering into a house of mirrors and never being able to find your way back out. Frames within frames could multiply like rabbits and take over your screen until nothing was left except scrollbars and itsy-bitsy windows everywhere.

In Drumbeat, the whole business of creating a frameset seems, fortunately, so effortless that you'll wonder what all the fuss was about.

Choosing a Prefab Frameset Structure

Drumbeat contains 11 prefab frameset configurations from which to choose. Just like those suburban prefabs with standard fittings that can be replaced with more expensive appliances and imported tiles, each frameset can be customized in various ways. If the rooms (frames) are a little small or you want to put in a glass door here or there, don't worry. Just pick the prefab with the basic structure you want, and you can customize it later (and it won't even cost you extra).

To create a new frameset:

1. **Click the Insert Page dropdown arrow and select Frameset.**

2. **In the New Frameset dialog box, select the frameset configuration you want to use, and click OK, as shown in Figure 7-1.**

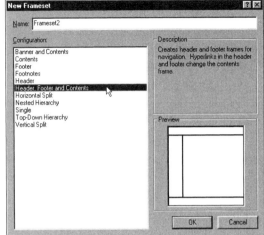

Figure 7-1:
Select a
frameset
from the
available
configura-
tions.

Browse through the frameset configurations in the New Frameset dialog box
and you see a preview of each frame setup. The frameset configurations also
include default targets for links in each frame that you can change as you
want.

Don't see a prefab you like? See the section "Building Do-It-Yourself
Framesets," later in this chapter, and our architect can help you come up
with your personal design.

Living the single configuration life

Wait — we want to show you one more model. Think of it as a cheap studio
apartment. The single configuration gives you just one frame in a frameset.

Why have a single-frame frameset? The single-frame frameset is available for
only one reason: to provide a workaround for one of the most irritating
browser differences that occasionally aggravates precise designers — the difference in default margins between browsers and the fact that, even if you try
to override these default margins, you're still left with a little padding around
the edge. You can use a single frameset and set the border attribute to 0, and
the problem is solved. Clumsy? Yeah, but until somebody gets these browser
developer folks to talk to each other better, you're stuck with this type of
workaround occasionally. (Until you save up the down payment, you could
be stuck with a studio apartment, too. As a recent U.S. President once said,
"Life just isn't fair.")

Furnishing the house

A frameset is like a house that's just beginning construction. Although the framing is in place, the house has no walls yet and no real rooms. After you have the frameset configuration, you have to provide pages for each frame.

You can see the Frameset structure on the Site tab. Simply click each frame under the frameset and insert a page. Or drag an existing page into the frame. When you're done, your frameset looks something like Figure 7-2.

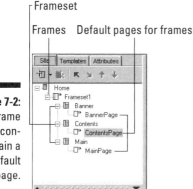

Frameset

Frames   Default pages for frames

Figure 7-2:
Each frame
must con-
tain a
default
page.

You can drag multiple pages into a frame if you want so that you can get the big picture on where everything belongs as you work on your site. The first page listed in the site tree under a frame is the default page for the frame — the one that loads into the frame when the frameset first loads. To get the other pages to appear in the frame, however, you must set up a link to the page with a target to the correct frame.

Targeting links

When you use framesets, creating targets for each link becomes very important. An ordinary link without a specific target simply loads the new page over the old one, in the same window. With frames, you often want a link to open a page in a different frame. Click a link on a menu on the left, and a new page loads into the window on the right, for example. The target of the link is the window on the right.

The default frameset configurations often include appropriate default targets for links from certain frames in the set. The default target is indicated on the Attributes Sheet for the frame. (It doesn't always work in earlier versions of Drumbeat, so if you haven't upgraded Drumbeat to include Service Pack 2, you may have to set the targets yourself.) The default targets for framesets merely reflect the imagination of the developer, who figured that you would probably want to use this frameset to do this kind of site. It doesn't mean that you're stuck with that target for your links.

To target links to frames, in the Link dialog box, click the Target dropdown list and select the name of the frame you want to target, as shown in Figure 7-3.

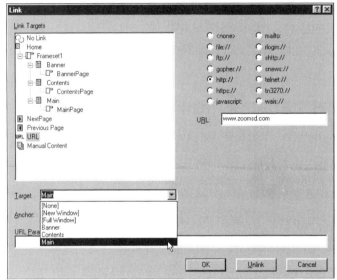

Figure 7-3:
Select the
target frame
for the link
from the
dropdown
list.

You can also create links that target specific anchors within a page. You can make almost any element on a page into a target for links: Simply check the Anchor box on the Attributes Sheet for the element. For example, if you want to create a link to a text element, select the text element on the Layout and check the Anchor option on the Attributes tab. To make the link easy to iden- tify, give the element a name that makes sense. The next time you make a link to that page, the name of your anchor is on the Anchor dropdown list. Just select the anchor to make it the target of the link.

Customizing Your Frameset

Look at frames presentations on the Web these days, and you notice that nobody much likes those original clunky framesets with borders and scrollbars all over the place. They're usually much more subtle, like modern houses with open construction, including partial dividers and glass walls. All frames (and most houses) usually have to be customized a bit to make them come out as nice as you really want them.

Both framesets and frames have attributes that control the way the frames are displayed. Actually, framesets have only one attribute, which is Border, as shown in Figure 7-4. You can set the border to a numerical value in pixels. A border value of 0 means no border. This value isn't really sufficient on its own, however. To truly erase borders, you must also set the border attributes for each frame.

Figure 7-4:
Set the
border
width for
a frameset
on the
Attributes
tab.

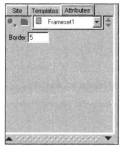

The attributes for frames are where most of the real control resides. To change frame attributes:

1. Select the frame in the site tree on the Site tab.

   Frames don't show up on the Templates tab. Only the pages placed under them show up there.

2. Click the Attributes tab.

The attributes for frames are shown in Figure 7-5 and explained in Table 7-2.

Figure 7-5:
Control
frame
display
attributes
such as
border
color,
scrolling,
and default
targets
for links.

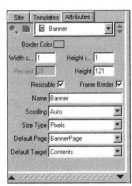

Table 7-2	Frame Attributes
Attribute	*What It Does*
Frame Border	Indicates yes or no (for no border). Even if you set the border to 0 on the Frameset Attributes tab, you still have to disable borders in this check box to make them disappear completely. If you want borders, you can choose their color.
Margins	Sets the width and height of the margins within the frame. The margin is the space between the edge of the frame and the contents.
Resizable	Lets you decide whether you want users to be able to resize frames by dragging them.
Name	Identifies the frame to make targeting the frame with links easier. The name may also be used in scripting, so changing the name to something identifiable makes your life easier.
Scrolling	Turns scrolling on or off or lets you leave it set to Auto, which means that scrollbars appear only when necessary.
Size type	Designates the method used for sizing the frames: Pixels, Percentage, or Leftover. *Pixels* give maximum control for frames containing images. *Percentage* keeps the frame sizes relative to each other. *Leftover* means that this frame gets what's left after the other frames take their share of the screen.
Default page	Loads first in this frame whenever the frameset loads.
Default target	Specifies the default target frame for links in this frame. You can also target Full Window (get out of frames altogether), New Window (make a new browser window for the link), or Parent (supersedes the parent frame in a nested frameset).

Resizing frames

Resizing frames, fortunately, is much easier than moving the walls in your house. To resize a frame in Drumbeat, all you have to do is drag the frame border on the layout area to the size you want. Use the ruler to gauge the width or height precisely. Ignore the space taken up by the scrollbar in the layout area if you're turning off scrolling. The horizontal scrollbar usually doesn't appear on the browser screen anyway, unless you use unusually wide content in a frame. To get a precise size for your frames, set the Size Type option on the Attributes Sheet to pixels and enter a number for the Width (for a vertical frame) and Height (for a horizontal frame) options.

While working in the layout area, you may have to drag the frame to a larger size than you intend it to be in the end so that the scrollbar doesn't get in your way. Be sure to drag the frame back to the actual size you want before publishing. Another useful trick is to turn off the display of scrollbars. To get rid of them, right-click in a frame and choose Scrollbars or press Ctrl+PgDn.

If you're not intimidated by a little code, you can also change the frame sizes on the file that controls the original frameset configuration.

Making glass walls (or invisible frames)

Invisible frames are the fashionable way to wear your frames these days. Invisible frames do not reveal their borders, so they appear as one seamless page, even though they may actually be three or four pages in a frameset. They can help cut down load time for repetitive content, such as banners and menus. (The initial loading time for the frameset may be longer, however, because you have to load several pages).

Because the differences in what a browser displays can make creating a truly invisible frameset that works the same in both browsers a frustrating enterprise, you may have to play around with the frameset settings. Be sure to check the results in multiple browsers to be sure that you get what you intend.

To make an invisible frameset:

1. **Select the frameset in the site tree. Click the Attributes tab and set the Border attribute to 0.**

2. **Then select each frame on the Site tab, click the Attributes tab, and uncheck the Frame Border option.**

Figure 7-6 shows the Banner and Contents frameset after turning off borders and doing some cosmetic touch-ups. Scrolling has been set to No for the top frame, which contains only images, and a background color has been added to the Contents frame for the menu.

If you want to ensure that under no circumstance does a border appear, set Scrolling to No for all frames. This method is advisable only if you're absolutely sure that your contents will not overflow the space provided. (Remember to be kind to your visitors by using large fonts or high-resolution monitors.) If you use only an image in the frame, overflow shouldn't be a problem. Otherwise, leave the scrolling setting to Auto, and the browser uses a scrollbar only if necessary.

Figure 7-6: With borders turned off, this Banners and Contents frameset (which contains three frames) looks seamless.

When you look at a frameless frameset in a Netscape browser, you sometimes see a seam between the frames where the margin is. To make sure that borders and margins don't make visible seams between frames, set the border color of the frame to the same color as the background color of the page or pages in the frame.

Building Do-It-Yourself Framesets

So you don't like any of the prefab framesets? Whatsamatta U? Some people just have to have things their own way.

Okay, Bigshot, you can make your own frameset configuration and add it to the ones already available in Drumbeat. Making your own takes a little minor coding work, although it's no more confusing than figuring out a frameset in HTML, if you're familiar with that process.

Here's the secret: The information for each default frameset in Drumbeat is in an .inf file that you can find in the Framesets directory of the Drumbeat program files (C:\Program Files\Drumbeat 2000\Framesets with the default installation). You can open any one of these .inf files in Notepad (or any text editor) and inspect it. For example, here's the .inf file for the Banner and Contents frameset (bantoc.inf), which you can see in Figure 7-6 in the preceding section:

```
 [info]
title=Banner and Contents
description=Creates a banner frame at the top, with a con-
            tents and main frame.  Hyperlinks in the banner
            change the contents frame.
noframesURL=
layout=[R(64,*)F("Banner",[C(150,*)F("Contents","Main")])]
```

The last line contains the information for the frameset configuration. The code is straightforward:

- ✔ **R:** Rows
- ✔ **F:** Frame
- ✔ **C:** Column

Brackets indicate the major divisions. Here's the interpretation of this frameset:

- ✔ **R(64,*):** Sets up the main horizontal division into two rows. The first row at the top is 64 pixels high, and the second row takes the rest of the screen after the 64 pixels are subtracted from the top (* means "the left-over amount").

- ✔ **F("Banner"):** Proclaims the name of the first frame to be Banner, the name used for targeting links.

- ✔ **[C(150,*):** Sets up the vertical division of the second row into two columns. The beginning of the subdivision is indicated with the open bracket. The first column is 150 pixels wide, and the second takes the leftover amount (*).

- ✔ **F("Contents","Main")]:** Proclaims the names of the two frames in this row to be Contents and Main. The brackets at the end close this row.

The easiest way to make your own frameset configuration is to find a frameset that's close to what you want, open the .inf file for that frameset, and then edit the instructions to produce your altered version. Save the frameset under a new name with the .inf extension in the Framesets directory.

To show you how it's done, we show you how to alter the Banner and Contents frameset. You can split the top frame into two frames, where the upper-left frame is a small window in which you can put one of those flashy animated ads. The ad image is 167 x 73 pixels, so make the first row 73 pixels high and the first column 167 pixels wide, to fit it precisely. The total frameset includes two rows of two columns each.

Here's the code for the new .inf file:

```
[info]
title=Ad Banner Contents and Main
description=Creates a small ad frame top left plus banner
           frame top right, with a contents frame and main
           frame below.
noframesURL=
layout=[C(167,*)F([R(73,*)F("LTop","LBottom")],[R(73,*)F("RTo
         p","RBottom")]
```

After you save your new frameset in the Framesets directory, Drumbeat adds it to the default configurations and even gives you a preview version of the new frameset, as shown in Figure 7-7.

Figure 7-7:
A new frameset shows up in the Frameset chooser.

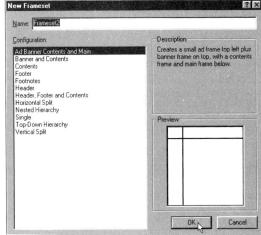

Making Links Do Double Duty in Frames

A link in one frameset normally produces a change of contents in another frame, which you choose as a target for the link. However, sometimes you may want to change the contents of two frames at one time with a single click. You can do that by adding a simple JavaScript `onClick` action to the link.

The frames presentation made from the new configuration is shown, slightly jazzed up, in Figure 7-8.

Figure 7-8: A four-frame presentation with flashing ad banner.

Suppose that you want the contents of both lower frames to change when a user clicks one of the navigational buttons in the upper-right frame. The menu on the left changes, along with the contents of the main frame. We show you how to make both frames change at one time.

To set up the double link action on one image button:

1. **Link the image button first to a page that targets one of the other frames.**

   Which frame you choose really doesn't matter. The thing that does matter is that you select the appropriate Target frame.

   You link the Sellers image button to the SellersContents page, targeting the LBottom frame, as shown in Figure 7-8.

2. **Right-click the image button and choose Edit Script⇨onClick.**

   The Script Center opens in the attic, with the image button selected as the object, and the `onClick` event selected on the Event dropdown list. (You can read more about the Script Center in Chapter 16.)

3. **In the scripting window, enter the following two lines of code:**

```
parent.RBottom.location="Sellers.html"
parent.LBottom.location="SellersContent.html"
```

You can see this action being set up in Figure 7-9. To do it yourself, substitute for `RBottom` and `LBottom` the names of the frames you want to change. Substitute for the html pages in quotes the filenames of the pages you want to link to. You can use a fully qualified URL instead, if you want. That's all it takes!

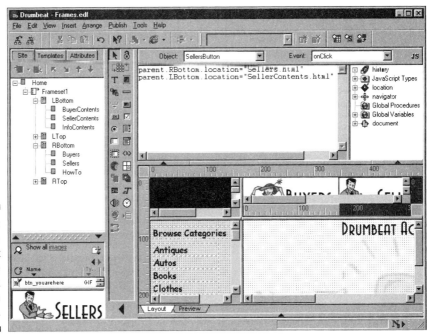

Figure 7-9:
Creating the
JavaScript
for the
`onClick`
action for a
button.

Chapter 8

The Lazy Designer's Guide to Quick Changes and Instant Design

In This Chapter

▶ Getting things lined up and spaced out

▶ Thematic changes

▶ Making things draggable

▶ Positioning in 3D

▶ Adding pop-up notes, scrolling, calendars, and date and time functions

*W*e call this chapter a "lazy designer's guide," but that doesn't mean that we think you're sitting out there in a rocking chair on your front porch, having a cold drink. (It would be nice, though, wouldn't it?) As the designers of all those WYSIWYG interfaces out there have come to realize, however, we're all just a bit lazy when we're confronted with a choice between sitting down with a calculator and doing things by dragging and dropping.

If you don't exactly think of yourself as lazy — just overworked and over-booked — this chapter has some interesting tricks to help you leap tall buildings in a single bound. Many of the spiffy tricks that Drumbeat makes easy — like rollover buttons, animations, and style sheets — are well covered in earlier chapters. Later chapters show you more tricks of the trade involving PageSets, databases, and forms.

Think of this chapter as a cornucopia of Drumbeat design tricks that have nothing in common except that it's time you knew about them.

Toying with Aligning and Spacing Tricks

In Chapter 4, we explain the use of the jargon term *snap* in relation to the grid that's on the Drumbeat layout area by default and the guidelines you can set up when you need precise alignment of SmartElements, such as images. Sometimes, these conveniences can seem to be an annoyance, or can even seem to fight each other, unless you know some tricks of the trade.

Align 'em, size 'em, space 'em

Figure 8-1 shows the cascade of Arrange menus as you never see them — all at one time.

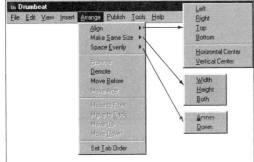

Figure 8-1:
Take a look
at all the
Arrange
submenus.

Figure 8-2 shows the Arrange Elements button with its dropdown variants. The button doesn't "light up" until at least two SmartElements are selected, and when you use a certain variant of it, it stays in that mode until you change it.

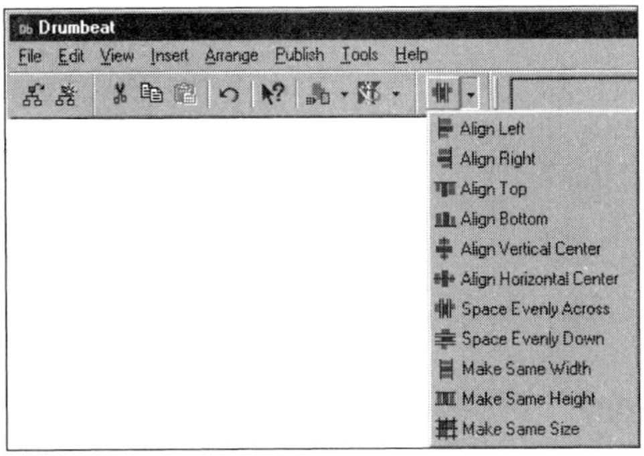

Figure 8-2:
Whoa!
Eleven vari-
ants of the
Arrange
Elements
button.

The menu and the button obviously offer the same choices, even if they're presented differently. We must confess to being somewhat iconically challenged, although we recognize that many people interpret these pictograms with no difficulty whatsoever. It's a left-brain, right-brain thing.

All these alignment, sizing, and spacing options apply when you have a set of elements in the layout area that need neatening up. Start by marquee-selecting the entire set — or if other elements are in the way, Ctrl+click them each in turn.

The *last* object to be included in the group becomes the *reference element* — the one the others will align with. If your selection ends up with the wrong one as reference, just Ctrl+click the one you want to elevate to this high office.

Figure 8-3 shows a collection of objects that have been slapped down in the layout area all higgledy-piggledy — a button, a line of text, and two mis-matched images.

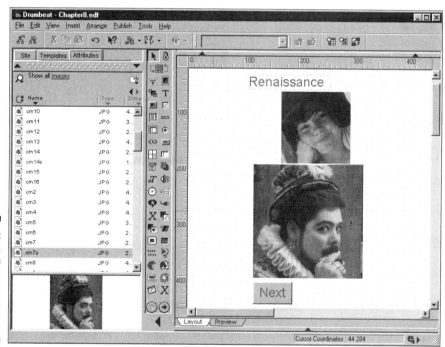

Figure 8-3:
This page is in need of help from the aligning and sizing aids.

If you were faced with the same problem, here's how you would fix things:

1. **Select the two images, with the smaller as reference.**

2. **Click the dropdown arrow on the Arrange Elements button and choose Make Same Size.**

3. **Select all four elements, with the button as reference.**

4. **Click the dropdown arrow on the Arrange Elements button and choose Align Vertical Center.**

5. **With all elements still selected, choose the Space Evenly Down option.**

The process of resizing images is a little perilous. A far better technique is to "resample" them in a graphics editor — for demonstration purposes, we were making the image smaller, which is not too bad. Resizing an image larger than the original by that amount is guaranteed to give poor results.

The other options on the Arrange dropdown menu are, first, the functions for rearranging the site hierarchy (repeating what you can do with the four Promote/Demote/Move page arrows in the Site Manager (refer to Chapter 2), and then the controls for the Z-Order of stacked elements, which we explain with pizzazz later in this chapter, in the section "Layering objects."

Note the underlined capital letter in each of the option lines, indicating the keyboard method for making something happen. For example, with a set of SmartElements selected, pressing Alt+A,S,W means "make same width."

Making a composite image

Composite images are often used to create one image from many pieces, with different link destinations associated with each image piece. The images are often used rather than image maps because they let you associate different alternate (ALT) text with each piece of the image. Most modern browsers display image ALT text as a ToolTip when the image is moused over, which helps indicate the link destination.

Here's a quick-and-dirty way to make a composite image, without having to get out a calculator to figure out all the positions:

1. **Place on the layout area the pieces that make up the first row of your image, slightly overlapping one another.**

2. **Select them all, click the dropdown arrow on the Arrange Elements button, and choose Align⇨Top.**

3. **With all elements still selected, click the dropdown arrow on the Arrange elements button again and choose the Space Evenly⇨Across option, as shown in Figure 8-4.**

   All your images should snap into place, abutting one another, as shown in Figure 8-5.

Dealing with Changing Content

Getting everybody to make up their minds about a Web site at one time can be kind of like holding a conference on world peace in the gorilla cage at the zoo. (Come to think of it, that's not much different from doing it in the U.N. Security Council chambers.)

Figure 8-4:
Choosing
the Space
Evenly
Across
command to
create a
seamless
banner from
four sepa-
rate images.

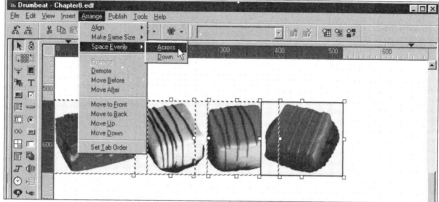

Figure 8-5:
The com-
pleted
banner. Dig
in!

Drumbeat has several handy ways, short of declaring war, that you can deal with the problem of late artwork, changing design, and fickle clients.

Making instant design changes with themes

When you're placing elements on a page from a Content Table, we advise you elsewhere just to drag the stuff from the Content Table and drop it wherever you need it — and that's definitely the most intuitive way to go. However, you can also do it the other way around and assign static content on the element's Attributes Sheet. Figure 8-6 is a reminder of the dialog box that pops up so that you can assign the content to row X, column Y of Content Table Z.

Hang on — what's that option to assign to Current Row all about? It's a clue to another bit of behind-the-scenes magic that Drumbeat offers. The *current* row is the row that's selected in the Content Table — indicated by its label cell being much darker than the others, as shown in Figure 8-7.

Figure 8-6:
Assigning
static
content.

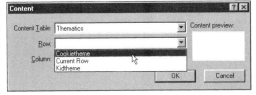

Darker color of label indicates current row

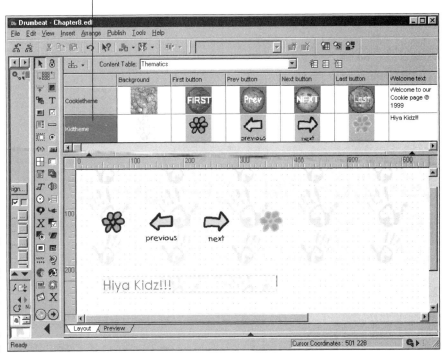

Figure 8-7:
A Content
Table holds
alternate
thematic
artwork.

The darker appearance means that you can set up a Content Table with rows representing complete alternate sets of content and switch everything with one click of the mouse.

The two rows you see in Figure 8-7 represent two completely different graphical treatments for the page. Background image, button renderings, and even formatted text — everything's set up in thematic rows.

If the content of all that stuff is assigned to the current row, the whole she-bang takes on the appearance of whichever row you click in the Content Table — instantly.

The only assignation that's a little tricky is the background image. You assign it in the BkgndContent area of the page's Attributes Sheet, and you first have to "disinherit" background content from the controlling template. Click the Inherit button (the "crop circle" icon) in the upper-left corner of the Attributes Sheet, and uncheck the BkgndContent option in the dialog box that pops up.

Why would you want to use the "current row" feature? We can think of a few reasons: to make a quick presentation of design options to a client, to indicate seasonal changes to a commercial site, or to facilitate the rapid switching around of multimedia components.

Using color (backgrounds and box properties)

Don't have time to create special buttons for a site? Or maybe you're still waiting for the designer to catch up with you, but you want to show the client something a little more stylish than just gray buttons.

Create a style that includes a fancy font, a background color, and a color border. It's a nifty way to create quick effects. (Of course, it works in only 4.0 browsers and later.) Choose Tools⇨Styles and choose to create a new style or edit an existing one.

On the Background tab, you can choose a color for the button:

1. **Select the Fixed option for the background color.**
2. **Click the color bar and select a color.**

On the Box tab, you can add a border of a different color:

1. **Select a style from the Style dropdown list. (Solid is the only one that works reliably across browsers.)**
2. **Select the Fixed radio button for box color, and then click the color bar and select a color.**
3. **Enter a number (1) for the border width.**

On the Text tab:

1. **Choose a font that pleases you and designate its size (10 or 12 pt) and weight (400 for regular, 700 for bold).**
2. **For text color, choose Fixed, and then click the color bar to select a color.**

You can preview what the style will look like. Save the style, and then apply it to your buttons. Voilà! — instant buttons that look like graphics, as shown in Figure 8-8.

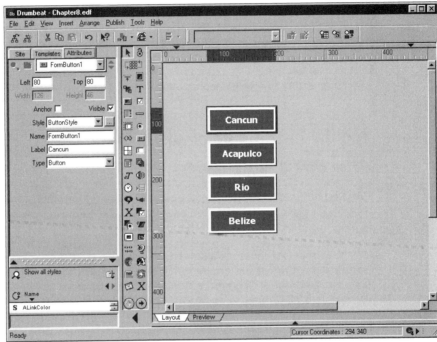

Figure 8-8: A complex style is applied to a set of navigation buttons.

Using SmartElement Collections

Sometimes you can spend a great deal of time getting things just right on a page — lining up those navigation graphics with all their rollovers, for example. You want to reuse them on different pages or even in different sites you're building. How do you copy them easily and preserve all that work?

A SmartElement collection is just the ticket. Follow these steps to make a reusable collection out of those navigation graphics:

1. **Select the whole bunch at one time (marquee-select them in the layout area by drawing around them with the mouse).**

2. **Right-click any one of the selected elements and you see the option Add to Element Library. Select it.**

3. **In the pop-up dialog box, give the collection a name (in Figure 8-9, it's** CandyButtons**).**

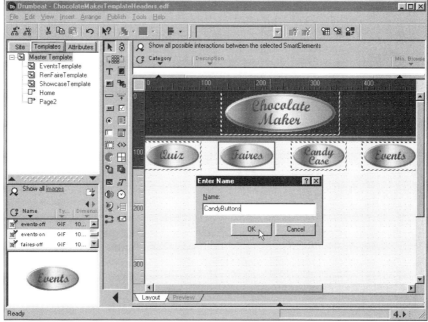

Figure 8-9:
Making a
Smart-
Element
collection
from a
group of
buttons.

Now, how do you use the new collection? You can get at it in two ways:

1. **In the Asset Center, click the Locate Assets button and choose SmartElements⇨Show All SmartElements. Or, you can refine the filter to Show All SmartElements Using Custom Technology and then click Custom and change it to Element Collection.**

2. **Find your custom collection on the list and drag it to the layout area of a page.**

   Positioning the collection exactly on the page at the same coordinates as it was on the original page is easy if you use guidelines where you want to place the collection (perhaps on a template) and let it all snap into place at one time.

If you plan to use this collection frequently, you can add it to your SmartElements toolbar:

1. **Click the Element Library icon on the SmartElements toolbar.**

2. **Select the Element Collections tab, and put a check mark next to the collection.**

3. **If you want to select a custom icon for this collection, click Edit. In the Element Collection Properties dialog box that's displayed, click the Appearance option and then the Change Icon option.**

When you close the Element Library, your new collection appears on the SmartElements toolbar. The ToolTip uses the name you assigned.

A SmartElement collection can include all the interactions assigned to the elements in the collection — as long as you remember to include the elements that participate in those interactions. If the collection includes database interactions, remember to select the recordset (or recordsets) that's involved, too, and make it part of the collection.

Taking Some Time for Dynamic HTML Tricks

Drumbeat seldom refers (wisely, we think) to Dynamic HTML (DHTML) as such. The term is used (and abused, sometimes) to describe so many things that it becomes more and more diffuse with passing time. The differences between the two major Web browsers are more accentuated in their view of dynamic effects than in any other respect, which all helps to reinforce the view that nobody really knows what Dynamic HTML really is.

One thing's for sure, though: Sometime in 1997, when Version 4 of both major browsers was released and Cascading Style Sheets (CSS) became fully accepted, Web designers could suddenly make their pages interact with their users in ways that provided both excitements and dangers.

An enhanced user interface

Drumbeat groups a bunch of contracts by using dynamic effects under the "Enhanced UI" category:

- ✔ Add/Remove Border
- ✔ Brighten
- ✔ Dim
- ✔ Flip
- ✔ Glow
- ✔ Hide
- ✔ Show

You can apply most of these effects to text or images with equal ease. Most are interactions between two SmartElements, although some can take effect whenever the Web page loads or a timer expires.

Brighten, Dim, Flip, and Glow are special filters built into Internet Explorer 4.0 and later and have no meaning to Netscape.

Show and Hide are the most useful because they enable all sorts of interesting pop-up and dynamic footnoting effects. Figure 8-10 shows a rather sober but undeniably useful page, enabling the user to make instant sense of those horrible acronyms that occur throughout official texts such as NASA historical documents. We coined a new word to describe these pop-ups: deacronymizers.

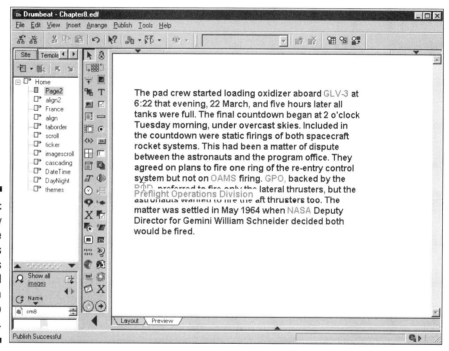

Figure 8-10:
Decode any of the acronyms on this technical page with a pop-up message.

Here's how we made the Preflight Operations Division (POD) deacronymizer. We created a separate text object with just the acronym POD as its content, imposed a special highlighted style, and named the object POD. We layered the object on top of the original acronym in the block of text. The translation, Preflight Operations Division, had its own text object, using the same style, named `PODpopup` and given the attribute Invisible. The interaction is `Show PODpopup when the mouse moves over the word POD`.

HTML purists may cringe at this technique because it's worse than useless for users who prefer to override design fonts and use their own. We'll be diplomatic and say that this technique is useful for in-house documentation on a LAN. Other ways to make use of pop-up effects remain valid when a user takes control of text formatting.

We hardly ever use the Internet Explorer-specific filter effects, but we must admit that they're quite fun. Figure 8-11 shows the glow effect used on an image and a text word. Images glow only if they have some areas of transparency to glow in.

Figure 8-11:
Holy glow-
worm! It's
the glow
effect in
Internet
Explorer.

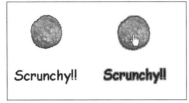

Making things movable

One of the most fun aspects of Dynamic HTML is the document-level event capturing introduced in JavaScript 1.2. Before that concept came along, JavaScript functions could be triggered only by events associated with a specific page element, such as a mouse click on a button. Now, a mouse click can be captured no matter where it occurs (Microsoft achieves this with a semi-compatible technique called event *bubbling*). Together with the absolute positioning of page elements in three dimensions, this advance makes possible some startling effects, including drag-and-drop of page elements, that both the main browser types can show equally well. Although getting drag-and-drop to work by straight JavaScript programming is quite a sweat, Drumbeat makes it a point-and-click operation.

Drumbeat has two ways of implementing drag-and-drop — "drop anywhere," and "dropzone only." Because the latter makes use of Microsoft's event bubbling, it's valid only on sites rated for Internet Explorer 4.0 and later. Don't worry: The difference between the two becomes clear very soon.

Figure 8-12 shows an animal picture puzzle in the making. A picture of a leopard has been chopped into 15 tiles. Each tile has been placed on the lower part of the page in scrambled order and has had the simple activation `Drag the image [imagename] around the browser window` applied to it. Right-click any image and choose Possible Activations, and this one is in the Interactions Center — it's the "drop anywhere" technique.

A container frame of the right size has been provided for the user to drag in the leopard pieces, attempting to reconstitute the picture correctly.

By way of helping out frustrated puzzlers, the complete picture is also in the frame, although it's invisible. If users want a helping hand, they can mouse over the text above the frame to temporarily reveal the whole picture with whatever tile they're moving superimposed, as shown in Figure 8-13.

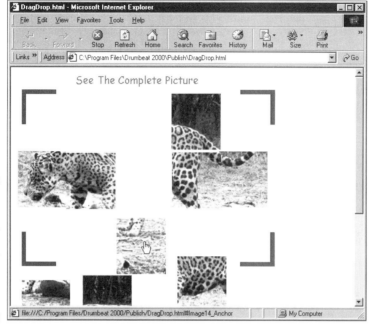

Figure 8-12:
This animal puzzle is being created by dragging and dropping.

Document-level event capturing allows dragging-and-dropping of text elements, too, although Drumbeat restricts this activation to images.

Figure 8-14 shows the other type of drag-and-drop contract, using a *drop zone,* being applied.

The drop zone is a registered SmartElement. Add it to your SmartElements toolbar by opening the Element Library, selecting the Custom tab, and checking the option for DropZone V10_30.

The drop zone is put into action as an interaction between itself and an image. As long as the site is targeted for Internet Explorer 4.0, the interaction `Set Drop1 the drop zone for Image1 is available.` Also visible in Figure 8-14 is the Attributes Sheet of one of the drop zones. In addition to being able to set the normal positioning and sizing attributes, you can set the border thickness and control both border and highlight color and visibility. If the Show Border option is checked, the drop zone is visible on the page (unless it's obscured by some other element) as an open rectangle. If Show Highlight is checked, the drop zone outline appears when the image that interacts with it overlaps the zone.

This page is an idea for a simpler version of the animal puzzle, in which every tile of the puzzle has its appropriate drop zone with a visible highlight so that the user can easily see where each piece belongs by dragging it around until a highlight appears.

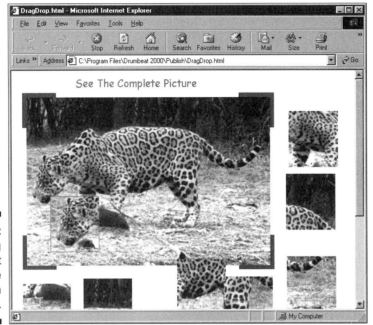

Figure 8-13:
Mousing over the text reveals the picture as a guide.

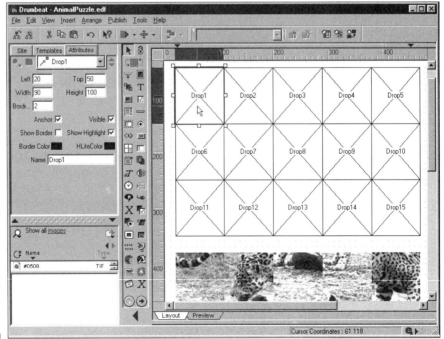

Figure 8-14:
Using drop zones to make the puzzle easier to solve.

Here's a description of the drop zone's behavior:

- ✔ You can drag an image linked to a drop zone anywhere in the browser window, but it will not settle outside the drop zone.
- ✔ If the user attempts to drop it outside the drop zone, it snaps back to its starting position, whether or not the starting position was within the drop zone.
- ✔ The image can settle in any position in which it overlaps the drop zone.
- ✔ The drop zone cannot absolutely determine the final position of the image except in the highly theoretical case in which both drop zone and image are a single pixel.

Figure 8-15 shows the drop-zone version of the puzzle in use.

Layering objects

When we say that Dynamic HTML allows for the positioning of page elements in three dimensions, we don't quite mean that a Web page can be a VRML experience, like flying through downtown Chicago or a canyon on Mars.

Page elements can, however, overlap — and as soon as you have overlapping, you have to have some way of deciding who overlaps whom.

Because the dimensions across and down the page are thought of mathematically as the x and y axes, respectively, it makes sense to think of the third dimension, coming straight out at your face, as the z axis.

The position of any page element in relation to others that it overlaps is known as its *Z-Order*.

In the conventions of absolute positioning, numbers are assigned to positions on the z axis, with higher-numbered elements overlapping lower-numbered elements. Drumbeat doesn't make you aware of any numbering system, however, instead offering you four choices for Z-Order:

- ✔ Move to Front
- ✔ Move to Back
- ✔ Move Up
- ✔ Move Down

You make these choices by right-clicking the element and choosing Z-Order from the pop-up menu or by choosing the same options from the Arrange menu with the image selected.

Drop zone highlight shows when file is in range

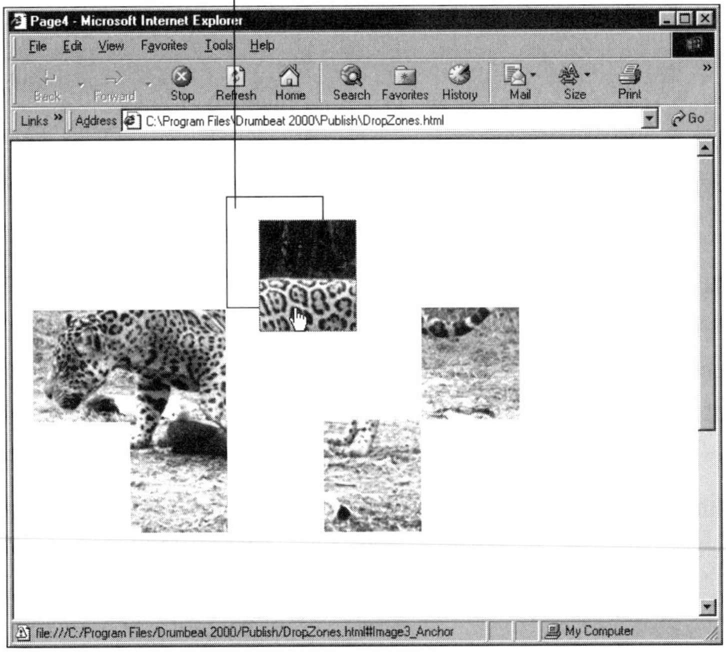

Figure 8-15:
Drop zones
make this
puzzle
almost too
easy to
solve.

That's exactly what we had to do to make the first "animal squares" puzzle work out. On a first attempt, tiles kept disappearing behind other images. The frame has to be at the back of the stack, and then the complete picture (normally invisible) comes next so that any tile overlapping it has a higher Z-Order. The 15 tiles have an assigned Z-Order determined by the order in which we placed them on the page (the first one on the page goes to the bottom of the stack), but you don't really care about that.

Whenever you're dragging images from the Asset Center to the layout area, you can't drag images you want to stack directly on top of one another. If you drag image B directly on top of image A, Drumbeat assumes that you want to replace image A with image B, and you see this dire warning message: "The current content will be lost." If stacking is what you really want, drop image B in some vacant spot in the layout area and then drag it on top of image A.

May we have the scroll, please?

Remember when it was considered an achievement just to get text scrolling through the status bar?

That's old hat, now that Java applets are freely available to scroll stuff in more creative ways. Drumbeat offers three applets as standard SmartElements: text scroll, ticker tape (sideways scroll), and image scroll. These applets run just as well in Netscape 4.0 and later as in Internet Explorer 4.0 and later, although users need to have Java capability.

Wanna get your prompt text on the status bar anyway? An activation for that in the Miscellaneous category puts a short message down there when some SmartElement is moused over. Now, the bad news: You have no way to make a longer message scroll sideways. You have to dig out those old JavaScripts and open up the Drumbeat Script Center (see the section "Using the Script Center," in Chapter 15).

Scrolling text

Scrolling text is clever and lots of fun. Basically, this applet enables you to put much more text into a text element than will fit vertically and have it scroll through at a speed you decide. You can enter text into the SmartElement directly in the layout area, but because of the overflow, it's much easier to use the Content dropdown list. Content may be derived from an external text file — if you use one, be sure to post it to the server.

Advanced features allow a great deal of user control. A user can grab the scrolling text and "throw" it (we tell you what on Earth this means in a minute), change its speed, and even resize it on the fly.

Here are the unfamiliar attributes:

- **Frame Rate and Pixels/Step:** Between them, these two control scrolling speed. The frame rate is the number of steps the text moves per second. For smooth scrolling, set the frame rate to 30 at 1 pixel per step. The same overall speed would be achieved in a more jerky style if the frame rate were 10 at 3 pixels per step.

- **HorzAmplitude and HorzPeriod:** Between them, these two control a nauseating side-to-side motion of the text. The amplitude is a measure of the amount of sideways movement, and the period is an index of the speed of movement, with a longer period meaning slower movement. Have an airsickness bag handy when you try this one out.

- **Drag:** If this option is checked, it enables users to drag the text vertically by using the mouse pointer. Responsiveness of the scroll to throwing is controlled by the Drag Strength option.

- **Throw:** If this option is checked, it enables users to accelerate scrolling with a sharp vertical movement of the mouse. Responsiveness of the scroll to throwing is controlled by the Friction index. Thrown text is arrested by the next mouse click.

- **Scale:** If this option is checked, it enables users to resize text on the fly by dragging horizontally.

Ticker tape

This applet is a right-to-left text scrolling applet, with some snaky effects as options. The effects are not quite as nauseous as the text-shakers of the vertical scroller.

Figure 8-16 shows one wave effect being tested in the Drumbeat preview window, and you can also see the settings of the Attributes Sheet that made it happen. The Wave Height and VertPeriod options have been set to create the shape of the wave. You set the Waves/Sec option has been set to a low number to keep the text reasonably readable.

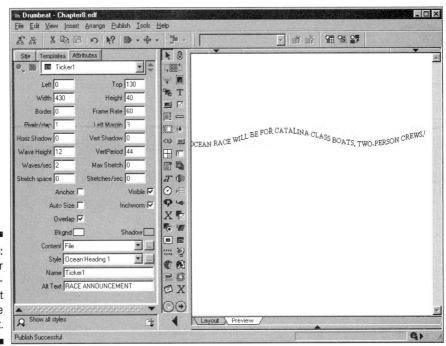

Figure 8-16: The Ticker Tape Smart-Element with a wave effect.

The other effect is text stretch, controlled by the Stretch Space, Stretches/Sec, and Max Stretch options. If you check the Overlap option, letters are allowed to overlap as they stretch.

As for the scrolling text, the Frame Rate and Pixels/Step options control the scroll rate between them. A combination of wave and stretch, with the Inchworm option checked, makes the text perform. Of course, you can ignore all the fancy effects and simply create a normal, sane, readable, ticker tape effect.

Do *not* use both single and double quote marks in the text of this applet. If you do, the first single quote is interpreted as the beginning of a comment, and text from that point on is invisible.

Both the vertical and horizontal scroll applets have a space for alternate (ALT) text. Putting something in there for the sake of users who don't have Java enabled is a really good idea.

Scrolling images

By comparison with the text-scrolling applet, the image scroller is conservative. No shimmy, no shake, no wave, no stretch. It's just a SmartElement into which you can place any image and have it scroll repeatedly in any direction.

The scrolling image is a so-called Standard SmartElement, but it's not on your SmartElements toolbar by default. To use it, open the Element Library and check this SmartElement on the Standard tab.

Scroll speed, controlled by the Delay and Pixels/Step attributes, doesn't seem happy at less than 3 pixels per step.

The Border attribute is supposed to put a black border around the picture, but this option appears to be faulty.

Chapter 9

Quick-and-Dirty Design
with PageSets

In This Chapter

▶ A poor person's database

▶ Coherent design

▶ All-at-once publishing

▶ Updateables

Database info presented on the Web can be classified in many ways: interesting versus boring, too much versus too little, baffling versus simple. The distinction we need to make for this chapter, however, is static versus dynamic. These days, everyone raves about dynamic data, or data that's derived "on the fly" and so conforms automatically to the database as it changes day by day, hour by hour, minute by minute.

The obsession with updatedness is driven by e-commerce, of course. If you're running a Web site of real estate listings or the prices of computer memory SIMMs, yesterday's data is about as interesting as yesterday's fresh fish. Many, many data sets don't need that kind of immediacy, however. Scientific data such as lists of flora and fauna, change only at the speed of evolution, although they're likely to reside in databases nonetheless. Educational data such as course syllabi don't normally need to be dynamic. A dynamic lookup would be an extravagance for a language translation database. All these things involve *static data* that changes so infrequently that it may be less trouble to remake a set of Web pages on the rare occasions when the data changes than to maintain a dynamic link.

Drumbeat has a special way of creating a set of Web pages derived from static data. This *PageSet,* like an AutoTable, can be generated only if a Content Table (we talk about them in Chapter 6) already exists. PageSets find plenty of applications in commerce as well as in science and education because much commercial catalog information changes on rare and predictable occasions, and republishing a PageSet is not hard. Let's face it: You may have a "bottom line" reason to go for static data even on a catalog site. This type of data is quicker and often cheaper to set up than a dynamic database link.

Some special types of PageSets even turn out to be partially dynamic after all because they're generated by links to ODBC data tables. But we're getting ahead of ourselves.

Creating Client-Side PageSets

Regardless of where the data you use to create your PageSet comes from — from the back of an envelope, an Access database on your PC, a 100 MB corporate database on a mainframe, or just out of your head — it has to be organized in a Drumbeat Content Table before it can go anywhere else. At the top of Chapter 6, we write that a Content Table is "just another way of organizing data," and that's what we mean.

The Chocolate Maker gets a database

We hint in Chapter 2 that a PageSet may not be a bad idea for the Candy Case page in the Chocolate Maker's Web site. Sure enough — somebody over there got his fingers out of the chocolate icing for long enough to provide a CSV file giving details of their wares. Here are the header and the first line:

```
ProductNum,ProductName,ShowName,ChocType,Description,Price,
          Keywords
599,Chocolate Mint Crunch,"Jack o' the Green",Mint with White
          Chocolate,Creamy White Chocolate with
          Mint,$16.00,mint
```

Figure 9-1 shows the dialog box used to import this entire file into a Content Table. Display this dialog box by exposing the Content Center and clicking the New Content Table button. Note that the Use First Line for Column Names option is checked because that's obviously what the first line is.

Figure 9-2 shows part of the resultant Content Table, all imported in a flash.

By default, every column is designated for the content type Formatted Text, which is fine with us because that's what we need.

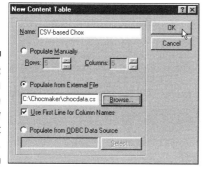

Figure 9-1:
Import a
CSV file into
a new
Content
Table.

A column for images will be inserted here

Figure 9-2:
The first
eight items
in the
chocolate
maker's
Content
Table.

Cleaning up the Content Table

What's missing from the CSV file are the mouthwatering pictures of the
chocolate specialties. Not that it would have been impossible to provide
them — a column containing the exact path to each picture could have been
used as static content for the images in the layout area. The table looks *so*
much prettier, though, if you import the actual images.

To add a new column for images, select the header of the column to the right of the intended insert point, and then *either* click the Add Row/Column button on the left end of the Content Center toolbar *or* right-click and choose Insert from the pop-up menu. Because you want this column to contain images, you have to tell Drumbeat about it, in the dialog box shown in Figure 9-3.

Figure 9-3:
Designate
the media
type of an
inserted
column.

Having created the column successfully, it's now just a matter of filling it with stuff like triple-chocolate and chocolate mint crunch by double-clicking each cell in turn and browsing to the appropriate image. Yummm (see Figure 9-4). The images are .jpg files, sized in proportion to the width of the pieces, and with backgrounds matching the template background color so that they seem to float on the page. Notice that we replaced the generic labels of each row with appropriate names — this has no effect on the appearance of the PageSet but makes life easier when it comes to making links to a page in the PageSet, because you can pick the row and column by name. (To find out how to create links to pages within the PageSet, see the section "Linking to and from pages in PageSets," later in this chapter.)

For the Chocolate Maker, we had to do one more tweak before we could pour all this data into a PageSet. The so-called "show names" of the chocolate articles are the names used as sort of subtitles for displays at Country Faires, and we needed them to appear on the page in quotation marks. Because quotes are considered to be the default "text qualifiers" for CSV files, they fail to import. Because Drumbeat (in common with most database applications) just considers them as unwanted delimiters, we had to add them back into the Content Table column by hand, one pair at a time.

If you're in control of the CSV file itself, you can always use the HTML entity format **"** for a literal double-quote.

It's time to make pages

After you have a Content Table looking right, making the PageSet is amazingly simple:

1. **Open the Site Management Center and click the Site tab.**

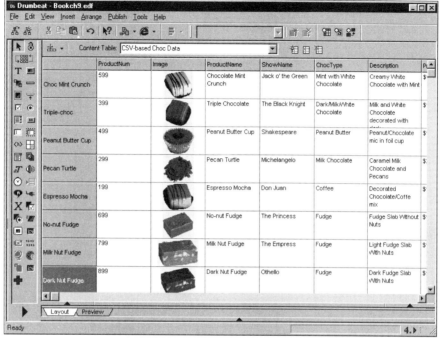

Figure 9-4:
The Content
Table is
finished
except for
one slight
tweak.

2. **Select the page you want the PageSet to be subsidiary to; in this case, Home.**

3. **Click the Insert button to display its variant menu, as shown in Figure 9-5, and choose the PageSet option.**

4. **In the Web Page Properties dialog, give the PageSet a name and select which Content Table to use from the dropdown selector.**

Bingo!

Figure 9-5:
The Insert
Page button
becomes an
Insert
PageSet
button.

Designing PageSets

The first time you create one of these things, you may be disappointed at how drab it looks. Figure 9-6 shows the immediate result of creating a PageSet from the Chocolate Maker's CSV file — it's certainly not impressive. The PageSet may very well have information in it that you don't want, none of it styled or positioned as you want it, and you see only the first of the many items in the Content Table — in this case, the chocolate mint crunch.

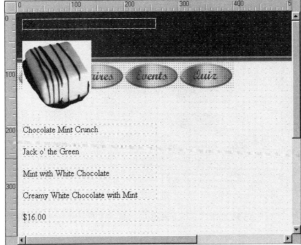

Figure 9-6:
A first look at the Candy Case PageSet: Hmmmm.

Quit worrying — the PageSet exists, but you haven't done any page design yet. Here are some immediate things to do:

- ✔ Select and delete fields you don't need on the page (in this example, `ProductNum`, `ChocType`, and **keywords**).

- ✔ Move the fields you do want into approximate position.

- ✔ Make sure that the Auto Size option is checked on the image's Attributes Sheet.

- ✔ Add any other art the page needs (the header .gif file, in this example).

- ✔ Step through each page of the PageSet by selecting each row of the Content Table in turn (click the row label cell).

That quick review of the whole PageSet may be an early warning of design problems. You may as well pick your favorite chocolate, though (we have to vote for the fudge), and design around that. Any design you do with that page is repeated exactly in the entire set.

Hold on to this thought: No matter how many pages are in a PageSet, there is only one design.

You may want to publish and preview at this point, just to satisfy yourself that those First, Prev, Next, and Last buttons really do work. Yes, they're ugly. Be patient, we soon show you how to fix them up.

A PageSet *always* has one specific Content Table as its primary source of content. In designing pages, however, you're not restricted to having only elements from that table on the page. You may bring content in from any of the usual places, *including other Content Tables.*

The point to bear in mind when you're publishing PageSets is that they really *are* sets of pages. If 36 items are in the Chocolate Maker's catalog, 36 separate pages are published. They're given the kind of names you would expect a computer to hand out, such as these:

```
CandyCase_1_36.html
CandyCase_2_36.html
CandyCase_36_36.html
```

Those pages are served up just like any other HTML page. After they're on the server, they're divorced from the underlying CSV file and the SQL query that allowed the file and the PageSet to join hands at design-time. That's the reason Drumbeat refers to the content of pages or elements as *static* content when it comes from a Content Table.

The SmartSpacer: Taking care of the variables

Figure 9-7 shows the design of the PageSet taking shape — if you're following along in this chapter with your own PageSet project, you've imposed some special styles on the various text blocks and pushed things around until everything's satisfactory. In the Chocolate Maker site, another run-through revealed a typical problem of PageSets: Even though you may think that the data rows are standardized, they are only to a point, and the nonstandard ones can ruin a design unless you know how to cope.

In this case, the image of the chocolate pecan turtle is a good deal taller than the rest (214 pixels, compared to an average around 120). Of course — the turtle is much bigger than the others in real life, too. Figure 9-8 shows how this situation creates a bad effect by making that particular image overlap the navigation buttons.

Figure 9-7:
The Candy
Case
shapes up.

Figure 9-8:
Uh-oh —
problems
with the
pecan turtle.

Image and button overlap

The answer is a *SmartSpacer* — a standard SmartElement whose contribution to page design is invisible but almost magic. The SmartSpacer's job is to keep other page elements vertically separated, come what may. Set a SmartSpacer on the page, and nothing can overlap it. Try to move an element down over it, and you simply push the SmartSpacer down too, together with any other elements that lie below it on the page. Try to move an element up over the SmartSpacer, and the element either stubbornly stays below or pops above it.

This behavior is, in fact, exactly what you need to maintain separation between the image and the navigation buttons in this page design. If you absolutely must make the site available to Version 3.x browsers, you're out of luck — although 4.0 browsers can use the refined CSS positioning techniques on which the SmartSpacer depends.

Adjust the height of a SmartSpacer, 20 pixels by default, by dragging on its handles. You can also adjust its height and origin on its Attributes Sheet. *Origin* means its "original" position — a SmartSpacer can never float higher on the page than its origin.

Fixing up buttons

It's time to do something about those ugly navigation buttons. We had a set of nice chocolatey buttons designed, but how to substitute them for the default buttons without losing their functionality?

The clue is to figure out what's really going on to make the navigation buttons do what they do. Right-click the First button and choose Assigned Interactions (Ordered) from the pop-up menu. The Interactions Center opens, and you see this interaction listed as applied:

```
First: When First is clicked go to the first page in PageSet
```

Click each of the other three in turn and you find similar applied interactions. Now you've lifted the hood and seen how the engine works.

The point is that the appearance of the buttons is nothing special. You can simply delete them and substitute four image button SmartElements on the page, with whatever images you want. Then it's simply a matter of reapplying those same interactions to produce the same functionality. Follow these steps for each button:

1. **Delete the button.**

2. **Substitute the decorative image you want.**

3. **On the Attributes Sheet for the image, give the image an appropriate Name: FirstBtn, PrevBtn, NextBtn, or LastBtn.**

4. **Right-click the image and choose Possible Activations from the pop-up menu. The Interactions Center opens up with a list of possibilities.**

5. **Scroll to the activations in the Pageset Static category and select the one you want.**

6. **Double-click the activation. The icon at the left end of the line changes from blue to red, indicating that the activation is applied.**

Figure 9-9 shows the last of the four activations being applied: `When LastBtn is clicked go to the last page in pageset.`

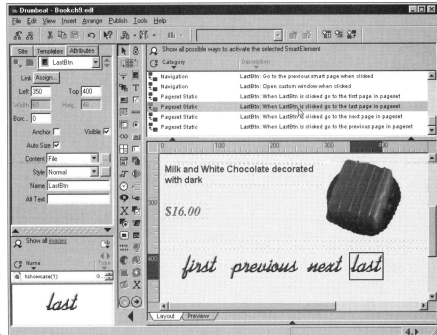

Figure 9-9: Making chocolate navigation buttons not just attractive but also functional.

Linking to and from pages in PageSets

Even though a PageSet is considered one page from the point of view of site structure, incoming hyperlinks may be targeted at any page within the set. By that, we mean that a hyperlink can be set up from some Web page external to the PageSet, pointing to one of the pages within the set. Figure 9-10 shows an incoming link being pointed at the first of the fudge pages — and now you know why we took the trouble to show you how to label the rows of the data table.

Hyperlinks within PageSets don't work, however. You cannot create links from the chocolate turtle page to the fudge page or from the peanut butter cup page to Next Page. The buttons you use to navigate are considered to be all you need.

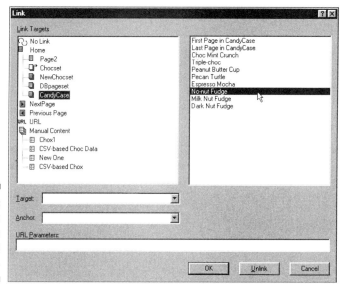

Figure 9-10:
Creating a
hyperlink to
the fudge
pages.

You can create outgoing hyperlinks in the normal way. Any additional elements you bring in to the layout area as hyperlink sources appear on every page in the PageSet. If you want to create a hyperlink from a phrase on *only* the peanut butter cup page, you can do it as long as the phrase originated in the Content Table. With the PageSet in the layout area, expose the Content Table in the Content Center, select the peanut butter cup row by clicking its label cell, and then make your link on the peanut butter page.

Making An Updateable CSV-Derived PageSet

The PageSet we're using as an amusing illustration in this chapter, the Chocolate Maker site, is pretty much committed to static data, on the assumption that the catalog of goodies wouldn't change often enough to justify a dynamic data link. But suppose that the Chocolate Maker objects and demands dynamic data? Hang the expense!

We write about real database connectivity in Chapter 10. However, a kind of intermediate step enables you to create an updateable type of PageSet using ODBC connections but without a database as such.

ODBC, or Open DataBase Connectivity, normally refers to an agreed-on standard allowing any commercial database application to offer its data sets to any other application, using an *ODBC driver.* The driver software is specific to each database format — Oracle, dBASE, and FoxPro, for example — and you normally have to be a registered user of the database type to be able to install its driver.

However, every user of Windows 95 or Windows 98 automatically has a sort of generic ODBC driver: the *Microsoft Text Driver,* which uses plain old ASCII files with extensions such as .txt, .asc, and .csv as its data sources. Setting up connectivity to a real database (described in Chapter 10) involves creating a *Data Source Name (DSN)* that references the database in SQL, the ODBC language,.

Confused? Life's about to get easier because we step you through the process of making your .csv files *appear as though* they are the tables of a real database. You do it by making a DSN out of not a database, but rather the folder in which the .csv files reside.

The result will be an actual set of pages, one for each record in the data file. The relationship between the PageSet and the data file is dynamic only at design-time. The data file doesn't even get published because it wouldn't get used.

So what's the point? Only that this technique separates the responsibility for data update from that for site design — and that may well reflect the setup where you work.

Making the Content Table

You've heard of a 12-step program? This procedure goes four steps better:

1. **Open the ODBC Data Source Administrator by double-clicking the ODBC Data Sources icon in your Control Panel.**

   Figure 9-11 shows what the Data Source Administrator looks like.

2. **Select the System DSN tab, and click Add.**

   You see the Create New Data Source dialog box, which lists all the ODBC drivers you have installed. Figure 9-12 shows what ours looks like — your mileage will certainly vary, but if you don't have the Microsoft text driver available, something is seriously amiss with your system.

3. **Select the Microsoft text driver and click Finish.**

   Now you see the ODBC Text Setup dialog box. Expand it by clicking Options. It looks like the dialog box shown in Figure 9-13.

Figure 9-11:
The Windows 95 ODBC Data Source Administrator. Official-sounding, isn't it?

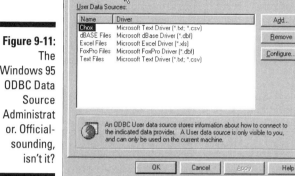

Figure 9-12:
Select the Microsoft text driver for a data source.

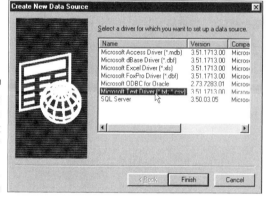

Figure 9-13:
The ODBC Text Setup dialog box.

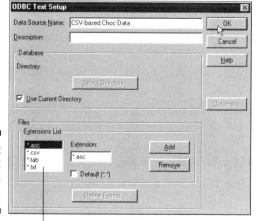

File extensions list

4. **Enter a name and (optionally) a description of the data source — in this case,** CSV-based Choc Data **— and make sure that .csv is listed on the extensions list, in the lower-left corner.**

   Note that you can equally well access .txt and other file types in this way, but the data fields still must be comma-separated.

5. **Uncheck the Use Current Directory option and instead click Select Directory.**

6. **In the Select Directory dialog box, browse to the folder that contains your data,** as shown in Figure 9-14.

File names are grayed out because the folder, not the file, is the data source

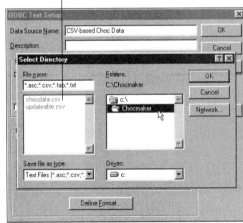

Figure 9-14:
Select a
folder as a
source for
the text
driver.

7. **Click OK, click OK again, and then close the ODBC Data Source Administrator by clicking OK one more time.**

8. **In Drumbeat, click the Add Assets button, select Queries to open the Query Manager, and then click New.**

   In the SQL Query dialog box, you should now find on the dropdown list of data sources the data source you just created.

9. **Select the Data Source from the dropdown list. All files with .csv extensions that are in the folder the DSN points to are listed in the Tables window.**

10. **Select the one that has the data you want to use.**

   The column names are listed in the window to the right, as shown in Figure 9-15.

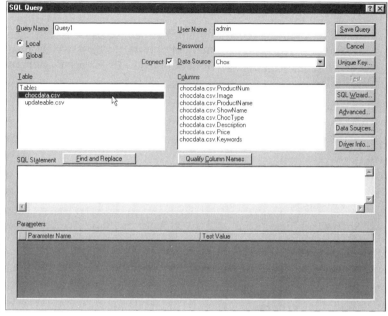

Figure 9-15:
The CSV file is brought into the Drumbeat SQL Query dialog box successfully.

11. **Write a SQL statement in the SQL window that selects the columns of data you need. (For more information about creating SQL statements, see the section "Oh, say, can you SQL?" in Chapter 10.)**

    If you want to import them all, just write **SELECT * FROM [filename].csv**.

    For the Chocolate Maker PageSet, we wrote the following because we knew that we did not need some of the columns:

    ```
    SELECT Image,ProductName,ShowName,Description,Price FROM
            chocdata.csv.
    ```

12. **Click the Test button to make sure that the SQL statement is understood. If the test produces a query error, something is wrong with the SQL statement.**

13. **Give the query a name in the Query Name box in the upper-left corner (something to replace the default and make more sense to you), and click Save Query.**

    The Query Manager reappears, with your new query listed.

14. **Make sure that the new query is selected and click Create Table.**

    The status bar in the dialog box indicates that Drumbeat is creating the table.

15. **Close the Query Manager by clicking the Done button. Open the Content Center and select the table from the dropdown list to see your new Content Table.**

Notice that the CSV file you used, unlike the old one, has a column for the images. Not the images themselves — that would be impossible in an ASCII file — but rather the paths to them. You cannot edit an ODBC Content Table the same way you can edit a manual Content Table — which means that you cannot add rows or columns or add items to the Content Table by dragging and dropping.

To make the images appear on the pages of your PageSet, you merely need to use an Image SmartElement rather than the text field that's automatically generated.

1. **Make a PageSet from the Content Table.**

2. **In the layout area, delete the text element that contains the path to the image.**

3. **Drag an I Image SmartElement from the SmartElements toolbar to the layout.**

4. **On the Attributes Sheet for the image, select Static Content for the content of the image. In the Content dialog box, assign the Content Table column containing the image path.**

Now you can go about the business of page design as before.

Make sure that the Auto Size option is checked on the Attributes Sheet for the image so that the image size adjusts as necessary on different pages.

Updating the PageSet

The difference — an important difference — between this PageSet and the one we started this chapter with is that if the underlying CSV file changes, the PageSet changes too. Does a change to the data file show up immediately in the PageSet in Drumbeat? Ah, well — that just depends. Here's the deal:

✔ Every time you open the site in Drumbeat, the PageSet is remade to conform — so, yes, you see the latest content in the CSV file for the PageSet.

✔ If the site's already open in Drumbeat — no, the PageSet won't change. To refresh the content, you have to reconnect to the data file.

To refresh the content of the PageSet, click the Edit Content Table button and click OK in the dialog box. The PageSet changes to show the new content. To update the PageSet on the server, however, you still have to republish.

Here's the only point that truly matters: After the site is published, the PageSet does *not* get updated unless somebody makes the effort to update and republish.

Part III

Creating Server-Side, Database-Driven Pages

The 5th Wave   By Rich Tennant

"I'm not sure I like a college whose home page has a link to The Party Zone!"

In this part . . .

Find out how Drumbeat builds Active Server Pages or JavaServer Pages faster than any product on the market. As the DataForm Wizard performs his abra-cadabra, you'll have a database-driven web site before you can blink. This part explains how to hook up your database, use the wizard to create your pages, and then customize your database pages with special form elements and interactions.

Chapter 10

Hooking Up to a Database

· ·

In This Chapter

▶ Figuring out your database setup

▶ Naming your database (setting up a DSN)

▶ Deciding what you want to use in your database (creating a query)

▶ Viewing and using your data in Drumbeat

· ·

*W*e can come up with lots of fashionable reasons to build Active Server Pages: They make you look totally with-it and up-to-date. They get you invited to cool Microsoft seminars where you get free T-shirts. You can put "ASP programmer" on your résumé and up your ante in the techie employment stakes.

Using database content on your Web site, however, is the only rational reason for using ASP. Sure, you can make Active Server Pages without ever using a database. But that's kind of like buying an airplane and sitting in the cockpit and making raspberry noises as you pretend to fly. If you want to earn your ASP wings, you first have to get a database together and get it connected. You have to tell Drumbeat where to find it so that you can build your ASP pages, and you have to tell your Web server about it so it can serve up the data on your Web site.

We know of no way to talk about databases without getting temporarily tongue-tied with acronyms. Fortunately, the ones you need are fairly limited, so let's get all the acronyms used in this chapter out of the way quickly:

> ✔ **ODBC:** The translator that enables different database applications to connect to different applications
>
> ✔ **DSN:** The nickname you give to your database so that it comes when you call
>
> ✔ **SQL:** The language you use to get information out of your database

Whew! That's it. In this chapter, you learn what you need to know to use a database in Web pages and how to set up your database so that you can build Active Server Pages in Drumbeat.

Setting Up a Database Scheme

If you're lucky, you already have a database hanging around that you want to use to build your Active Server Pages. Maybe you built it awhile back for some other use — your grandmother's precious cookie recipes, perhaps. Or maybe it's already part of your mighty organization's copious files and your task is to make it accessible to a Web-based intranet. In that case, you may need to understand only a little about how the database is organized before you start to build your Active Server Pages.

On the other hand, the idea of a database-driven site may just be a gleam in your eye. You have some idea of the content you could put in a database and how you could use it to make your Web site more efficient, although you're not quite sure how to organize the material. Although we can't give you a complete course in database management here, we can give you some basic understanding and guidelines before you begin.

First off, all databases are not alike. That's a fact of life we can't do much about. Some database applications use one set of terms for things, others another. Some let you see the big picture. Others, especially those used in big corporate applications, limit what you can see to just a little porthole view of the vast sea.

If you're new to databases, a good resource to get you started is *Intranet & Web Databases For Dummies,* by Paul Litwin (IDG Books Worldwide, Inc.).

Oh dee, be see, please

The first question you have to determine is whether your database is fully ODBC compliant. ODBC stands for Open Data Base Connectivity, a standard that enables databases of different origins to talk to each other and be accessed by other programs. Although most professionally oriented databases on the market today are ODBC compliant, a few aren't. Some of the small "desktop databases" that have become popular in the last ten years, as wonderful and easy to use as they are, aren't ODBC compliant.

If you want to build Active Server Pages, you must have an ODBC compliant database. That's because other programs (Drumbeat and your Web server included) have to get access to your database to obtain the data they need to run.

So what if you have a little baby database you love dearly but it's time for it to grow up and go to ODBC academy? Not to worry. Almost all database applications, even dinky ones, enable you to export your database files in one form or another and import files from other formats. If you can't import your database directly into the new application, you should at least be able to export the tables from the original program separately as TXT or CSV files. These files can then be imported into your new ODBC program, where you can reset up any necessary relationships.

Understanding databases

If you're just getting started with creating your database you need to sit down and think about the kind of data you're presenting and how to organize it most efficiently. Before you try to put your entire CD collection on your new home page, decide whether you want to organize it by artist, musical genre, or by the boyfriend or girlfriend you had when you bought it.

If you're using an existing database, you need to be familiar with how that database is organized. Here's a quick rundown of database essentials:

Tables are the primary organization pieces of a database. Every database has at least one. Big, important databases have lots.

- ✔ A "flat-file database" is a database that has only one table. All the information is presented in one grid. A spreadsheet file, such as an Excel file, is an example of a flat-file database.

- ✔ A fully relational database contains a number of tables — anywhere from two to several thousand — which relate to one another in various ways. Each table organizes discrete parts of the much bigger database puzzle.

- ✔ Each row in a data table is known as a *record,* and each column represents a different type of information. The terms *column* and *field* are often used interchangeably.

Primary keys: A primary key is simply a field (or column) that is *guaranteed* to be different in every record. It uniquely identifies each record, in other words. You could use the first names of your friends as a primary key for your Rolodex database only if you had a miserably small circle of friends. It would surely fail because everybody is destined to have more than one John in their lives. Some data tables have natural primary keys, although more often a key field of sequential numbers is created with its sole purpose in life to be a unique identifier for the record. The same key fields are sometimes *foreign keys* when used to relate multiple tables or views to one another.

Queries are the logical statements that select the data you want to use for a particular function. You can construct queries in your database application using a visual interface, write them by hand if you know SQL, or construct simple queries directly in Drumbeat with the SQL Query Wizard (see the section "SQL the wizard's way," later in this chapter).

Views are pretty much the same as queries. Most big, industrial-strength database applications use the term *view* rather than *query*. Also, in many large corporate databases, users do not have access to the tables behind the database applications. Users are allowed to access only different Views that have been set up by the database administrator, often with secure access.

Stored procedures are compiled SQL subroutines that can be stored in the database and called from your application to process or retrieve information from the database.

Calling your database by name

If you've never worked with databases, the idea of setting up a Data Source Name (DSN) for it may seem a little confusing. It's really no big deal, though. A DSN is just a nickname you create for your database.

This unique name identifies the database to your own computer and gives it the basic driver information it needs to make a connection to the database from any other application. When the DSN is created, the path to the database is mapped and stored with it.

If you're working with a personal database on your own computer, whenever you're ready to publish your site, you have to transfer your database up to your Web server. Then you (or somebody) have to create a DSN for it on the server, too. The DSN used on your machine and on the Web server must be identical. Although the path to the database is inevitably different, the server has no trouble finding it if it's using the right nickname.

If you're using the JSP version of Drumbeat 2000, you may think that creating a DSN for ODBC connection shouldn't apply to you — but it does! Drumbeat uses ODBC for design-time display of database elements. You have to create an ODBC DSN if you want to see what you're doing. JDBC takes over after you publish. You also must take the extra step of setting up the JDBC connectivity to your database, which you do from the SQL Query builder. Click the JDBC button to get to the JDBC setup options.

DSN, DNS — whatever

If you've been hanging around the Web awhile, you may be likely to confuse DSN with DNS — or think that your eyes are playing tricks on you. We can't blame you. We often say one when we mean the other, too. A DNS is a Domain Name Server, which is responsible for resolving Internet domain addresses like `uspo.gov` and `amazon.com` on the host server. When your domain name (for example, `me.com`) is set up on your Web server, the relationship between `me.com` and the boring numerical IP address (`199.2.50.5`, for example) is created within the DNS. It has everything to do with whether people can find their way to your site, although it doesn't really have anything to do with your database.

If you're publishing to a remote server, you may have to rely on your ISP to set up your DSN on the server after you've transferred the database. Some ISPs, however, have special setups that make it possible for you to create your own DSNs on the server. This ability can be useful if you intend to do a great deal of work creating different database-driven sites. If you're in the market for an ISP to host your ASP site, you may want to look for an ISP that offers this service rather than rely on someone else to get around to your requests in her own sweet time.

Setting up the DSN

Setting up the DSN for your database is something that's done outside of Drumbeat, in the Windows or Windows NT ODBC Data Source Administrator. (If you have an ODBC database installed on your system, you have the ODBC Data Source Administrator.) After the DSN is set up, Drumbeat and other programs can access the database. Other programs include Personal Web Server if you're testing your Active Server Pages locally. Drumbeat lets you access the ODBC Data Source Administrator from within Drumbeat (from its SQL Query Builder). Because there are so many other steps to get there and back and such a maze of dialog boxes to wander through, though, it's probably easier to do it from Windows. That way, you can better understand where you've been and be able to find your way back if necessary. (One reason you may have to find your way back is if you move your database; in that case, you have to reconfigure the path to the database.)

To get to the ODBC Data Source Administrator, choose Start⇨Settings⇨ Control Panel⇨ODBC.

As shown in Figure 10-1, you can set up three types of DSNs:

 ✔ **User DSN:** Available only to an individual user on a computer and stored in the user's personal settings

 ✔ **System DSN:** Available to anyone who uses the computer on which the DSN is defined

 ✔ **File DSN:** Created as an independent file that can be easily moved from one system to the next

A system DSN does fine for most purposes, so that's what we use for illustration, although the process of setting it up differs little from the other methods.

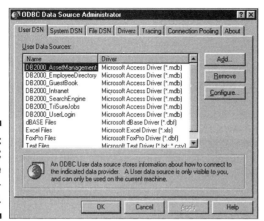

Figure 10-1:
The ODBC
Data Source
Adminis-
trator.

If you've set up a file DSN correctly, you may be able to use it to set up the DSN on the Web server itself so that it doesn't have to be re-created on the server. You have to check with your Web server administrator before attempting this procedure, however.

To set up a new DSN:

1. **Click the System DSN tab. Then click Add, as shown in Figure 10-2.**

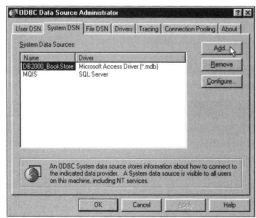

Figure 10-2:
System
DSNs are
listed on the
System tab,
where you
can add a
new one or
reconfigure
an existing
one.

2. **Select a driver for your database, and then click Finish.**

    The driver you select matches your database application. If you're using a Microsoft Access database, you select the Microsoft Access Driver, as shown in Figure 10-3. (If you're using a DB2 database for the JSP version of Drumbeat, the setup is slightly different.)

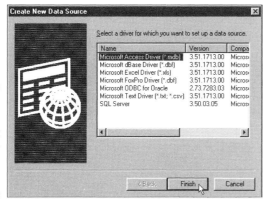

Figure 10-3:
Select the
correct
driver for
your data-
base.

Next, you have to name and select the database you want to access.

3. **Type the nickname you want for this database.**

You can add a description in the Description field if you want, although it's not necessary.

4. **Click Select to browse to the location of the database, and then choose it.**

You're back on the System DSN tab with the path to your database correctly showing in the dialog box, as shown in Figure 10-4.

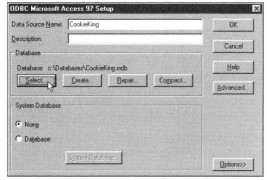

Figure 10-4:
Give your
data source
a name and
select it by
browsing.

5. **Click OK.**

You're done setting up your DSN. Back on the System DSN tab in the ODBC Data Source Administrator dialog box, you see your new DSN listed.

6. **Click OK to close the dialog box.**

You're ready to use your database in Drumbeat!

When Drumbeat is installed, it automatically creates DSNs for several of the databases included in the Starting Points files. (See the section "Creating a Site," in Chapter 2, for more info about Starting Points.) These DSNs, listed on the System DSN tab, all begin with DB2000. You can select one of these (for example, DB2000_AssetManagement) and click Configure to see how it's set up.

Chocolate chip or white chocolate macadamia nut?

For the rest of this chapter, we talk about cookies — no, not the annoying little notes that Internet merchants write on your hard drive, but rather the crunchy, munchy things produced by that collection of Nana's recipes we mention earlier in this chapter. To make an interesting database to play with, assume that a busy kitchen is turning out orders on schedule in a businesslike manner. This database — named CookieKing — has four related data tables:

- The orders for batches of cookies you've received
- The types of cookies you make
- The exact recipes for each type of cookie you bake
- The list of cookie ingredients you have on hand and which recipes use what

Figure 10-5 shows the CookieKing database tables, neatly organized in Microsoft Access.

The Cookie King database, which is used in this and the next two chapters, is provided in the sample files on the CD. Install the sample files in your Drumbeat directory. Then, using the instructions in the section "Setting Up the DSN," earlier in this chapter, set up the DSN "CookieKing" to the database in C:\Program Files\Drumbeat 2000\ASPSamples\CookieKing\CookieKing.mdb. (If you have the JSP version of Drumbeat, substitute JSPSamples for the ASPSamples directory.)

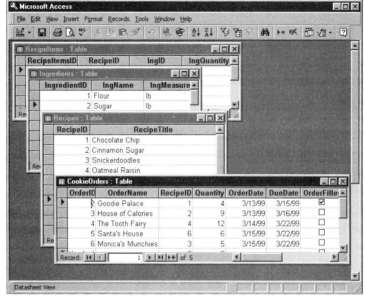

Figure 10-5:
The
CookieKing
Database
details
require-
ments for
cookie
orders,
recipes, and
ingredients.

Creating a Query

To build database-driven pages in Drumbeat, you have to first construct a query. You may not have to do this procedure quite from scratch: If you've already constructed in your database application some queries you want to use or have had them constructed for you, you can race right through this section. The process of accessing those queries, however, still requires you to go through the Drumbeat SQL Query Builder, so start it up and take a look.

To get to the SQL Query Builder:

1. **Click the Add Assets button in the Assets Center and select Queries, as shown in Figure 10-6.**

   The Query Manager, shown in Figure 10-7, lists the queries that have already been built for this site. Empty? That's because you're just getting started.

Figure 10-6:
Opening the
Query
Manager.

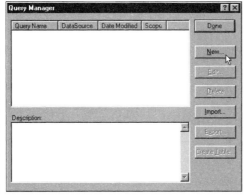

Figure 10-7:
Begin to
create a
new query
or edit an
existing one
in the Query
Manager.

2. **Click New to create a new query.**

   The SQL Query Builder is where you get down to business.

3. **Select the data source to use from the Data Source drop-down list.**

   If you've created your DSN to the CookieKing database, you'll find it on the list, as shown in Figure 10-8.

If you haven't yet created your DSN, you can take a little trip through the looking glass to the Windows ODBC Data Source Administrator to create it from here. Click Data Sources and the ODBC Data Source Administrator pops up over the Drumbeat screen. When you finish with the ODBC Data Source Administrator, you return to the SQL Query Builder.

After you've selected your Data Source, the tables and views (if any) in that database are visible in the left Tables window. You can peruse the structural content of a table or view by clicking any name. The column names from the database appear magically in the Columns window on the right. If you've forgotten or don't know the names of columns in a table, this reminder is a helpful one. Don't confuse what you see in this display with what you do in selecting a table for a query, however! Drumbeat's just trying to be helpful in showing you the content of your database.

In the SQL Statement window, you construct your actual SQL query. There are three means to this end:

  ✔ You can type a SQL statement directly in the window.

  ✔ You can copy and paste a SQL statement from another application into the window.

  ✔ You can use the SQL Wizard to construct a SQL statement for you.

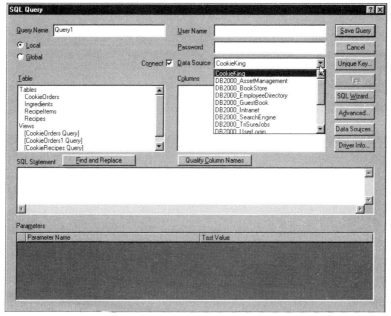

Figure 10-8:
Select a
data source
from the list
of DSNs in
the SQL
Query
Builder.

If you know how to use SQL, you may prefer to use the first option. In that case, you can skip the next couple of sections. If don't want to re-create work you've already done, however, look at the section "Using a preexisting query or view," later in this chapter, to see how to use these features in Drumbeat. When you're finished, don't forget to name your query and save it.

Drumbeat uses ODBC for design-time display of databases. JDBC is used at runtime, when you access your JavaServer Pages through the server. If you're using the JSP version of Drumbeat 2000, you have to set up the JDBC/ODBC connectivity before the database can be properly accessed. Drumbeat allows you to create your queries, but the proper connection isn't established until you provide the JDBC Connectivity information. To set up JDBC connectivity, click the JDBC Connectivity button in the SQL Query Builder. Select the database from those available or click Add to add a new one, and provide the information required for your server and connection.

Oh, say, can you SQL?

SQL, short for Structured Query Language, is the Esperanto of database languages: No matter what internal language the database application understands, it's supposed to understand and respond to SQL when it's spoken to.

The basis for almost all SQL statements you need is the `SELECT` statement.

We don't intend to teach you all about SQL here, although a simple working knowledge of the SELECT statement takes you a very long way. We diverge from cookies from a moment to give you an example.

To select a table named Animals in your database and include all the fields, you can just enter this line:

```
SELECT * FROM Animals
```

The asterisk means "all," so the preceding line would be the same as this one:

```
SELECT ALL FROM Animals
```

If you want to select fields from more than one table, you can extend this SQL statement a little:

```
SELECT * FROM Animals, Vegetables
```

If these two tables are related in some way — if Animals has a field named FavoriteFood, for example, that looks up a corresponding value in the field VegetableID in Vegetables — you have to say what that connection is:

```
SELECT * FROM Animals, Vegetables
WHERE Animals.FavoriteFood=Vegetables.VegetableID
```

You can easily see where extracting data with SQL statements can get much more complex. You may want to add a qualification that you want only animals that live in Africa, or maybe vegetarian animals that live in Africa whose adult weight is more than 500 pounds. Or, you may want to specify SELECT * FROM Animals, Vegetables, Minerals and then use your database to derive the minimum daily requirement of calcium for elephants. For that, you may need a stored procedure, which we talk about later in this chapter, in the section "Using stored procedures."

The "ID" tacked on to the end of VegetableID, you may notice, is a dead giveaway that you're dealing with a primary key that's probably auto-numbered.

By the way, whether you call it "ess-cue-ell" or "see-quel" — it's all the same to us. We prefer the latter because it's easier to say (and it makes the title to this section work).

If you plan to design a large number of database-driven sites, probably the most useful thing you can add to your knowledge is SQL. A good introduction to this topic is *SQL For Dummies,* by Allen G. Taylor (IDG Books Worldwide, Inc.).

SQL the wizard's way

Assuming that you have a fairly simple query you want to create (from one to three tables with some simple WHERE clauses), you can use the SQL Wizard to build it for you, with a little prompting. The following steps show you how to create a query to the CookieKing database to extract the orders information, using the SQL Wizard:

1. **Choose a Data Source in the SQL Query Builder.**

2. **Click the SQL Wizard button.**

3. **In the From Tables dialog box, check the table or tables you want to include in the query.**

   You need data from both the `CookieOrders` and `Recipe` tables, which are already related by the key field `RecipeID`. You check both tables, as shown in Figure 10-9, and click Next.

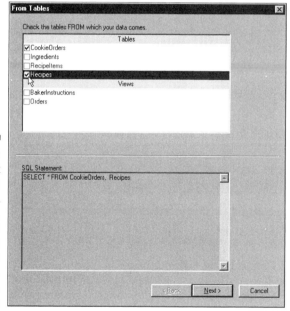

Figure 10-9:
In the first dialog box in the SQL Wizard, select the tables to include in your SQL statement.

4. **In the Select Columns dialog box, check the columns in each table you want to include in the query. Then click Next.**

   Note that only the tables you've selected in the preceding dialog box appear in this one. Each table is expanded to show all the available fields. In this example, you want all the fields from both `CookieOrders` and `Recipes` because you want to use the real name of the cookie (which is in the Recipes table) and not just the numerical value RecipeID, which relates the two tables. In Figure 10-10, you can plainly see how the appropriate SQL statement gets created automatically.

The order in which you select the columns determines the order they appear in the SQL statement and in the Content Table you generate. This table is based on the query and the order in which the columns get placed on the page when you use the DataForm Wizard. It isn't critical because you can move things around later, but it can be a timesaver to select them in the order you think you want to see them on a page.

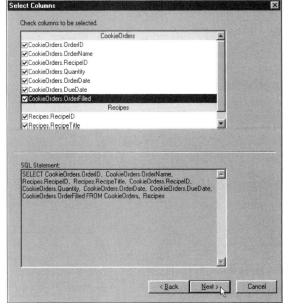

Figure 10-10: Select the columns from each table to include in your SQL statement.

5. **In the Select Unique Key Columns dialog box, check the columns that are the primary keys in your database tables.**

   Because this data selection is relational, Drumbeat needs to know which fields are the primary keys in each data table. In this example, OrderID in CookieOrders and RecipeID from Recipes are the primary keys. If you're not going to — ahem — lose your cookies as this data is imported into Drumbeat, you need to state the relationship between the two tables in the next dialog box, named Where Clauses.

6. **In the Where Clauses dialog box, click in the Expression 1 box and select** CookieOrders.RecipeID **from the drop-down list. Click in the Qualifier box, and then select = from the drop-down list. Click in the Expression 2 box and select** Recipes.RecipeID **from the drop-down list. Figure 10-11 shows the results.**

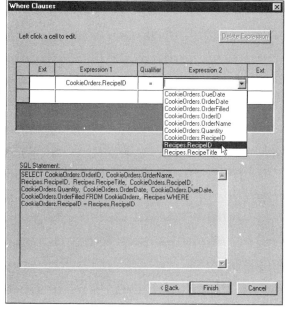

Figure 10-11:
In the
Where
Clauses
dialog box,
define the
relationship
between
your tables
and any
qualifiers for
your SQL
statement.

Nothing stops you from filtering your data in more complex ways using this dialog box. You could restrict the data to only unfilled orders, for example, with `WHERE CookieOrders.OrderFilled = FALSE`. However, because the Drumbeat ASP handling allows just such data filtering within the page, you may prefer to do it there.

7. When you're done, click Finish.

The SQL Query Builder returns to the screen, where you see the SQL statement you just built, as shown in Figure 10-12.

If you have duplicate column names — that is, the same name appears in two different tables, such as the `RecipeID` field that relates the two tables in the example — you have to qualify your column names so that Drumbeat knows which column belongs to which table. When you click Save Query or the Test button, you're prompted to do so before the results can be saved or displayed. Or, you can take care of it right away yourself by clicking the Qualify Column Names button, as shown in Figure 10-13.

Click the Test button to preview the results, as shown in Figure 10-14. This action not only lets you know whether any problems occur with your query before you try to use it but also makes you feel more secure.

If you see an error message, you can go back and edit the query and click Test again until you get it to work.

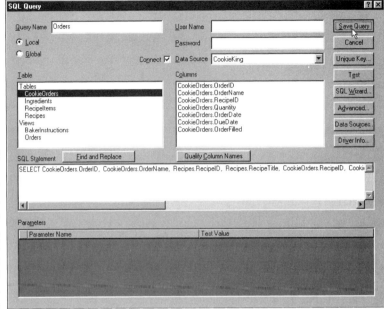

Figure 10-12:
When your
SQL state-
ment is
complete,
test it and
save it in
SQL Query
Builder.

8. **Click Save Query to get back to the Query Manager.**

Your new query is listed. As a final step, you should create a Content Table based on the query while you're there.

9. **Select your query and click Create Table. Then click Done to close the Query Manager.**

It may not be immediately clear that Drumbeat is doing anything when you click Create Table, but you see the results in the Content Table later, as explained in the section "Creating an ODBC Content Table," later in this chapter.

Using a preexisting query or view

SQL queries to large databases can be way too complex for you to be happy about having to create them all in Drumbeat. Also, the irksome fact is that many database applications have their own little dialects of SQL or their own peculiar syntax they want you to adhere to. Except for simple SQL statements like those we show you how to create in the preceding section, you're better off using a query or view that's built in the original database application.

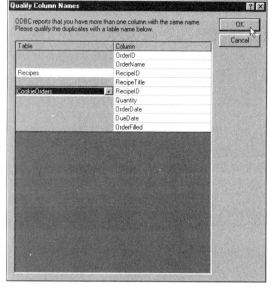

Figure 10-13:
Qualify the columns with duplicate names by choosing the correct table for each.

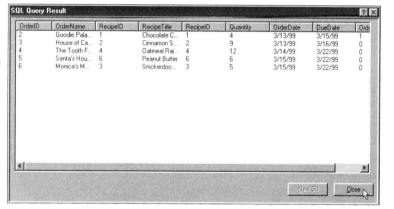

Figure 10-14:
View sample results of a query, and make sure that it works by testing it.

Drumbeat very deftly handles queries built in other applications by putting them in a little wrapper so that rather than have to accept and interpret the Drumbeat-generated SQL, the database interprets it in its own native fashion.

To use a predefined view:

1. **Click the Add Assets button and select Queries. In the Query Manager, click New.**

2. **In the SQL Query Builder, select your Data Source.**

3. **Create a `SELECT ALL` statement to your view, as shown in Figure 10-15.**

You can easily complete this step by typing this line in the window:

```
SELECT * FROM [ThisView]
```

Replace [ThisView] with the name of the View listed in the Table window you want to access.

If you really hate typing, you can use the SQL Wizard to create a SELECT ALL statement to your view. Whiz right through this procedure like so:

1. **Select the view in the From Tables dialog box, and then click Next.**

2. **Skip over the rest of the dialog boxes by clicking Next, Next, and then Finish.**

When you're finished, don't forget to name your query and save it.

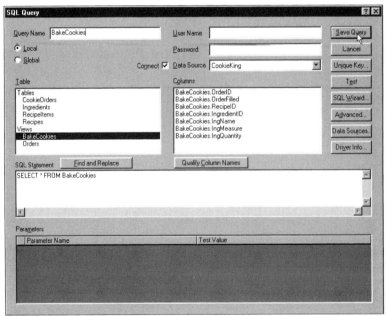

Figure 10-15:
Create a query to a view in your database.

Creating an ODBC Content Table

After you've created your queries to your database, you have to do just one more thing to make the data available for use in designing your pages in Drumbeat: Create a Content Table. Chapter 6 explains how you can use Content Tables as a convenient way to store assets you use over and over in your Web site. ODBC Content Table are a little different.

An ODBC Content Table looks the same as manual and CSV file-based tables, but serves a different purpose. It lets you visualize the database content so that you can use it for design purposes and gives you a visual way to make connections to the data and define interactions with the database.

Each ODBC Content Table is connected to a query you have already defined in Query Manager. You can create an ODBC Content Table in two ways:

- ✔ In the Query Manager, after you've defined your query, select the query and click the Create Table button.

- ✔ In the Content Center, click the New Content Table. In the New Content Table dialog box, select the option Populate from ODBC Data Source, and then click Select, as shown in Figure 10-16. Select the Query in the Query Manager, click Done, and then click OK.

Figure 10-16:
Create a new content table based on an ODBC data source you've defined in a query.

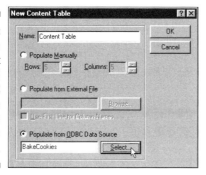

To see the contents of the Content Table, open the Content Center and select the table from the dropdown list, as shown in Figure 10-17.

Figure 10-17:
A content table made from the Orders query to the database.

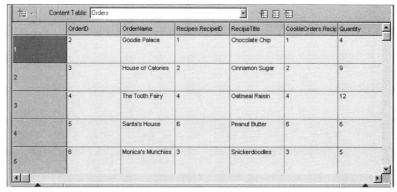

One important thing to remember about ODBC Content Tables is that you cannot edit an ODBC Content Table directly, although you can edit its underlying query.

When you're working with large databases, things go much faster if you limit the number of results displayed. On the Content tab of your Drumbeat Preferences (choose File⇨Preferences⇨Drumbeat). Although Drumbeat normally displays 50 results, you can reduce the number to something smaller. If you don't need to see results in your design, you can turn off the display of SQL results entirely, by checking that option box.

You have to repeat these steps each time you create a new site using ASP or JSP in Drumbeat:

1. **Create a DSN for your database (if it doesn't already exist).**

2. **Create queries to access the data.**

3. **Create an ODBC Content Table for each query.**

Chapter 11

Creating Active Server Pages Fast

. . . .

In This Chapter

▶ Preparing to use the DataForm Wizard

▶ Creating search and browse pages with the DataForm Wizard

▶ Creating Insert and Update pages

▶ Using a new recordset to customize a dropdown list

. . . .

*T*he DataForm Wizard is in many ways the ringmaster of Drumbeat's three-ring circus. Although the Drumbeat styles and scripting features are pretty cool, it's the database action that's the high wire act. We're willing to bet that you didn't buy the Drumbeat software or this book because you need another HTML editor but rather because you want to start building database-driven Web sites. Or, if you already do that for a living, you may want to find a tool that makes the process a whole lot easier.

Meet the DataForm Wizard. He's going to be your friend in this learning process. Although you can build database-driven pages in Drumbeat without the wiz (we show you how to do some of that in later chapters), he makes it so easy that you'll probably rely on him a great deal.

Getting Ready for the DataForm Wizard

Click the Site tab. Next to the Insert Page button is another button with a starburst on it. Has the sun come out on your button, or does it look cloudy and gray? If the sun's out, you can go out and play (skip right on over to the following section). If it's not, just choose File⇨Preferences⇨Site to make that button shine: In the Server Application Support box, click the arrow and select ASP (or WebSphere for JSP). Then click OK.

Notice that the browser support is set for Navigator 3.0. One of the benefits of server pages is that they work even in generic browsers, so you don't have to be concerned about designing only for 4.0 browsers or higher unless you want to include other features that are 4.0 and higher only.

Back on the Site tab, you should see the New DataForm button light up. You're now allowed to go play with the DataForm Wizard.

We may as well get one more thing out of the way right now because we know that you will want to look at your pages in the browser after you've created them, and you can't do that until you've set up your publishing settings properly:

1. **Choose Publish⇨Publish Settings.**

2. **In the Publish Settings dialog box, enter the path to the directory to which you will publish on the server.**

   If you're using Personal Web Server or IIS, the directory is named something like C:\Inetpub\wwwroot\mysite. (For C, substitute the drive you're publishing to on your computer or your intranet.)

3. **Click the ASP tab. For the Alias option, enter just the name of the directory to which you are publishing. In Step 2, the directory is mysite.**

4. **For the Default Page option, click Select and select the page you want to start from in the site. Then click OK.**

You may want to leave the last step until you have created your DataForm pages so that you can choose one of these pages for your default page. We cover the process of setting up for publishing in more detail in Chapter 2, so if you haven't done any of this before and can't quite figure out what we're talking about, flip over there and have a look.

Doing Your Database Homework

DataForm Wizard is pleased as punch that you're ready to play. However, he hopes that you know the rules of the game when it comes to databases. Here's another spot test:

1. **Click the New DataForm button on the Site tab.**

   The DataForm Wizard pops up, with a window in which you're supposed to select a data source, as shown in Figure 11-1. Is anything listed there? If you have one or more Content Tables or recordsets listed, good. (You can cancel and get back to the game in the next section.)

2. **If the box is empty, click New Content Table. In the New Content Table dialog box, which already has the Populate from ODBC Data Source option selected, click Select.**

   The Query Manager pops up, as shown in Figure 11-2. Is anything listed there? If so, it means that you've created your query but neglected to create an ODBC Content Table for it. Every query needs an ODBC Content Table to get started.

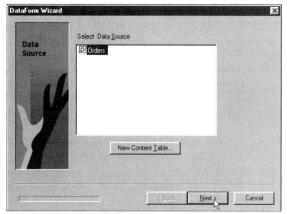

Figure 11-1:
Got Content
Tables or
recordsets
listed here?

3. **Just select the query and click Done. In the New Content Table dialog box, name the Content Table** Orders, **and then click OK.**

You're back in business!

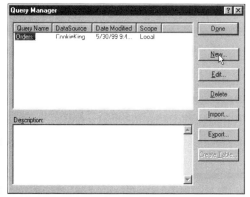

Figure 11-2:
Got a query?

If no queries are listed in the Query Manager, you have some homework to catch up on. Click Cancel and go read Chapter 10 to find out how to set up SQL queries and ODBC Content Tables. Here's what you have to do:

1. **Hook up your database (create a DSN).**

2. **Create your queries to the database in the Drumbeat SQL Query Builder.**

3. **Create an ODBC Content Table.**

After you're caught up with the information in Chapter 10, come back and we'll play ball.

The Wizard's Way

The Drumbeat DataForm Wizard automatically creates for you five different types of database-driven pages, which it calls DataForms. The Wizard builds these pages for you at your bidding:

- ✔ **Detail:** Includes the details of each record in your database. Usually, you have one record per page. However, you can also choose to use a data loop, which enables you to display a set number of records per page (whatever you specify).

- ✔ **Search:** Lets you set up a search operation by choosing the field or fields you want to search in your database.

- ✔ **ResultList:** Creates a list of results matching a search. The results are presented in table format. You can create links from each record to its detail page for more information.

- ✔ **Insert:** Enables you to insert new records into your database. You can use form elements of different types for each column in which you want to insert data.

- ✔ **Update:** This page enables you to edit and update existing records, typically by clicking an Update button on the detail page for a record.

In addition, you can add a Delete option. If you check the Delete option, the wizard adds a button to the Detail page that enables you to delete the current record.

Although it may be tempting to create all five DataForm pages at one time, we suggest that you keep it simple the first time around and just create the detail, search, and result list pages, for two reasons:

- ✔ You most likely will want to separate the display and maintenance functions of the site so that site visitors can view and search records, although only the users you approve of can have access to the underlying database for inserting and updating records.

- ✔ You may need to use different queries for the Insert and Update pages, depending on your database application and database structure.

With these principles in mind, return to the CookieKing's kitchen to see how things are going and whip up a batch of DataForm pages.

You can follow the recipes in this chapter exactly by installing the ASPSamples files on the CD. Two versions of the CookieKing database — one in Microsoft Access for ASP and one in DB2 for JSP — are included in the CookieKing folder. Create a DSN named CookieKing to the database of your choice and then open the CookieKing starter file. For ASP, use CookieKingASP11_1.edf; for JSP, use CookieKingJSP11_1.edf.

Making the Display Pages

Take a look at the query to the CookieKing database we set up in Chapter 10. (It's the same query that's set up in the CookieKing starter file, if you use the file on the CD.) The database contains information about cookie orders, cookie recipes, and ingredients. You create a query that would enable you to look at the outstanding orders. This query uses information from the COOKIEORDERS and the RECIPES tables, which are related by the key field RecipeID. Here's the complete SQL statement (for you SQL mavens):

```
SELECT COOKIEORDERS.OrderID, COOKIEORDERS.OrderName,
         COOKIEORDERS.RecipeID, COOKIEORDERS.Quantity,
         COOKIEORDERS.OrderDate, COOKIEORDERS.DueDate,
         COOKIEORDERS.SalesTypeID,
         COOKIEORDERS.PackagingID,
         COOKIEORDERS.OrderFilled, RECIPES.RecipeID,
         RECIPES.RecipeTitle
FROM COOKIEORDERS, RECIPES
WHERE COOKIEORDERS.RecipeID = RECIPES.RecipeID
```

You saved this query as Orders and created an ODBC Content Table of the same name. Now you're ready to create some pages to search and display the orders.

To run the DataForm Wizard:

1. **Click the New DataForm button on the Site tab or choose Insert⇨DataForm.**

2. **Select the ODBC Content Table on which to base your DataForms and then click Next.**

For now, select the Content Table named Orders so that you can get on your way.

The first thing you have to do is decide which pages you want to create. In this first run-through, you don't create the Insert and Update pages yet, so uncheck these options and the Delete option in the Form Feature Selection dialog box. Leave the Search and Result List options checked, as shown in Figure 11-3. Notice that you don't get any choice whether you want a Detail page: A Detail page is always created.

Give your DataForms a name in this dialog box too, to avoid using the default name DataForm#. Although you can change the name of your pages later, if you name it here, the wizard uses this name as you step through the wizard. We named ours Display because that's what this section of the site is for.

The Messages dialog box, as shown in Figure 11-4, asks whether you want to create custom messages for your detail and search results pages when you get to the end of the records. You can enter THE END and Sorry, Charlie! Try `again!` if you're so inclined. We know a better way to handle browsing records, which prevents people from navigating past the end of the records, which is to hide the navigation buttons when you get to the end of the records, so we don't care what this message says. (See the section "Vanishing tricks," in Chapter 13.)

Figure 11-3:
Check the pages you want to create and name your DataForm.

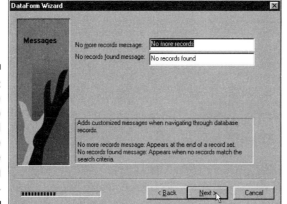

Figure 11-4:
Choose messages to be displayed when the database has nothing to show you.

Detail page

You can choose from several options for your detail page:

- ✔ The columns you want to display
- ✔ The type of SmartElement you want to use for each column
- ✔ What page you want the output to be on (whether you want to create a new page or use an existing page)

✔ Whether you want navigation buttons for browsing

✔ The number of records to display per page (if you want a data loop)

In the first dialog box for the detail page, check the columns you want to include on the page — or more precisely, uncheck those you don't want, because they're all checked by default. You don't want to show the `OrderID` or the two `RecipeID` fields because they're just numbers the database uses to keep track of things, so uncheck them, as shown in Figure 11-5. Rather than `RecipeID`, you want to show the `RecipeTitle` field from that table.

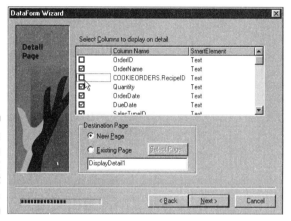

Figure 11-5: Uncheck the columns you don't want on the page.

The default display for each item on a detail page is a simple text box. However, you can choose the type of form element you want to use for each field. If your database includes a URL path to an image, for example, you can choose an Image SmartElement to contain the image; otherwise, only the path is shown in a text box.

The CookieKing database contains one field, `OrderFilled`, which is a true/false (yes/no) field (known as a Boolean field in technical jargon). The convenient way to display such a field is with a check box: checked for order filled, unchecked for unfilled. Choose a Checkbox SmartElement for this field by clicking the SmartElement column next to `OrderFilled`. A dropdown list box appears. Click the arrow to expand it and then select Checkbox from the dropdown list, as shown in Figure 11-6.

Notice that the name of the page is created for you in the Destination Page area, using the name you created for your DataForm with `Detail1` tacked on. You can change the name if it's not pleasing, although it does help to know which pages are part of the same set if they share part of their name. (Think of them as family siblings with the same last name if you want.) However, you can also choose to use an already existing page for the Detail page. If you're the kind of person who thinks design first and function second, you may have already designed some pages to hold the data. To place the detail output on an existing page, just select the Existing Page option and click Select Page. Then, you can select the page you want from your site tree.

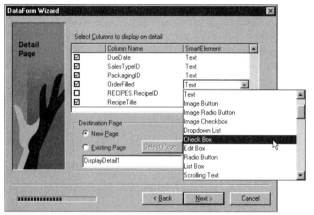

Figure 11-6:
Choose a
check box
for a
Boolean
field.

Click Next and you see even more options for the detail page, as shown in Figure 11-7.

Navigation buttons let you browse through your records using First, Previous, Next, and Last buttons. If you have in mind the thought of using your own custom image buttons for this task, you'll be tempted to uncheck this option — but we recommend that you don't. The reason is that DataForm Wizard creates all the client-side scripting for you on these buttons. Even if you want to replace them with your own buttons, if you let the wizard do his thing, you'll be able to copy the same interactions on your own buttons. (We have more to say about this subject in the section "Prettier buttons," in Chapter 13.)

Another option you can choose is the number of records you want to display per page. By default, that's just one. If you want to display multiple records per page, however, you can specify the number or select All Records. (If you select All Records, we hope that your database is very small.)

That's it for the Detail page. Click Next to move on to the Search page.

Search page

In the Search Page dialog box, you get to select the field or fields on which you want to be able to search. In this case, only one column is selected initially, and — wouldn't you know it? — it's the least useful column to search because it's the autonumber field of the table. You can uncheck that one right away. Now think about what you *do* want to search on.

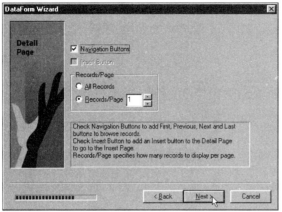

Figure 11-7: More options! Pick your navigation buttons and the number of records per page.

Being able to search for a customer's name so that you can find their order would be nice. It would also be nice to search by the cookie name so that you can see all the chocolate chip cookie orders at one time. Check the OrderName and the RecipeTitle fields because those are the appropriate ones for that information.

Again, you can select the Existing Page option if you want, but leave it alone for now and let the wizard create a new page for you. You may want to consider one more option: Single Edit Box. If you check this box, you also enable the Search type dropdown list. Although Drumbeat doesn't give you much explanation about what these things mean, they're not difficult to figure out.

If you select the Single Edit Box option, you get one edit box on the search page for multiple search fields — for example, if you want to allow searches for both the first and last name columns in a database from a single entry, without having to specify which column to search. If you also check the Search Type Dropdown option, you get a dropdown list box on the search page that lets you choose how you want the match to be made, with choices including *equal to, begins with,* or *contains.*

Although that method would work well for your customer name search, you have to find another way of doing that later because, on this search page, you're setting up a search on columns of different types, so the single edit box won't work. What you *do* want is a dropdown list for the cookie recipes so that you can pick from the list of cookies you have rather than have to type the full name. Select a Dropdown List SmartElement for the RecipeTitle column, as shown in Figure 11-8.

One last choice you get before moving on, because you chose multiple search fields, is the type of operator you want for the search: AND or OR. Choose AND if you want search results to be returned only if a match is made in both search fields. Choose OR to match either field.

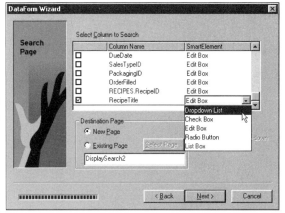

Figure 11-8:
Choose a
dropdown
list for the
search
column.

If you choose AND, you can search for things like `The Tooth Fairy` AND
`Oatmeal Raisin`, which gives you only the tooth fairy's orders for oatmeal
raisin cookies, but not orders by the tooth fairy for snickerdoodles.

You want to choose OR because you don't really want to limit your search
results that way. You're more likely to be searching *either* customer orders *or*
cookie names.

Result list page

For the Result List page, you can choose the columns you want to appear on
the page that displays the results of a search. Normally, you want to show
just an abbreviated list of matches, with links to the details on each record.
The DataForm Wizard creates a result list that is displayed in a table format.
The finished page is shown in Figure 11-9 to give you the mental picture of
what you're working toward.

To get a result list page that looks like this, choose the columns `OrderName`,
`RecipeTitle`, `Quantity`, and `DueDate`, as shown in Figure 11-10. That seems
about right to keep track of things. Notice that if you try clicking the
SmartElement column in this dialog box, you get nowhere. AutoTable is
the only option.

You can create sorting and display options for the result list next. If you
select the Create SmartElements for Sorting option, as shown in Figure 11-11,
you get a dropdown list, which lets you sort the display by any column in the
table. The Records/Page option lets you choose the number of records you
want to display at one time in the table. The Back and More buttons shown in
Figure 11-9 are used for navigating records if more results are returned than
can be displayed at one time.

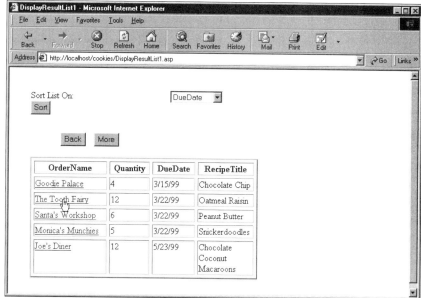

Figure 11-9:
A typical
result list
page, with
links to
detail
pages.

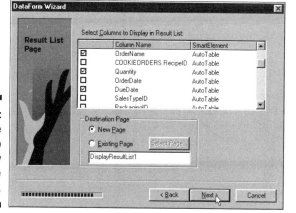

Figure 11-10:
Choose the
columns to
display
in the
result list.

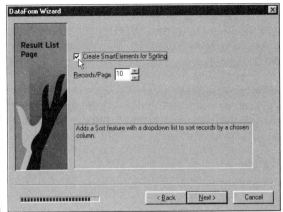

Figure 11-11:
Select the
column to
link to the
detail page.

The last dialog box in this set lets you set the Select Columns to Link to Detail option. It enables you to go from the display list directly to an individual record detail page for more information. Choose the `OrderName` column.

If the primary keys (or *unique keys*) for the database have not already been selected in the query, you're confronted with one more dialog box. You must indicate the primary keys so that the proper link can be created. In this case, the unique keys are `OrderID` and `RECIPES.RecipeID`. Check both these columns, as shown in Figure 11-12.

Before you click Finish and let the wizard do his abracadabra, you may want to review what you've chosen for your pages. You can click the Back button to go back through the dialog boxes and change anything you want. You can also change things later if necessary, so don't get stage fright. Whenever you're ready, click Finish and go for it!

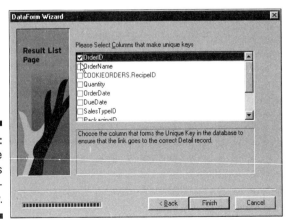

Figure 11-12:
Select the
unique keys
in the data-
base query.

Publishing and Revising Your DataForms

In this section, you take a look at what the wizard hath wrought. On the Site tab, you see three new pages. Click each one to take a look. The output is fairly standard — even kind of boring — but don't worry: You can fully customize the pages, including renaming and resizing field labels, rearranging elements, adding text styles, prettying up the buttons, and adding design features.

Before we get to that, you're probably dying to see how your pages really work. To do that, you have to publish and browse them in your browser.

Publishing your DataForms is simple (just click the Publish button), although it doesn't work unless you've taken the time to set up everything.

To publish your pages, you need

- ✔ A publishing directory on the server
- ✔ An alias for the site, which is usually just the name of that publishing directory
- ✔ A default page designation, which is the entry point for the site

Now may be the time to check the Publish Settings dialog box and choose onc of your DataForm pages as the default page:

1. **Choose Publish⇨Publish Settings.**

2. **On the ASP tab (WebSphere tab for JSP), next to the Default Page option, click Select and select your default page from the site tree.**

If you choose the search page as your default, you can do a complete tour of your site by entering a search, going to the result list page, and clicking a link to go to a detail page. From there, you can browse through your records.

Choosing the ResultList as the default page is sometimes useful because you can then check to ensure that all your records are being displayed and verify that the database connection is good. If you go directly to the ResultList page without first conducting a search, the list displays all records by default (or the first x number of records, according to the number you've specified per page — you can change the number on the Attributes Sheet for the AutoTable that holds the results).

Take a look at the site in your browser. Figures 11-13 and 11-14 show two of the pages you just created with the DataForm Wizard.

You've published the site, and the Drumbeat status bar reads Publish Successful! When you click the Browse button, however, you're staring at a blank page. Chances are that you left the default page set to Home and the home page in your site has nothing on it and no links to get anywhere. Duh! (Don't worry — we do this all the time.)

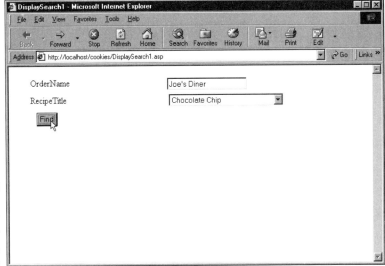

Figure 11-13:
Search for
the order for
Joe's Diner.

Search, schmerz

Suppose that you have noticed that your search page isn't quite perfect.
First, you have to enter its full name in order to match an entry in the
`OrderName` category. Second, the cookie type dropdown list doesn't include
all the types of cookies — only the ones that have been ordered and some
types are listed twice. That's because the information is coming from the
`CookieOrders` table. Plus, because no blank option is on the dropdown list,
it always includes a cookie name in the search, whether you want it or not.
The search page is probably the first one you'll want to mess with to make it
perform like you want. To do that, you have to read a little bit about recordsets (see the following section).

Recordsets

Bring any one of your DataForm pages into the layout area and you see a
couple of items in the basement, below the layout area. Each page has a form
and a recordset — something that looks like a keg of beer. (All those cookies
must be making us thirsty.) Each of the three pages has the same recordset
on it, named Recordset1.

The recordset, created by the DataForm Wizard, represents your database
query on the page. You should rename this recordset now, to make identifying it easier when you do other operations with it.

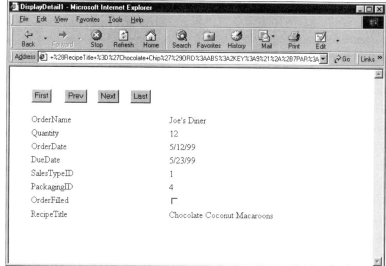

Figure 11-14: Joe's order for chocolate coconut macaroons.

To rename the recordset:

1. **Select the recordset in the basement of the page and click the Attributes tab.**

2. **In the Name field, enter a new name.**

The recordset is renamed on all the pages on which it is used. You may notice some other attributes here. The most important one is the Content Table to which the recordset is bound. The same message-display options displayed in one of the dialog boxes in the DataForm Wizard are shown, and you can change them here.

Recordsets and DataForms are site-level elements, which means that they are server-side elements and persist from page to page within the Web application (whereas ordinary page elements live and die unremembered from page to page).

In the Asset Center, set the filter for Site Elements by clicking the Locate Assets button and choose Site Elements⊅Show All Site-Level Elements.

You can create your own recordsets based on queries without going through the DataForm Wizard, which can be useful for building pages manually and for adding related database content from other queries. After you have created a recordset (or after DataForm Wizard has done so for you), you can also have multiple DataForms based on the same recordset. This method is much more efficient than creating new recordsets for the same query.

We get back to the subject of recordsets in a minute; but this is a convenient place to tell you how you can get back to the wizard to edit your DataForms if you want to change something.

The DataForm Wizard, in another guise

When you want to revise a set of DataForms the DataForm Wizard has generated for you, you can kick up the wizard again in another form. Rather than insert a new DataForm from the Site tab, you have to edit the properties of the existing DataForm.

To rerun the DataForm Wizard to revise a set of DataForm pages:

1. **In the Asset Center, filter for Site Elements. Choose either Show All Site-Level Elements or Show All Dataform Elements.**

2. **Double-click on the list the name of the DataForm you want to edit (or right-click and choose Properties).**

The DataForm Properties dialog box contains all the information about your DataForms. The same options are available on the tabs in this dialog box as are available in the DataForm Wizard, except in more compressed form. On the General tab (shown in Figure 11-15), you can choose to add new pages by checking the box next to the page. (Uncheck a box to have the page and all its components deleted for you.)

The Data Source tab shows the selected data source: either the ODBC Content Table or a recordset. Each page you have created is represented on a separate tab. You can change any of the options for a page on its tab.

Here are some common changes you may want to make:

- ✔ Add or delete a field from the page.
- ✔ Change the detail page to have a data loop.
- ✔ Change the SmartElement to use for a field.
- ✔ Add or delete navigation buttons.
- ✔ Add or delete a page from the set.

If you click OK on the DataForm Properties tab, the DataForm Wizard automatically reruns and regenerates your pages. It doesn't hurt anything, if you haven't made any changes. If you've added new elements to the pages manually, the wizard leaves them as they are. If you've replaced form elements on the page, however, you may see that the original ones have been added back to the page. (All you have to do is delete them.) If you don't want to rerun the wizard, close the window rather than click OK.

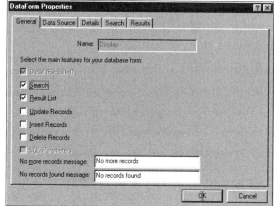

Figure 11-15:
Change the
page
options
and rerun
the wizard
from the
DataForm
Properties
tab.

Making Maintenance Pages

Suppose that you want to be able to maintain your database easily from your web pages. Rather than teach your cookie bakers to use a separate database application (an idea they'd probably resist), you can use web pages to make entries and update the database. Call it the maintenance side of the CookieKing site.

If you have a fairly simple database and no joins in the query used to create the display pages of your site, you can just add the Insert and Update pages to the site by editing the DataForm properties to include the Insert and Update pages and then choosing your options. This method may work fine for you if controlling access to the database is not a problem.

Creating Insert and Update pages with the same DataForm, however, may not be a good idea, for a couple of reasons:

✔ The display pages are meant for public consumption and are designed accordingly; the maintenance pages are private, however, and may include fields that you don't want to display on a public site.

✔ The query you use for the display pages is too complex to work with an insert/update operation on your database.

The CookieKing's database pages are so far really just designed for people within the kitchen and counting room to use. The query could cause problems, though, so you have to create a new one for the maintenance pages. The following section explains how.

A different type of query

Why can't you use the same query for your Insert and Update pages? Depending on your database application and the structure of your database, you may be able to. The biggest reason you can't, however, is that your database may not allow inserting and updating based on a query with a join (one that accesses more than one table).

Microsoft Access is fairly easygoing about this matter (as long as you have the latest database drivers), although many other databases, such as DB2, are much stricter in their rules. The safest thing to do is to create a simple query to the table to which you need to add or update records.

For the CookieKing, you need to create a query to the `Orders` table, without including the `Recipes` table this time. You also add a filter to show only orders that have not been filled:

1. **Click the Add Assets button and select Queries.**

2. **Click New to create a new query.**

3. **Select the CookieKing database for your data source.**

4. **In the SQL Statement window, enter this line:**

```
SELECT * FROM COOKIEORDERS WHERE COOKIEORDERS.
        OrderFilled=0
```

5. **Name your query** Orders2 **and click Save Query, as shown in Figure 11-16.**

6. **In the Query Manager dialog box, click Create Table.**

   To create the dropdown list display option on the Insert and Update pages, you need a separate query to the `Recipes` table soon, so create that now, too:

7. **Click New.**

8. **Select the CookieKing database for the data source again.**

9. **In the SQL Statement window, enter this line:**

```
SELECT * FROM RECIPES
```

10. **Name the query** Recipes **and click Save Query.**

11. **In the Query Manager, click Create Table and then click Done.**

You should now have three queries listed in the Query Manager and three corresponding ODBC Content Tables in the Content Center.

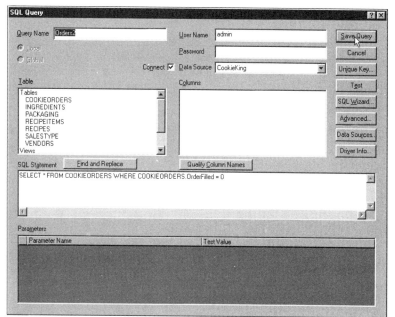

Figure 11-16:
Make a
new query.

Before you go to the wizard to generate the pages, you can do something that saves time later. If you generated the first set of DataForm pages described in this chapter, you may have noticed that the text labels on the pages are the same as the database column names. It would be nice to have them reflect something more comprehensible outside the database. If you rename the columns in the ODBC Content Table before using the wizard, the wizard uses the new column names for the labels.

1. **Open the Content Center and choose the** `Orders2` **table from the drop-down list.**

2. **Double-click the column header for** `Ordername`, **or right-click the column header and choose Properties.**

3. **In the Properties dialog box, type the name** `Order`.

Notice that the only thing you can change about an ODBC Content Table is the name of the column headings. The other options are all grayed out.

If you rename the columns in an ODBC Content Table *after* using the wizard to make your pages, the new column names automatically appear in the result list table. However, they do not appear on the other pages, where the labels show up as text boxes.

You can change the column names as shown in the following table (or make up your own names):

Database Field	Content Table Column
OrderName	Order
RecipeID	Cookie
OrderDate	Order Date
DueDate	Due Date
OrderFilled	Filled
SalesTypeID	Sales Type
PackagingID	Packaging

Bring back the wizard

To make the Insert and Update pages that will form the maintenance side of your site, you can use the DataForm Wizard again. Using the wizard to create Insert and Update pages is especially convenient because all the scripting necessary to interact with the database is created for you:

1. **Click the New DataForm button on the Site tab or choose Insert⇨ DataForm.**

2. **In the Data Source dialog box, select the** `Orders2` **table for your DataForm.**

3. **In the Form Feature Selection dialog box, uncheck the boxes for Search and Result List, as shown in Figure 11-17.**

   Leave the Update Records, Insert Records, and Delete Records options checked.

4. **Name the new DataForm** Maintain **(or something appropriate). Click Next and then Next again to skip over the Messages dialog box.**

5. **Select the options for the Detail page, as you did for the pages in the Display section earlier in this chapter, in the section "Making the Display Pages." Uncheck the** `OrderID` **field because it's not necessary to display this page. Choose a Checkbox SmartElement for the Filled column.**

6. **This time, for the Records/Page option, enter 5. The detail page then contains a data loop and shows five records at a time.**

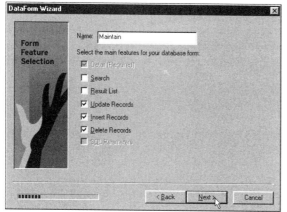

Figure 11-17:
Choosing
five records
per page
creates a
data loop on
the detail
page.

Update page

In the Update Page dialog box, you find a familiar set of options. First, you can select the fields you want to include on the Update page. They're the fields you want users to be able to edit or change. Don't include any primary key field that is autonumbered (or has a database trigger operation on it) because the database application handles it. Including these fields causes errors!

Uncheck the `OrderID` field and choose the Checkbox SmartElement for the Filled field again.

Insert page

The Insert Page options are basically identical to the Update page. You make the same choices there:

- ✔ Uncheck the `OrderID` field, which is an autonumber primary key field because the database application handles it.
- ✔ Select the check box labeled SmartElement for Filled.

Click Finish to let the wizard generate your pages.

Taking Another Look

To try out the insert and Update pages, you have to publish your pages. Before you do that, it's a good idea to change your default page to the new MaintainDetail1 page. Another approach is to set your default page to Home and create some links to the different sections of your site.

Adding an Insert button

An Insert button is the first thing that would be handy to help navigation from the detail page to the Insert page. To get to the Insert page, you have to add a button to link to this page on the MaintainDetail1 page. Don't ask us why the wizard doesn't create this button for you when you choose a data loop. It doesn't make much sense to us, really, but adding it yourself is easy.

Plop an image button (or a plain image — it doesn't matter) on the page. On the Attributes Sheet, click Assign Link and choose the Insert page for the link destination.

The next time you browse the site, you can try inserting a new record. When you do, you soon discover that it would be nice to have a few aids, such as a dropdown list from which to choose a cookie and maybe some radio buttons to simplify a few choices. Chapter 12 shows how to add these form elements and others and bind them to your database for proper insertion.

Adding an Update button to maintain state

One thing you need on your site is a button that takes you to the Update page. The button has to be placed next to the record shown in the data loop on the MaintainDetail page. When you browse the page, you see several records in the loop (as many as you specified that you want to display per page), so the button needs to know which record you want to update.

The way it does that is by a process called *maintaining state*. It sounds like a military parade maneuver, but it's a common requirement in database navigation and a surprisingly nonstandard situation on the Web. A Web server serves each page with no knowledge of which page it served previously, and still less knowledge of what interaction the user may have had with the page. The Web protocol is *stateless* — and that limitation obviously has to be circumvented when it matters very much which database record was just called up.

Drumbeat makes it easy by giving you an interaction you can apply to the image button that will maintain state as you follow the link to the Update page:

1. **Plop an image button (or a plain image) on the page to use as the link.**

2. **Select the image button and Shift+click to select the recordset too. Right-click and choose Possible Interactions.**

3. **In the Interactions Center, in the ASP Miscellaneous category, find and apply the interaction.** Go to [page] when [button] is clicked and show curr record of [Recordset].

4. **In the Parameters dialog box, click the Assign Page button, select the MaintainUpdate1 page from the site tree, and click OK. Then click OK again.**

Now you can publish the site again and try following the Update Button link and updating a record.

The table in the CookieKing database on which the Insert and Update pages are based has a field named Sales Type. This field is designed to take one of two options represented numerically: Wholesale (1) or Retail (2).

The Packaging field is also designed to take one of four values: Bulk, Boxed, Gift, or Standard. These, too, are represented numerically in the database.

Fixing the search

Remember that `Recipes` query you created earlier in this chapter, in the section "A different type of query?" You can use that query now to fix up the search page dropdown list in a jiffy:

1. **Select the search page to bring it into the layout area.**

2. **Select the Recordset element on the SmartElements toolbar and drag it to the layout.**

    The element looks just like the one the DataForm Wizard put into the basement of your page, only smaller.

3. **Select the new recordset that has appeared in the basement of the page and click the Attributes tab. On the Attributes tab, rename the Recordset** Recipes.

4. **Assign the Content Table from which the recordset gets its data. Click the dropdown button next to Content Table and select Recipes.**

5. **Select the dropdown list on the page. On the Attributes Sheet for the dropdown list, click the ellipsis button next to the Content attribute (the ToolTip says Assign Content).**

6. **In the Content dialog box that pops up, select Recipes for the Recordset option. For the column, select** RecipeTitle**. Now the dropdown list will get the list from the other recordset. Click OK.**

Just one more quick fix. You want to add a static option to the cookie dropdown list so that if you're searching for a customer name, you can leave the cookie dropdown selection blank:

1. **Click the dropdown list. Right-click and choose Possible Activations. In the Interactions Center, find in the Database Miscellaneous category the activation** Recordset1_RecipeTitle: Add static option to list

populated by a recordset. **(The name of the selected element precedes the activation.) Double-click the activation to apply it. In the Parameters dialog box that pops up, you can choose the message to be displayed at the top of the list for the static option.**

2. **Replace the default Option String with None. Leave the Option Value at 0. Leave the Selected box checked so that the prompt is the item that's displayed when the page loads.**

3. **On the Attributes Sheet for the dropdown list, choose None from the dropdown list for Selection so that when the page loads, the dropdown list does not take a value from the recordset but uses the static option instead.**

Change the default page to DisplaySearch1 in the Publish Settings dialog box so that you can browse this page directly (choose Publish➪Publish Setting, click the ASP or WebSphere tab, and click the default page Select button.) Republish and browse your pages again. Now your dropdown list is populated with the entire list of cookies in the Recipes table, plus a static option — None — as shown in Figure 11-18. Select any cookie to see the existing orders for that cookie type. Or type **Joe's Diner** to find Joe's order.

You still want to fix that edit box search so that you can just type Joe and have it find Joe's Diner. We show you how to do that in Chapter 12.

In fact, we'll let you in on a secret: The DataForm Wizard is a bit limited in its capability to create a search page. You can do a much better job of creating a search page starting from scratch — and it's not really all that hard.

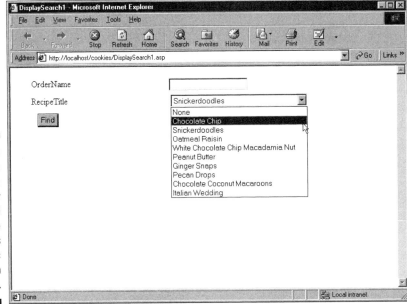

Figure 11-18:
The dropdown list now contains all the cookie names, plus a static option (None).

Chapter 12

Making Forms Follow Function

. . . .

. . . .

*J*ust in case you've never seen a form on a Web page, Figure 12-1 shows you a form. Whenever a user clicks a Submit button, the useful data goes somewhere. Jeez, now we know how airline cabin staff feel whenever they have to demonstrate how to buckle the lap belt.

Figure 12-2 isn't a form, although it sure looks like one. Crafty web designers these days often make use of list boxes for site navigation. Although the data doesn't go anywhere, a change to the list is captured by an embedded script and used to command a switch to a different page (in this case, a department of an online newspaper).

Drumbeat enables you to build forms, both real and unreal, on your pages, and it differs noticeably from other web site creation aids you may have come across, in the way it builds forms. Whereas the standard approach has been to get you to mark the beginning and end of a form section on a page and then populate it with whatever form input elements you feel the need for, Drumbeat skips the first step and lets you slap an input element down anywhere, on any page. The moment you do, the built-in logic assumes that you need a form on the page (even if you don't) and pops one into the basement, ready to be empowered with its ACTION and METHOD attributes. Alternatively, you can create the whole thing in one swoop with the DataForm Wizard. Chapter 11 does all that.

We start by showing you in Table 12-1 a quick list of all the form-related SmartElements and then describe most of them in more detail in the following sections so that you can pretty them up.

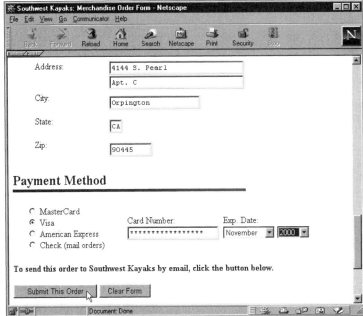

Figure 12-1:
Part of a
typical mer-
chandise-
ordering
form.

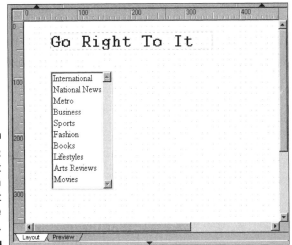

Figure 12-2:
Use this list
box form
element
for site
navigation.

Table 12-1	SmartElements That Are Specific to Forms	
Icon	*SmartElement*	*Description*
	Checkbox	Binary element (on/off or yes/no value).
	Dropdown list	Can be populated manually or from a Content Table.
	Edit Box	Standard text-input form element. To turn it into a multiline edit box (equivalent to the HTML form option TEXTAREA), check Multiline on its Attributes Sheet. If it's a password field, check Password to replace characters with asterisks as they're typed.
	Form Button	Form element to which you can give the status of Submit, Reset, or plain ol' Button.
	Hidden Form Field	Appears in the basement; its text is set and read by means of interactions with other SmartElements.
	Image Button	Container for a multiple image, usually used for a rollover button. You can activate it to submit the form. Not available for sites rated Generic.
	Image Checkbox	Drumbeat's own invention: a container for a set of three images that behave as a check box form element. Image 1 is the unchecked state; Image 2 is the mouseover state; Image 3 is the checked state. Not available for sites rated Generic.
	Image Radio Button	Another Drumbeat invention: a container for a set of three images that behave as a radio button form element. Not available for sites rated Generic.

(continued)

Table 12-1 *(continued)*

Icon	SmartElement	Description
	List Box	Similar to a dropdown list but with drag "handles" for you to expand it to show as many list items as you want. Also allows multiselect.
	Radio Button	Standard radio button type of form element. Meaningful only if part of a set.

Edit Boxes

The standard edit box enables users of the form to enter text in a free-form manner. Just as you do with all other form elements that are visible in the layout area, you place an edit box by clicking its button on the SmartElements toolbar and dropping the element on the page. You can cither drag and release or click the layout where you want to place the element. Also in common with the others, it can be repositioned at any time, using either the mouse (normally snapping to the grid) or the arrow keys (pixel by pixel). Although an edit box defaults to a width of 150 pixels, you can resize it at any time by dragging on the handles at the left and right ends.

Figure 12-3 shows the Attributes Sheet of an edit box. The usual position and width attributes provide another way of repositioning and resizing the element. The Max Length attribute may seem surprising at first glance — it looks as though the maximum length (100) is *less* than the default width. Not so — the maximum length is measured in *characters,* not pixels. We strongly suggest that you set a maximum length; otherwise, mischievous web surfers may spend all night entering nonsense in an attempt to flood your server. Edit boxes intended to have zip codes entered in them are often sized to accept five characters but are allowed a maximum of ten, for people who can remember their nine-digit zip codes.

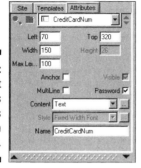

Figure 12-3:
Check out
this
Attributes
Sheet for an
edit box.

The Anchor and Visible check boxes have the same function as they do for text boxes. Check Anchor, and the element is available as a hyperlink destination (refer to the section "Targeting links," in Chapter 7). Uncheck the Visible option, and the element is invisible (although a dynamic effect you invent may later reveal it).

The other two check boxes enable you to change this element from a standard edit box to two other form input types. Check the Multiline option, and your edit box immediately sprouts more drag handles, enabling you to pull it into a multiline input window as wide and as deep as you want (known as a TEXTAREA by the HTML cognoscenti). If you click to check the Password option, the edit box becomes the type that echoes asterisks to the screen as the user fills it out so that passwords and other secret info aren't visible to snoops. (We show that in the example in Figure 12-3 because it's for a credit card number.)

Nine times out of ten, you don't want to assign any content to an edit box; on the tenth time, however, you may want to add some content, such as a prompt or the default answer to a question. Sometimes a form needs to be presented on a web page completely prefilled so that the work a user does is more like editing than creating.

The Content dropdown list enables you to assign content by either typing it in a text editor, referencing a Content Table (Drumbeat calls this *static content*), or linking to a server expression. A server expression may typically be a call to the ASP Request object, with the aim of retrieving text from dynamic activity elsewhere on the web site. We show a simple example later in this chapter, in the sidebar "Passing form data from page to page," and describe a much more complex one in Chapter 13, in the section about using hidden form elements.

You can give an edit box a style and, of course, a name. Try to remember to give names more interesting than Edit1 to your edit boxes because it makes activations and interactions so much easier to follow.

Because edit boxes are the most common type of form field, the DataForm Wizard uses edit boxes by default on your Update and Insert pages, unless you choose some other SmartElement for a field. If you want to replace an edit box with some other kind of SmartElement after the DataForm Wizard has generated the page, you can simply delete the edit box in the layout area and replace it with a new SmartElement. Then you must bind the new element to the same recordset content on the Attributes Sheet. That's exactly what you do to the CookieKing pages you create in Chapter 11.

If you've followed through with the demo exercise from Chapter 11, you can use the same file to follow this example. If you've just jumped into the middle of this discussion, you can find a starter file on the CD in the back of this book that includes everything to date. For ASP, use CookieKingASP12_1.edf. For JSP, use CookieKingJSP12_1.edf. You also need the CookieKing databases (in Access for ASP or DB2 for JSP) on the CD, and you have to set up the DSN for the database on your machine.

Check Boxes

A check box is almost the humblest of form elements. It transmits only a single bit of information: Yes or No, On or Off. Unique among the form elements, a check box passes no information if it's unchecked at submit time. No news is *no* news to the data interpreter.

Yes/no information is, of course, very useful in the real world. Do you want fries with that: Yes/No? Do you want to contribute a dollar to the Presidential campaign fund: Yes/No? Are you qualified for a student discount: Yes/No? Is this cookie order filled or not filled?

Although check boxes are fairly ubiquitous on forms, we don't have much to say about their attributes. You can decide whether a check box defaults to checked or unchecked, using — guess what? — a check box. You can push it around the page. That's about it.

The important point in the context of the CookieKing DataForm is that check box states can be determined from recordsets. When you created the CookieKing form pages in the DataForm Wizard in Chapter 11, we told you to take advantage of the option to have a check box used for the `OrderFilled` field. However, if you don't choose the check box option in the Wizard, replacing the edit box with a check box is an easy operation on the page.

To use a check box to display the value for a true/false field in a recordset:

1. **Drag a Checkbox SmartElement from the SmartElements toolbar to the page.**

2. **With the Checkbox option selected, click the Attributes tab.**

3. **On the Attributes Sheet, select Recordset from the Content dropdown list.**

4. **In the Content dialog box (which pops up automatically when you make the selection), select the recordset and the column with which the check box should be associated.**

5. **If your page is an Insert or Search page, check the option labeled Submit Only (Don't Get Content from Recordset). If it's an Update page, leave the box unchecked so that it shows the correct state (checked or unchecked) according to the database record.**

Figure 12-4 shows this process almost done.

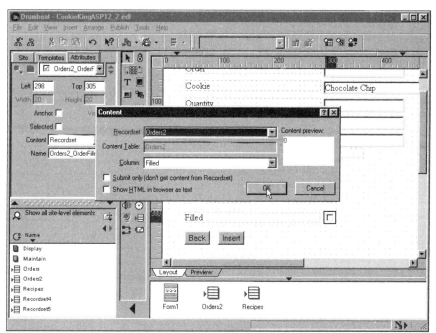

Figure 12-4: Bind the state of a check box to one column of a recordset.

If you're building a form page by hand instead of just revising the content of a page generated by the DataForm Wizard, you have to take some extra steps. You have to apply the interaction Use [Checkbox] data to update/ insert in [Recordset] when [Button] is clicked, which is in the Database Edit category. You must make sure that your form-submit interaction is the last one on the page. See the section "Setting up the Submit button," later in this chapter.

Radio Buttons

The purpose of a set of *radio buttons* is to enable the user to make *one* choice from a set of alternatives. Selecting option A implies that you're deselecting of B, C, and D, for example.

It makes no sense, therefore, to have a single radio button to transmit a user's decision. If users have only one option, they have no need for a button. (Henry Ford would have used a single radio button for the choice of color if he had had an e-commerce site for ordering Model Ts. He would have gotten a real kick out of that.)

The successful form designer thinks of radio buttons in groups. If you want to go two better than Henry, place three radio buttons, marquee-select them, and assign all three to the Color group. Then go back and assign them the values red, green, and blue. Figure 12-5 shows one of the Attributes Sheets.

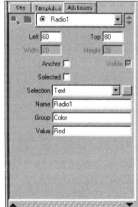

Figure 12-5:
The
Attributes
Sheet of a
radio button.

You should also mark one radio button in each set as Selected by default. Logically enough, selecting one deselects the others in the group.

The CookieKing site has two fields that could benefit from being displayed as radio buttons. The Sales Type field is a simple choice between Wholesale and Retail. The Packaging field is a choice of four packaging alternatives: Bulk, Boxed, Gift, and Standard. To keep your database information neat, use numbers to represent each of these options (Bulk=1, Boxed=2, and so on). Translating these numbers into radio button options is an easy process. We show you how it's done with the Insert page. You can use exactly the same process to set up radio buttons for selection on the Update page.

To replace the edit boxes with radio buttons:

1. **Delete the Sales Type and Packaging edit boxes from the page.**

2. **Double-click the Radio Button SmartElement on the SmartElements toolbar.**

   This step puts the tool in lock mode so that you can drop multiple elements on the page.

3. **Click the layout twice next to the Sales Type label to place two radio buttons. Click the layout area four times next to the Packaging label to place four radio buttons there.**

   You may want to rearrange the layout a little first to make room for your additions.

4. **Click the Lock tool on the SmartElements toolbar to unlock the selection.**

   Next, you create labels for each radio button to translate the selection into plain English.

5. **Place a text box next to each Sales Type radio button and enter** Wholesale **and** Retail, **respectively.**

6. **Place a text box next to each Packaging radio button and enter** Bulk, Boxed, Gift, **and** Standard.

To keep things tidy, you can resize all the boxes and reposition them. You can resize all text boxes at one time by sizing the longest one first. Then select all six text boxes by Ctrl+clicking each one in turn. Ctrl+click the one you resized last. Then click the Arrange Elements button and select Make Same Width. Adjust the position of the text boxes and radio buttons in the layout area appropriately, as shown in Figure 12-6.

Now that you have the radio buttons on the layout, with appropriate labels, you have to assign a group and a value to each button. Remember that each radio button must belong to a group. For now, all six buttons have been assigned to the default Group1. You can let the Sales Type buttons keep that default. Because the Packaging buttons belong to a different group, however, you have to change the default group name.

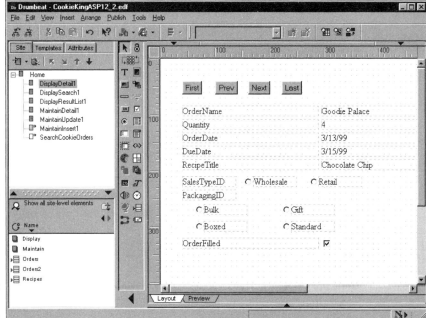

Figure 12-6:
Are you a
wholesale
business?
Would you
like that gift
wrapped?

Assign Selection, Group, and Value to radio buttons on the Attributes Sheet.
Selection is where the radio button gets its value, Group is the group name
of the set of radio buttons to which it belongs (same for all members of the
group), and Value is the value this button passes to the database if it's selected.
Because the Selection and Group are the same for each set, you can set these
values for all the radio buttons at one time:

1. **Ctrl+click both Sales Type buttons. Select the Attributes tab. On the
   Attributes Sheet, for the Selection option, select Recordset. In the
   Content dialog box, select the Recordset (Orders2) and the Column
   (Sales Type). You're inserting a new record from this page, so check
   the option Submit Only (Don't Get Content from Recordset).**

2. **Ctrl+click all four Packaging buttons; for Group, rename Group1
   to** Group2.

   The numbers are meaningless here — you could just as easily name this
   group Alligator, as long as it's called something different from the first
   group.

3. **For Selection, select Recordset. In the Content dialog box, select
   Orders2 as the Recordset option and Packaging as the Column option.
   Check the option Submit Only (Don't Get Content from Recordset).**

4. **Select the Wholesale button and, on the Attributes Sheet, check Selected so that it becomes the radio button selected by default. Do the same for the** Bulk **radio button.**

Now you have to assign the proper value to each button, as reflected in the database, and the buttons can no longer be assigned as a group. The following table shows the proper values to associate with each selection in the CookieKing database:

Radio Button	Value to Assign
Wholesale	1
Retail	2
Bulk	1
Boxed	2
Gift	3
Standard	4

Your mission, should you choose to accept it, is to do the same thing to the Update page. What, did we hear some grumbling? Did you say that's too much repetitive work? Okay, try this technique:

1. **Marquee-select all the radio buttons along with their labels. Press Ctrl+C or choose Edit⇨Copy.**

2. **Switch to the Update page. Delete the** SalesTypeID **and** PackagingID **fields and their labels. Then press Ctrl+V or choose Edit⇨Paste.**

Voilà! That's it. All the radio buttons, along with their proper assignments, are copied to the page. You can check the Attributes Sheet for each button to reassure yourself. You can drag them into the position you want and rearrange the other elements on the page so that nothing overlaps. There's just one thing you have to tweak to make sure that the Update page functions correctly: Click the ellipsis button next to the Selection box and, in the Content dialog box, uncheck the option Submit Only (Don't Get Content from Recordset). In this case, you do want the content to come from the recordset so that the selection shown matches what's in the database.

You can copy the radio buttons to the MaintainDetail1 page, too. Be careful, though, if you try to copy them to the DisplayDetail1 page. Because the page uses a different recordset, the recordset assignment for the buttons has to be redone. (The section "A different type of query," in Chapter 11, explains why these two sets of DataForms use different recordsets.)

You may be wondering why we didn't have you select a radio button for the SmartElement for these fields in the DataForm Wizard. We have two reasons — one benign, the other not so benign. The benign reason: Because the wizard has no way of knowing how many radio buttons you want, it would give you only one, and you would have to add the others yourself anyway. The not-so-benign reason: If you place the radio buttons on the page with the DataForm Wizard and then rerun the wizard later, the initial buttons default back to the Group1 setting. Because you placed them on the page manually, the wizard leaves them alone. It *does* generate a couple of extra edit boxes for these fields if you rerun it, although it's easier to delete those than to remember to reset the radio buttons.

List Boxes and Dropdown Lists

List boxes and dropdown lists are really the same element, with slightly different attributes. You can populate either of them with a list of elements of arbitrary length: the months of the year, the books of the Old Testament, the name of every car General Motors ever manufactured, or the 800 species of beetle identified in the Florida Everglades.

A dropdown list *always* shows just one list item in its passive state. In its active state, the list expands to show either the whole list or as much as will fit in the available screen height, and the user scrolls to make a unique selection.

A list box, by contrast, does not change its height when it's active. Instead, you can pre-expand it to show many items in its passive state, up to the complete list. A list box generally has both up and down scroll arrows, but if the complete selection list is displayed, no scroll arrows are displayed because there's nowhere to scroll to. You can collapse a list box to display only one line, in which case it looks much like a dropdown list — except that it has teeny-weeny up-and-down scroll arrows. (Some people call this configuration a *spin box,* perhaps because it reminds them of a slot machine.)

A list box, unlike a dropdown list, can be given a multiselect attribute: A user can make multiple contiguous selections by Shift+clicking and make noncontiguous selections by Ctrl+clicking, just as you do when you're selecting multiple files in Windows Explorer.

Figure 12-7 shows the Attributes Sheet of a list box. A dropdown list has the same attributes with the exception of the multiselect option.

Figure 12-7:
Another
Attributes
Sheet —
this one's
for a list
box.

Populating and defaulting a list box

More important than the presentation of the element, obviously, is the question of how the list gets its items — or how it's *populated,* in the jargon.

Drumbeat provides two built-in lists of oft-used things: the states of the Union (in their 2-letter U.S. Post Office standard abbreviations) and eight standard salutations, from "Mr." to "The Honorable." Hmmm, wonder why they left out "Monsignor" and "Excellency" — cardinals and ambassadors frequent our web pages all the time. You can grab these prefab lists by applying an activation to the list element on the page.

To use one of these preset lists:

1. **Place a List Box or Dropdown List SmartElement on the page.**

2. **With the list box selected, right-click and choose Possible Activations.**

3. **In the Interactions Center, find in the Forms Set Value category the interaction that says** Populate with Salutations **or** Populate with US States. **Double-click the interaction to apply it.**

Well, that was fun. If you're not collecting names and addresses, however, this procedure doesn't have much use. If you want to assign your own content to a list box, you can choose from several different possibilities. Check the Content dropdown on the Attributes Sheet and you see List/None/Server expression/Static content. If a recordset is present on the page, Recordset is also an option.

The List option means that it's up to you to create a list manually. Select this option and click the ellipsis button, and you pop up the List Content dialog box, as shown in Figure 12-8. Click the Add New Item line and start making your list. The best method is to type each item, press Enter to confirm it, and then click the down arrow to bring focus to the Add New Item line again.

Figure 12-8:
Enter your
own list
items here.

As usual, the Static Content option means that the list gets its items from a Content Table. In Chapter 6, we give an example of populating a list box from a Content Table containing multilingual months of the year.

List boxes can have default selections, which means that you can arrange to display a list of beetle species with Bembidion Quadrimaculatrum already selected by default (or even something that normal human beings can understand, if you insist). Set up a default if you need one, by using the Selection dropdown list. If your list is populated from a Content Table, you can specify the row and column of the default selection. Otherwise, your manual entry simply needs to match the list item you want as the default — and it's case-sensitive, so GET IT RIGHT, OKAY?

Populating the list of values

The content a user sees does not necessarily have to be what gets passed when the form is submitted, as is illustrated in the example of multilingual months set up in the section in Chapter 6 about putting things on the page. List boxes can contain *two* lists:

- **Content:** The list the user sees in the list box on the page
- **Value:** The corresponding value for each list item that gets passed as data

These two lists are defined by the Content and Value attributes on the Attributes Sheet for the list box. The values of a list item default to the same as the content, if you don't provide a value list. In the multilingual month example, the values list was numeric. Figure 12-9 shows a Content Table that dual-populates a list box with pizza toppings. Transmitting "onions, pepperoni, and anchovies" is wasteful when the pizza joint passes the order to the kitchen as O/P/A in any case.

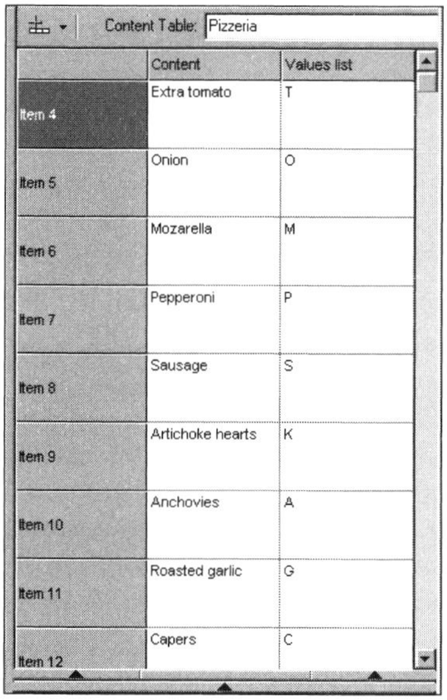

Content Table: Pizzeria

	Content	Values list
Item 4	Extra tomato	T
Item 5	Onion	O
Item 6	Mozarella	M
Item 7	Pepperoni	P
Item 8	Sausage	S
Item 9	Artichoke hearts	K
Item 10	Anchovies	A
Item 11	Roasted garlic	G
Item 12	Capers	C

Figure 12-9: This Content Table provides both content and values to a list box.

Although you can make up a values list manually, by setting the Value option on the Attributes Sheet to List and entering your own values, we seriously recommend using a Content Table for this task. That's the only way to be sure that your values and your contents match. Wouldn't want an order for pepperoni and cheese to get passed on as anchovies and artichoke hearts, would you?

Using a list box for navigation

If you've read the beginning of this chapter, you may remember that we point out that Figure 12-2 isn't a true form, even though it looks like one. If you were curious about how to use a list box for site navigation, this sidebar is here to satisfy your curiosity.

Make a site with several pages — or just pick one you already have. On the home page, set a list box (or a dropdown list) and name it **NavBox**. Populate it with a content list of the vernacular names of some of your pages and a matching values list of the *exact* published filenames, including extensions like .html or .asp.

Right-click the box in the layout area and choose Possible Activations from the pop-up menu.

In the Interactions Center, in the Navigation category, you see a list that includes this line:

```
NavBox: Go to NavBox's value
    when selection changes
```

Apply that activation. Publish. Notice that you aren't restricted to pages within the site — you can put any valid URL in the values list and it acts just like a hyperlink. You could, for example, turn this list box into a selector for 20 search engine sites. This type of navigation is becoming quite common on the Web.

Using list boxes with recordsets

A list box can also get its content dynamically from a recordset. Whenever a list box is used in conjunction with recordsets on a database-driven page, you have to pay attention to these three attributes:

- ✔ **Content:** What the user sees in the list box on the page
- ✔ **Value:** The corresponding value associated with each list item
- ✔ **Selection:** The value that is either retrieved from or passed to the database

The Selection attribute serves two purposes, according to the circumstance. If you're using an Update page, you want the value in the list box to be *retrieved* from the database so that the value shown when the page loads matches the current record. (Otherwise, users have to reset the list to the proper selection before resubmitting, and they'll probably forget and mess things up for you.) If you're using an Insert page, you want the value the user selects to be *passed* to the database.

To see how this process works, add a dropdown list to the Insert and Update pages on the CookieKing site:

1. **Select the Insert page in the site tree.**

2. **Select the edit box next to the Cookie label and press Delete to delete it.**

3. **Place a Dropdown List SmartElement on the page where the edit box was.**

   You want to be able to select from the list of cookie names for the list box. However, what's inserted into the database record is the corresponding number. To get the cookie names, you have to add the Recipes recordset to the page.

4. **Click the Locate Assets button and choose Site Elements⇨Show All Site-Level Elements.**

5. **Drag the Recipes recordset from the Asset Center to the basement of the page.**

   If you drag the Recordset to the page, the basement automatically pops open and the Recordset appears there.

6. **Select the dropdown list. On the Attributes Sheet, click the dropdown arrow next to the Content box and select Recordset. The Content dialog box pops up. For the Recordset option, select Recipes; for Column, select RecipeTitle, as shown in Figure 12-10.**

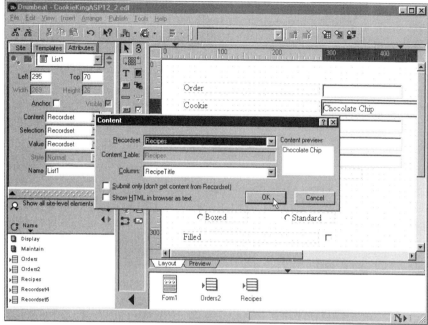

Figure 12-10:
Tell the
dropdown
list where
to get its
content.

The Content attribute dictates what a user sees in the box on the page. However, when the record is submitted, it needs to pass on a number, not a word. So now you have to set the number value for the selection.

7. **Click the Value dropdown arrow and select Recordset. In the Content dialog box, select Recipes for the Recordset option and RecipeID for the Column option, as shown in Figure 12-11.**

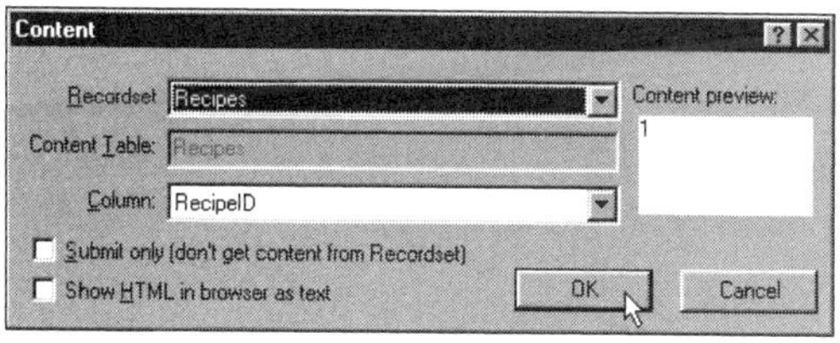

Figure 12-11:
Tell the
dropdown
list what
value to
send to the
database.

Finally, you have to set the Selection attribute. On the Insert page, Selection indicates the database column in which the data is inserted. The recordset you're inserting it into is Orders2.

8. **Click the Selection dropdown list and select Recordset. In the Content dialog box, select Orders2 for the Recordset option and Cookie for the Column option. Because this is an insert operation, click to check the box labeled Submit Only (Don't Get Content from Recordset), as shown in Figure 12-12.**

Figure 12-12:
Tell the dropdown list in which column to insert the data.

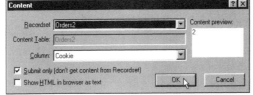

A lazy diversion

The setup for the Insert page cookie dropdown list is nearly identical to what you need on the Update page. The Selection attribute has a different meaning on the Update page, though: It takes its display value from the current record-set. The setup is the same, however. You can save yourself time now by copying and pasting the necessary elements on the Update page:

1. **Select the dropdown list and press Ctrl+C (or choose Edit⇨Copy).**

2. **If the site-level elements are not already showing in the Asset Center, click the Locate Assets button and choose Site Elements⇨Show All Site-Level Elements. Select the Recipes recordset and drag it to the basement.**

3. **Switch to the Update page in the layout area and delete the Cookie edit box.**

4. **Press Ctrl+V (or choose Edit⇨Paste).**

5. **Drag the dropdown list to the position on the page next to the Cookie label.**

You have to make just one little fix now. On the dropdown list's Attributes Sheet, click the ellipsis button next to the Selection attribute selector to open the Content dialog box. Uncheck the option Submit Only (Don't Get Content from Recordset) because, this time, getting its content from the recordset is precisely what you want it to do.

Form Buttons

A form generally needs some kind of OK button in order to send the data on its way, load the next page, exit from the page group — whatever. It's also considered a courtesy to users of a form to give them a Reset button that has the effect of clearing all entered text and restoring all defaults.

Drumbeat provides two standard SmartElements for use as form buttons: a standard-issue gray button and an image button you can decorate any way you want.

You can set the standard-issue button on its Attributes Sheet to one of three types: Submit, Reset, and Button. The low-maintenance varieties are the standard-issue Submit and Reset button. Put them on a page and they function immediately.

On the other hand, the Button-type button and the Image button have to be activated if you want them to do something, except that the Image button can also act as container for a rollover effect, as we explain in Chapter 3. They're activated by essentially the same set of activations, many of which allow redirection to another page.

You can relabel the non-image buttons however you want. The Submit button can be labeled Go For It! and the Reset button D'oh! if you're feeling whimsical. You can also impose styles on them, including the type of CSS paragraph style that specifies a box and a margin, so that you can spiff them up (refer to the section in Chapter 8 about using color).

If you intend to put a set of activations on a button that includes one for submitting the form, you're far better off with a button-type button than a submit-type button. If you add a submit action to a button that's already submitting as its natural behavior, you can cause problems.

Buttons can also participate in interactions with other page and basement elements, most interestingly with recordsets. There are around 30 interactions between a button and a recordset on the standard list, and, if you're handy with JavaScript, you can create scads more of your own.

Before you replace form buttons with images on pages generated by the DataForm Wizard, you should be aware that image buttons, because they depend on JavaScript, don't work for "generic" browsers. (They work only with Navigator 3 and later.) The form buttons the wizard generates work with all browsers.

To add a Reset button to the Insert page on the CookieKing site to enable users to clear all form fields with a click, follow these steps:

1. **Click the Form button on the SmartElements toolbar and place the button on the page.**

2. **Click the Attributes tab. On the Attributes Sheet, change the Type option to Reset by clicking the dropdown list. Change the label on the button to Reset or Clear or whatever you want.**

That's it. Publish and browse the page. Put a few items in the boxes on the page, and then click Reset to make them vanish. Easier than making a rabbit appear out of a hat!

To browse the Insert page directly, you can change your default page on the Publish Settings (Publish⇨Publish Settings⇨ASP) or WebSphere tab. Or you can enter the URL with the page name in the browser location window.

Form Attributes

The first time you place a form-related SmartElement on a page, a form element automatically turns up in the basement. You can click it and display an Attributes Sheet for the form, just as you can for other elements. Figure 12-13 shows the Attributes Sheet for a newly hatched form. Hmmm, not too much to play with there.

Figure 12-13: Look! — even the lowly form has attributes.

If a page has been created as part of a DataForm, you generally don't have to worry about the form element. If it hasn't, however, you may have to pay attention to the form's Action and Method attributes.

The Action attribute represents the page the data goes to when the form is submitted, and normally that page then loads into the browser. In other words, setting the action of a form is a bit like creating a sophisticated type of hyperlink that takes form data along for the ride.

When you click the Action Assign button, in fact, you see exactly the same dialog box as you do when you're creating a conventional hyperlink. The destination can be any page in the same site or any legitimate URL anywhere, including a CGI subdirectory if you're that way inclined.

The Method dropdown list offers a choice of Get or Post. Post is the default, and in most cases you probably won't want to change it. Although this choice between two different ways of transmitting the data may seem a bit technical, there are some everyday considerations, such as

- ✔ If the method is Get, the data gets stuck on the end of the destination URL as a query string and is visible in the browser destination window. If you have office privacy considerations, Post is preferable.

- ✔ Get is also inadvisable if a large amount of data may be generated in the form — a huge text input field, for example. Some UNIX servers have limited buffer space for Get data and truncate the query string.

- ✔ Get is terrific for the type of form submission users may want to do regularly, such as send their location to a weather forecasting site. After the form has been submitted, the entire URL and its query string can be bookmarked, and the user never has to fill out the form again.

We advise you to leave the Enctype dropdown list set at Default. The other option supports file transfer, which you can't do anyway without using some special components we don't bother with here.

Passing form data from page to page

On an ASP-supported site, a form page that's submitted becomes a so-called *request object* on the server. You can make use of that to pass user-entered data from page to page. Here's a simple demonstration:

1. **On PageA, place an edit box named editboxA and a Submit button.**

2. **On PageB, place an edit box named editboxB.**

3. **Return to PageA, select the form object in the basement, and expose its Attributes Sheet. Click the Action Assign button and assign a link to PageB.**

4. **Return to PageB, select the edit box, and expose its Attributes Sheet. Using the Content dropdown list, assign its content as a server expression. The Content dialog box pops up.**

5. **In the Expression window, type** Request("editboxA"). **Ignore the Design Text box — it's only there so that you can type "blah blah" and see it on the layout because the sensible text isn't available from the server.**

6. **Publish, enter something in editboxA, and submit the form.**

   Your browser displays PageB with your text already in the edit box.

Building a Search Page By Hand

After you understand Drumbeat-style form elements, you can ignore the some-what limited search page generated by the DataForm Wizard and design your own to have the features you want. The process gives you some insight into how Drumbeat handles forms and interactions with recordsets in general.

You can create a new search page for the CookieKing site to see how it's done. Add a new page to the site. (On the Site tab, click the Insert Page button.) Select the page in the site tree, press F2, and rename the page SearchCookieOrders. Because this process can seem lengthy, we break it down into four parts in the following four sections. Here are the steps:

1. Add the form elements.

2. Set up the edit box.

3. Set up the list box.

4. Set up the submit action.

Adding the form elements

To start building your search page, you need to add the pieces that the user will see in the browser. They include the form elements in which users will make entries or from which they will choose selections, and any instructions on how to use them to search the database:

1. **Place an Edit Box and a Dropdown List on the page.**

2. **Add two text boxes next to the form elements. In the first one, next to the edit box, enter the instruction** Search client orders. **In the second text box, next to the dropdown list, enter the instruction** Search Cookie Orders.

3. **Add a form button to submit the request. On the Attributes Sheet for the form button, you can replace the default label Button with** Search. **(If you want to be Microsoft-hip, you can enter Go instead.) Change its name to** Search, **too, if you like.**

What you have should look much like what's shown in Figure 12-14.

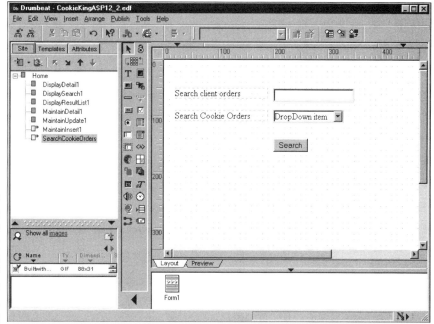

Figure 12-14:
Desperately
seeking
cookies: The
beginning of
the search
page.

Setting up the edit box

After you have the form elements you will use in the search page, you have to add the recordset you want to be able to search:

1. **Click the Locate Assets button in the Asset Center and choose Site Elements⇔Show All Site-Level Elements.**

   The Orders recordset is the one you want to search.

2. **Find the Orders recordset and drag it to the basement of the page.**

   It makes no difference whether you drag it to the page or to the basement — it appears in the basement anyway.

3. **Ctrl+click to select the edit box, the Orders recordset, and the Search button. Right-click and choose Possible Interactions.**

4. **In the Interactions Center, find the interaction** Add Edit1 edit box to filter of Orders when Search is clicked. **(It's in the Database Filter category.) Double-click the interaction to apply it.**

   In the Parameters dialog box, you have to set up which column is being searched.

5. **Select the OrderName column for the `Recordset` field. The Connector option determines whether you want this search to be an AND or an OR search. You're searching two different things, so make it OR, as shown in Figure 12-15. For the Operator option, select Includes; then you can search for a partial string (`Joe`) to find a match in a record (`Joe's Diner`). You can ignore the Clause Separator option in this box because it doesn't apply.**

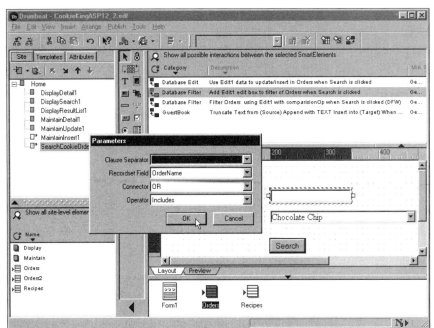

Figure 12-15:
Set up the
search and
go for it!

Setting up the dropdown list

The dropdown list on the Search page is so far a blank slate. You want to set up the dropdown list to show the names of all the cookies to select from. The Recipes recordset is the one that contains this information, as you see in a minute:

1. **Drag the Recipes recordset from the Asset Center to the basement of the page. On the Attributes Sheet, notice that the Content Table with which the Recipes recordset is associated is also called Recipes. If you open the Content Center and choose the Recipes table, you see the list of cookies you want.**

2. **Select the dropdown list on the layout. On the Attributes Sheet, click the dropdown arrow next to the Content box and select Recordset. The Content dialog box pops up. For the Recordset option, select Recipes. For Column, select RecipeTitle.**

The Content attribute dictates what the user sees in the box on the page. The value is the value it's looking to match in the Orders record-set. You have a matching `RecipeTitle` field in the Orders recordset because of the join in the underlying query, so you can simply match that text field.

3. **Click the Value dropdown arrow and select Recordset. In the Content dialog box, select Orders for the Recordset option and RecipeTitle for the Column option. Check the option for Submit Only (Don't Get Content from Recordset).**

   Add a static option to this list box, too, so that it's possible to have noth-ing selected if you want to search only for orders. Otherwise, the default selection on the cookie dropdown list gets added to the search, and the results would show not only all orders for Joe's Diner but also all orders for chocolate chip cookies.

4. **Right-click the dropdown list and choose Possible Activations. In the Interactions Center, find in the Database Miscellaneous category the interaction** Add static option to list populated by a record-set. **Double-click the interaction to apply it.**

5. **In the Parameters dialog box, select the message to display at the top of the list for the static option. Replace the default option string with** Select a cookie, **as shown in Figure 12-16. Leave the Option Value option set at 0. Leave the Selected box checked so that the prompt (**Select a cookie**) is the item that's displayed when the page loads.**

6. **Click the Attributes tab and, on the Attributes Sheet for the dropdown list, set the Selection option to None.**

   If you don't, the item that's displayed in the list when the page loads is whatever value is in that field in the first record in the database.

   Now that the content of the list is set up, you can add the dropdown list to the search filter.

7. **Ctrl+click to select the dropdown list, the Search button, and the Orders recordset. Right-click and choose Possible Interactions. In the Interactions Center, find the interaction** Add List1 dropdown list value to filter of Orders when Search is clicked. **(It's in the Database Filter category.)**

8. **Double-click the interaction to apply it. In the Parameters dialog box, select RecipeTitle for the** Recordset **field. Choose the Connector OR again. For Operator, choose =.**

   The operator this time is = (an equal sign) because you want to match the full name, as shown in Figure 12-17.

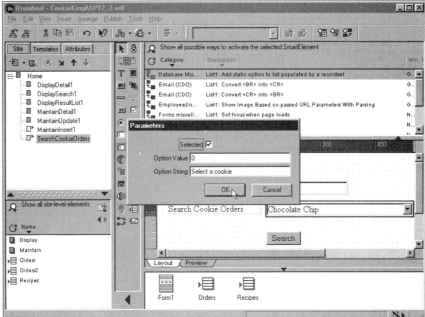

Figure 12-16:
Add a
static option
to the list to
eliminate a
default
selection
from the
search.

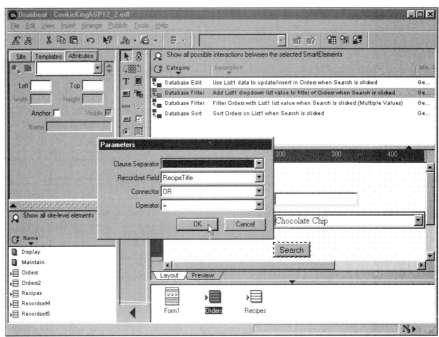

Figure 12-17:
Add the
dropdown
list to the
search filter.

Setting up the Submit button

The Search page is almost done. You have just one more thing to do to make the page work: Tell the button to submit the search when it's clicked and where to go to show the results:

1. **Click the Search button and the Orders recordset. Right-click and choose Possible Interactions. In the Interactions Center, double-click the interaction** Filter Orders when Search button is clicked **(it's in the Database Filter category).**

   Don't use the similar interaction that has (DFW) after it. That one is used by the DataForm Wizard, and because this page is being built by hand, you need the other one.

2. **In the Parameters dialog box, click the Assign button next to Go To Page and select the DisplayResultList1 page from the site tree.**

The page you choose to go to must contain the same recordset you use as the basis of the search. In this case, both the search page you just created and the Result List page generated by the DataForm Wizard have the Orders recordset, so everything should be fine.

Did you forget anything? Before you publish, you may just want to recheck to ensure that all the interactions are properly assigned. Right-click an empty area in the layout area and choose Assigned Interactions (Ordered). In the Interactions Center, you should see four interactions: one for the edit box, two for the dropdown list, and one for the form button alone, as shown in Figure 12-18.

The Submit action must be the last action to occur on the page. If for some reason you decide to create your page in a different order and the submit action is not the last one listed, you have to reorder it to get the page to work. Just select the interaction and drag it to the end of the list.

You can add more search fields to this page by using the same process. Each form element is added to the search with the same Add [source] to filter interaction. Just be careful to keep the submit action last.

Publish the new search page and try it out. You'll see that it functions exactly as you want.

What can go wrong will go wrong

Hey, what can we say? Sometimes things go wrong. Sometimes you misread an instruction. Sometimes the database is a mess. Sometimes you just get hung up on your own pigheaded thinking. Believe us, you're not alone; people who program things for a living learn to eat humble pie for breakfast, lunch, and dinner.

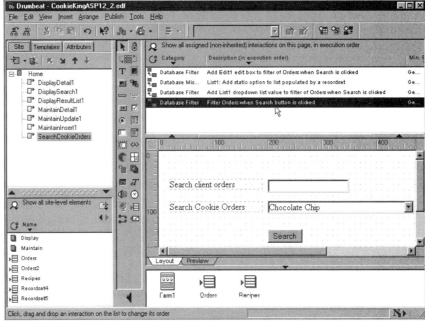

Figure 12-18:
All the inter-
actions are
listed on the
page in exe-
cution order.
(Wonder if
they shoot
'em all at
dawn?)

If you've built your DataForm page, like the hand-built search page in this section, and all it does is give you errors when you try it out in the browser, here are some likely things to check to find the problem:

✔ Check the Parameters you selected for the search. Right-click the page and choose Assigned Interactions (Ordered). Double-click any interaction on the list that has parameters to bring up the Parameter dialog box to check it and make changes, if necessary. Make sure that you're searching the right column and that the Operator option is correct for the type of search.

✔ Make sure that all the database column assignments are correct. Dropdown lists and list boxes are the trickiest things to get right. Recheck all the Content, Value, and Selection assignments you've made on the Attributes Sheet.

✔ Check the assigned interactions on the page to make sure that they appear in a sensible order.

For multiple elements on the page, set them one at a time and browse the page after each addition. You can even create separate pages for each one and test them all out separately. Then use copy-and-paste to bring all the elements together on the final page.

Chapter 13

Making Forms Smarter

*Y*ou've seen those forms on the Web that look like identical machine parts spit out of a factory: Useful, but not pretty. With Drumbeat, you don't have to be stuck with cookie-cutter form pages. After you have your DataForm pages, you can design them as you want.

You can also do a host of things to make your forms function better. This chapter explores some of the things you can do to tailor your forms for both beauty and practicality. Most tasks are easily accomplished by applying standard interactions from the Drumbeat Interactions Center.

Making Form Buttons Smarter

To get an idea of the suite of the scripting the DataForm Wizard generates automatically for you, you can take a look at the interactions on any page you've generated with the wizard. If you've followed the examples in Chapters 11 and 12, you can look at the pages you've created for the CookieKing site.

You can follow the examples in this chapter with any site in which you've generated database pages with the DataForm Wizard. If you've read and followed the examples in Chapter 12, however, you can pick up where you left off with the CookieKing site in that chapter. Or use the starter file for this chapter that includes all the examples so far on the CD: The file is either CookieKingASP13_1.edf for ASP or CookieKingJSP13_1.edf for JSP.

Click the Locate Interactions button (it looks just like the Locate Assets button in the Asset Center), and choose Show All Interactions on This Page from the pop-up menu. It's quite an interesting list. Figure 13-1 shows the interactions for the MaintainDetail1 page on the CookieKing site. You're peering "under the hood" to see the suite of relationships between the recordset and the button-scape, which the DataForm Wizard has already taken care of.

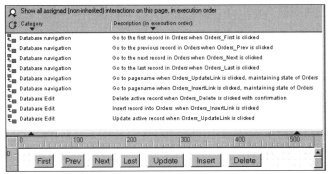

Figure 13-1:
These
interactions
make the
buttons
work.

The interactions on the detail page (except for one that was applied manually) all belong to the Database navigation category. If you take a look at the insert and update pages, you see interactions from the Database Edit category. Those that belong to the Database Edit category are the functions that delete, insert, and update the current record. They naturally belong to specific buttons by default. Database navigation means all the things that make the First, Prev, Next, and Last buttons work.

The DataForm Wizard is so efficient at setting up this whole engine that it almost seems a shame to pick it apart and remake it button by button, although that's what we suggest that you do. Having remade it, you can add some nifty refinements of your own in this chapter.

Prettier buttons

Here's another way to look at the interactions on the page — this time, button by button. Click the Locate Interactions button again, and choose the option Show All Assigned (Non-Inherited) Interactions on This Page, in Execution Order. Then, whenever you click a button in the layout area, the list is filtered to show only the interactions in which that particular button participates. Figure 13-2 shows the interaction for the Last button on the MaintainDetail1 page.

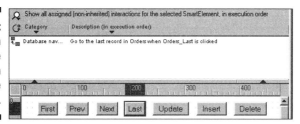

Figure 13-2:
Interaction
between the
Last button
and the
recordset.

You can delete these standard-issue gray buttons one by one, replace them with artier buttons, and then reapply the interactions that make the buttons work. In each case, you should investigate the interaction carefully, making sure that you understand any parameters it may have, before removing it and reapplying it to your arty button. To save you the trouble, Table 13-1 provides a reference to the interactions between the recordset and each button in a standard button-scape.

Table 13-1		DataForm Button Interactions	
Button	*Interaction*	*Participants to Select*	*Parameters to Set*
Detail page			
First	Database navigation: Go to the first record in [Recordset] when [button] is clicked	Button, Recordset	None
Prev	Database navigation: Go to the previous record in [Recordset] when [button] is clicked	Button, Recordset	None
Prev with Looper	Database navigation: Display previous set of records from [Recordset] in Looper when [button] is clicked	Button, Recordset	PageSize (number of records in looper), LooperName (automatically generated)
Next	Database navigation: Go to the next record in [Recordset] when [button] is clicked	Button, Recordset	None

(continued)

Table 13-1 *(continued)*

Button	Interaction	Participants to Select	Parameters to Set
Detail page			
Next with Looper	Database navigation: Display next set of records from [Recordset] in Looper when [button] is clicked	Button, Recordset	PageSize (number of records in looper)
Last	Database navigation: Go to the last record in [Recordset] when [button] is clicked	Button, Recordset	None
Last with Looper	Database navigation: Display last set of records from [Recordset] in Looper when [button] is clicked	Button, Recordset	PageSize (number of records in looper)
Insert	Database edit: Go to pagename when [button] is clicked, maintaining state of [Recordset]	Button, Recordset	pagename (of insert page)
Update	Database edit: Go to pagename when [button] is clicked, maintaining state of [Recordset]	Button, Recordset	pagename (of update page)
Update with Looper	Database edit: Go to page when [button] is clicked and show curr record of [Recordset]	Button, Recordset	pagename
Delete	Database edit: Delete active record when [button] is clicked	Button, Recordset	None

Button	*Interaction*	*Participants to Select*	*Parameters to Set*
Update and Insert pages			
Back	Database navigation: Go to pagename when [button] is clicked, maintaining state of [Recordset]	Button, Recordset	Pagename
Update	Database edit: Update active record when [button] is clicked	Button, Recordset	None
Insert	Database edit: Insert record into [Recordset] when [button] is clicked	Button, Recordset	None
Search page			
Find (single field)	Database Filter: Filter [Recordset] when [button] is clicked (DFW)	Button, Recordset	None
Find (multiple fields)	Database Filter: [Recordset] using [List box] with comparisonOp when [button] is clicked (DFW)	Button, Recordset	None
Result list page			
Back	Database navigation: Set/move AutoTable [Table] direction backward when [button] is clicked	Button, AutoTable	None
More	Database navigation: Set/move AutoTable [Table] direction forward when [button] is clicked	Button, AutoTable	None
Sort	Database Sort: Sort orders on [list box] when [button] is clicked	List box, Button	None

Follow these steps to replace the buttons on the MaintainDetail1 page in the CookieKing site, using the interactions described in Table 13-1:

1. **Select the MaintainDetail1 page to bring it into the layout.**

2. **Marquee-select (or Ctrl+click) the four buttons (First, Prev, Next, and Last) and press Delete.**

3. **Click the Locate Assets button and choose Media⇨Show All Images.**

4. **In the Asset Center, find the cookie button image. Drag it to the layout, above the looper. Click the Attributes tab and, on the Attributes Sheet, rename the button** First **(replacing the default Name).**

5. **Find the Prev, Next, and Last buttons and drag them to the layout too, and then rename them accordingly. To make assigning interactions easier, select the looper on the layout (click the dotted line) and rename it on the Attributes Sheet to just** Looper.

5. **Select the First button and the Orders2 recordset in the basement. Right-click and choose Possible Interactions.**

6. **In the Interactions Center, scroll down to the Database Navigation category and find the interaction** Go to the first record in Orders2 when Orders2_First is clicked **and double-click to apply it.**

7. **Select the Prev button and the Orders2 recordset and find the interaction** Display previous set of records from Orders2 in Looper when Orders2_Prev is clicked. **Double-click to apply it. In the Parameters dialog box, for the PageSize option, enter the number of records in the data loop (5) and the name of the looper on the page (Looper).**

8. **Select the Next button and the Orders2 recordset and find the interaction** Display next set of records from Orders2 in Looper when Orders2_Prev is clicked. **Double-click to apply it. In the Parameters dialog box, enter the number of records in the data loop (5) for the PageSize option.**

9. **Select the Last button and the Orders2 recordset and find the interaction** Display last set of records from Orders2 in Looper when Orders2_Prev is clicked. **Double-click to apply it. In the Parameters dialog box, enter the number of records in the data loop (5) for the PageSize option.**

Figure 13-3 shows the job of button substitution halfway done on the MaintainDetail1 page in the CookieKing site. Because this page is the one with the data loop on it, you have to pick the interactions that apply to the looper. If you replace buttons on another site that doesn't have a data loop on the page, pick the plain version of the contracts, as described in Table 13-1. The words in brackets in the interactions are replaced with the names of the selected elements when the possible interactions are shown.

Because image buttons are not natural submit buttons, like the form buttons are, you have to take an extra step to apply a submit action to each button in order for them to function correctly.

To apply the submit action:

1. **Select the button (the First button, to start) and the Form element in the basement.**

2. **Only two interactions are available in the Interactions Center, and they're in the Forms Submit category. Apply the interaction** Submit Form when First is clicked. **In the Parameters dialog box, uncheck the Validate Form option and leave the edit box blank.**

3. **Repeat these steps for each of the other image buttons on the page.**

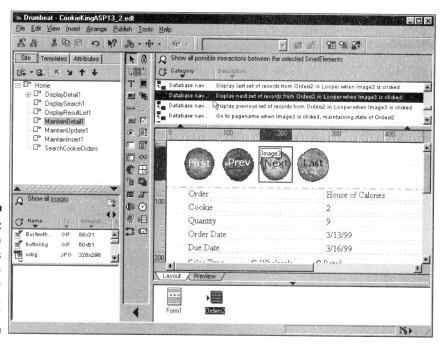

Figure 13-3:
Replace the form buttons with some tasty image buttons. Got milk?

Because the interactions the DataForm Wizard creates are server-side scripts, they work for all browsers. The interactions you apply to go with your arty buttons are client-side JavaScript interactions, so they're not supported by generic browsers.

Vanishing tricks

If you've taken the time to replace your form buttons with image buttons, as described in the preceding section, you've probably noticed many other possible interactions for buttons in the process. To see all possible interactions for a button, select any form button and the recordset, and display the possible interactions between those two elements. You see a list that encompasses more than the Database Edit and Navigation functions you've already met.

There are some interesting interactions in the Database Miscellaneous category. Figure 13-4 shows the list filtered for these. To filter the list of interactions for this category, click the Locate Interactions button in the Interactions Center and select Show all possible cookie interactions between the selected SmartElements. Then click the underlined word *cookie* and, from the category list, select Database Miscellaneous.

Figure 13-4: Database miscellaneous interactions between a form button and a recordset.

The first five, beginning with Do not create Image1 if Orders2, suggest ways of refining your page. In plain English, there's no point in having a First or Prev button if you're already looking at the first record, and no point in a Next or Last button if you're already looking at the last record.

To make the buttons disappear when they're not needed, simply apply the appropriate interaction to make it disappear. On the CookieKing site, you can do it this way:

1. **Select the First button and apply the interaction** Do not create Orders2_First if Orders2 is on the first set of records in Looper. **(On a page without a data loop, apply the generic interaction** Do not create [button] if [Recordset] is on the first record.**)**

2. **In the Parameters dialog box, for the PageSize option, select the number of records displayed in the data loop. In this case, set 5 records per page. You also have to specify whether the buttons appear above or below the looper.**

3. **Select the Prev button and apply the same interaction and the same parameters as you did for the First button.**

4. **Select the Next button and apply the interaction** Do not create Orders2_Next if Orders2 is on the last set of records in Looper **with the same parameters. Apply the same interaction to the Last button.**

Keeping count

Look again (or maybe for the first time) at Figure 13-4. It lists some of the possible interactions between a form button and a recordset. The eighth item on the list is Database Miscellaneous: Replace [token] with number of records in Orders2. That might give you an idea about how to make the page more informative for users — it certainly gives us one.

The preceding section explains ways to signal the beginning and end of data on a Detail page, but what about some guidance in between? Wouldn't it be nice to be able to include on every page a label that reads Record number X of Y? Token substitution is the way to achieve that, although the interaction listed in Figure 13-4 is not what you want. Instead, follow these steps:

1. **Find a nice cozy spot on the DisplayDetail page and place a text box. Name the text box** RecCount **on the Attributes Sheet.**

2. **In the text box, enter** Record number [X] of [Y].

3. **Click+Shift+click to select the text box and the Orders recordset. Right-click and choose Possible Interactions.**

4. **Apply the Database Navigation interaction** Replace Tokens in RecCount with current record number of Orders, **as shown in Figures 13-5 and 13-6.**

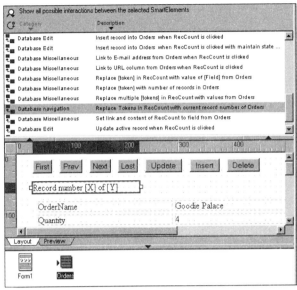

Figure 13-5:
Which is the
right token
replacement
interaction?

We have to admit that the token replacement interactions are pretty confusing. Figure 13-5 shows the interactions sorted so that the token replacement ones are all together and the one you want to apply is highlighted. It isn't clear from the wording, but this contract replaces *two separate* tokens in the text box — one for the current record and the other for the total records.

Just what the doctor ordered. In Figure 13-6, the token substitution is being defined, and in Figure 13-7 it's operating on a published page.

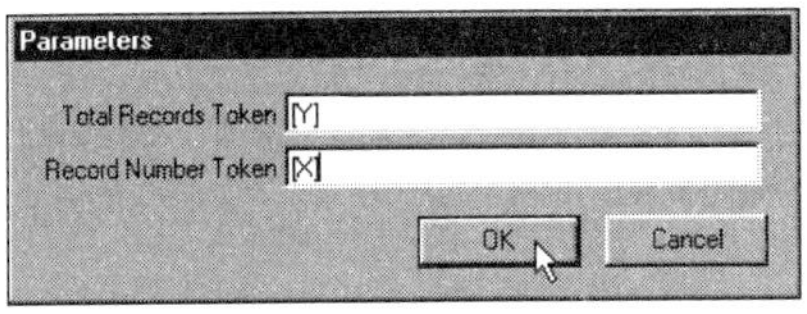

Figure 13-6:
Applying
the double
token
replacement.

Unfortunately perhaps, the same trick can't be performed on the MaintainDetail1 page. Because it has a data loop that displays several records, the concept of a "current record" is lost. However, if you're a JavaScript guru, or have one handy, you could create a new interaction to keep count of records that would take account of the maintain state requirement in the data loop. The section in Chapter 15 about writing a new contract gives you some hints.

Extra information added by token replacement

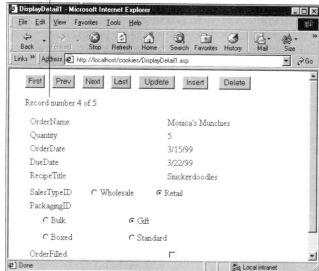

Figure 13-7:
The token
replacement
interactions
look like this
on the pub-
lished page.

Feeling Insecure?

Perhaps you should be: The default DataForm site kind of assumes that the users and the administrators of the database are the same people. Although that assumption may sometimes be accurate, it's more often the case that you want to make the detail and search pages available to any riffraff and reserve access to the insert, update, and delete functions to only trusted souls. Otherwise, the riffraff could get in and trash the entire database with total ease.

The obvious way to keep the riff-raff from where they aren't supposed to be is to password-protect the relevant pages.

Adding password protection

To add password protection to the insert and update pages: Right-click any-where in empty layout space, and choose Possible Activations from the pop-up menu. The list of ten or so activations you see in the Interactions Center represents ways to activate the page. At the bottom, you see `Place client-side password protection on this page`.

Go ahead and apply that activation. We'll cover our eyes while you enter the secret password in the dialog box. The Redirect on Failure window is where you put the name of a page to go to if the password a user enters is wrong (a page on which you write something like "Aha! Caught you!").

If you haven't created the redirect page yet, you may want to back out and do that first. Enter the full name of the redirect page (with the .asp file extension) in the Parameters window when you apply the interaction. Figure 13-8 shows client-side password protection in action.

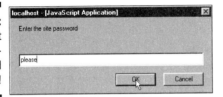

Figure 13-8:
Guard that
password-
protected
page!

You may have noticed that other password interactions are available that are more sophisticated than this one. They require that you set up a database with usernames and passwords. You can assign access based on group names, too. Stick with the easy one for now.

An example of how to password-protect pages using a database with group access rights is provided in DrumNote No. 3 on the CD in the back of this book. The example uses the Login Starting Point, which ships with Drumbeat (so you have all you need). Users are redirected to the appropriate page based on their login ID access rights. For more info about DrumNotes, see Chapter 17.

Not so fast!

If you choose the option to create a Delete function in the DataForm Wizard, you see that a Delete button is added to the detail page that's generated by the wizard. This button allows you to delete the current record you're browsing.

To test the Delete function, you can add a Delete button to the DisplayDetail page in the CookieKing site by changing the DataForm properties and rerunning the wizard. Click the Locate Assets button and choose Site Elements⇨ Show All Site Elements. Right-click the Display DataForm to bring up the DataForm Properties dialog box. Check the Delete box, and then click OK. DataForm Wizard regenerates the pages and adds the Delete button to the bottom of the page. (It also adds back some of the form elements you replaced earlier. Just delete the extra form elements and move the Delete button to the top of the page.)

Assuming that you have made a detail page with a Delete button, publish it and test to see whether your Delete button works — no — *wait!* Don't! The standard Delete button created by the DataForm Wizard is an instant-delete, here-you-go — poof! — it's-gone button with no "Are you sure?" warning box.

We don't much like that, and we discovered that Drumbeat does have an alternative contract that creates an interaction named `Delete active records when [button] is clicked with confirmation`. If you prefer that one, remove the interaction between the Delete button and the recordset and apply the confirmation version instead.

That, however, does not take care of the security problem. Because the Delete function doesn't have a page to itself, you have nothing to password-protect. Or so it seems.

Go to one of the pages you just password-protected and again right-click anywhere in empty layout space. This time, choose Edit Script⇨onLoad from the cascading pop-up menus.

Ignore the top two lines and the bottom two lines — they're merely markers. The actual JavaScript that makes the passwording happen is the six lines in between. Select all those six lines and copy them to your clipboard by pressing Ctrl+C.

Editing the Wizard's JavaScript

Bring the detail page into the layout area (the DisplayDetail page if you're using the CookieKing sample site), right-click the Delete button, and choose Edit Script⇨onClick from the pop-up menus. Figure 13-9 shows what you see in the Script Center.

Figure 13-9:
JavaScript
for the
"delete with
confirma-
tion"
contract.

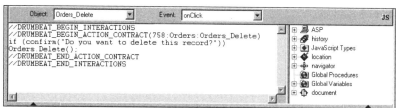

Again you see the same marker lines at the top and bottom. Although you cannot edit any script between those markers, you can add script above and below them. Create a new line *above* the confirm script, and paste the passwording script you copied in the preceding section into the new line. With a little editing, the whole thing looks like this:

```
pw = prompt("Admin password needed for delete");
if (pw != "Aubergine")
{
  alert("Incorrect password");
  window.location.href = "PasswordFail.asp";
}
//DRUMBEAT_BEGIN_INTERACTIONS
//DRUMBEAT_BEGIN_ACTION_CONTRACT(758:Recordset1:
        Recordset1_Delete)
if (confirm("Do you want to delete this record?"))
Recordset1.Delete();
//DRUMBEAT_END_ACTION_CONTRACT
//DRUMBEAT_END_INTERACTIONS
```

D'oh! We just gave away the password!

Although the script works as shown here, JavaScript mavens would want to wrap an ELSE clause around the confirm action so that the whole thing would become:

```
pw = prompt("Admin password needed for delete");
if (pw != "Aubergine")
{
  alert("Incorrect password");
  window.location.href = "Wrong.asp";
}
else
{
//DRUMBEAT_BEGIN_INTERACTIONS
//DRUMBEAT_BEGIN_ACTION_CONTRACT(758:Recordset1:
        Recordset1_Delete)
if (confirm("Do you want to delete this record?"))
Recordset1.Delete();
//DRUMBEAT_END_ACTION_CONTRACT
//DRUMBEAT_END_INTERACTIONS
}
```

Validating Form Entries

If you've spent any time making commercial online forms, you're familiar with the idea of validation. If not, it isn't hard to explain. Simply put, validation is an effort to save users from the consequences of their own stupidity.

Validation traps users who enter e-mail addresses with no @ character, zip codes with only four digits, dates and times that aren't possible, invalid credit card numbers, and such minor commercial sins. It looks as though the Drumbeat programmers had a great deal of fun with the validation business Table 13-2 shows all the validation contracts they've come up with.

Table 13-2   Form-Validation Contracts Available in Drumbeat

Validation	*Criteria*	*Parameters*
Alert if two form fields are identical	Field comparison	Case Sensitive, Error Message, Required
Alert if two form fields are not identical	Field comparison	Case Sensitive, Error Message, Required
Credit card no.	Field is all digits, dashes, spaces, periods, and passes Mod-10 Check, Required	
Custom	You supply the template	Alphanum Char, Error Message, Format, Letter Char, Number Char, Required
Date	Field date-formatted as recognized by JavaScript	Format, Required, When
Entry length	Field length between specified max/min	Error Message, Max Length, Min Length, Required, Strip Spaces
E-mail	Field contains @	Required
Fixed point	Limits number of digits after a decimal point	Decimal Places, Max, Min, Required
Floating point	Field is floating-point number	Max, Min, Required
Huge integer	Field is integer	Max Digits, Min Digits, Required
Integer	Field is integer (size limited)	Max, Min, Required
International phone number	At least 6 digits; punctuation allowed but not letters	Required
Non-blank	Field contains something other than spaces	Error Message
Social Security No.	Nine digits; spaces, dashes, and periods allowed	Required
Time	Field time is formatted as recognized by JavaScript	Required

(continued)

Table 13-2 *(continued)*

Validation	Criteria	Parameters
URL	Field starts with recognized URL protocol	Required
US phone number	7 digits, 10 digits, or 10 digits preceded by a 1; punctuation allowed but not letters	Required
Selection made from list	Item selected is not the first	None
Zip code	5 or 9 digits; punctuation allowed but not letters	Required

The following few sections describe some validations you might impose on the Cookie Order Insert page.

Preventing blank entries

Even fairly attentive users may occasionally slip and forget to enter something in a form field before submitting it. If the new baker's assistant tried to enter a cookie order without giving it a name, for example, it just may cause tantrums in the kitchen and possibly trigger resignations in the ranks of the master bakers. To prevent chaos in the kitchen, you ought to apply a non-blank validation to the Order Name field:

1. **Select the OrdersRS_Ordername edit box, right-click, and choose Possible Activations from the pop-up menu.**

2. **In the Interactions Center, scroll to the Forms Validation category to find the activation** Non Blank validation on OrdersRS_Ordername.

3. **Double-click to apply it (or right-click and choose Apply).**

   The Parameters dialog box pops up. The only parameter of this activation is the text of the error message.

4. **Enter something somewhere along the politeness scale from "Please give this order a name" to "Name it, stoopid!"**

As an additional incentive to users, because this edit box is the first on the form, it would be useful to set the focus on this field when the page loads so that the cursor appears immediately in the box. The Forms Miscellaneous category has an activation for that: Set focus when page loads.

Validating integer entries (and other database faux pas)

Databases can often be thrown into conniptions when users try to enter information of the wrong type in a field, such as alphabetic characters in a numerical field. Because orders for fractional numbers of cookies are even more likely to lead to tantrums in the kitchen, an integer validation on the Quantity field is appropriate in the Cookie King site.

Note that you can specify upper and lower limits to acceptable integer input. Like many of the validation contracts, this one has a Required option. If that option were not checked, a blank field would be counted as valid. In other words, a "required" field forces a user to enter something.

Validating date entries

Date fields can also be finicky in a database, and often require their own format. A nice refinement to the two date fields may be to have the Order Date default to today's date and the Due Date checked to ensure that it's a valid date and a later date than today. *Tantrums* would hardly be a strong enough word to describe the reaction from the kitchen if an order comes through for 500 macadamia nut cookies on Friday that were due last Monday.

Defaulting the Order Date field to today's date involves an activation in the Forms Set Value category, not Forms Validation. The interaction is `Set to today's date in different formats`. Its parameters allow for setting dates in the European style of the form DD/MM/YY, together with nine other formats.

You can apply the regular Date validation activation in the Forms Validation category to the `Due Date` field. This activation also includes the formatting options as well as allowing you to specify whether the date is Past, Future, or Any Date. Better set that one to Future to keep the kitchen happy.

Making custom validations

Suppose that you work for a bureaucratic organization that refuses to handle online inquiries from vendors unless they enter their correct vendor ID in a form field. (Perhaps you do!) The ID format looks like 123456/2000-A — 6 digits, a slash, the year, a dash, and a letter.

Figure 13-10 shows how to set up validation for that field in the Parameters dialog box for the custom validation activation. The # character stands for any digit; the A, for any letter; and the ? for any number or letter (not needed in this example). It works great — just be sure to change the parameter when the year 2001 rolls around.

Figure 13-10:
Custom
validation.

Knowing when to validate

If you publish an insert or update page with validations along the lines we suggest in the preceding few sections, it's a shock to discover that none of them appears to work.

That's because the effect of applying the validation contracts is to add each one to something called the *validate array,* waiting to be implemented. The validate array is not put into effect until the form is submitted, and then only if you take the extra step of applying an activation to *the form itself* (the icon in the basement). The activation is simply `Validate when [form] is submitted`.

This concept is a little confusing because the fact is that a typical insert or update page created by the DataForm Wizard never is submitted in the true sense. The insert or update action does something to the recordset, but, if you look at the list of interactions and activations on the page you don't see "submit form" anywhere. Nevertheless, the fact that the Insert/Update buttons are the submit type is good enough, apparently.

If you've replaced the standard form buttons with image buttons, you need to apply the submit interaction yourself because an image button doesn't have a submit type (type isn't even an attribute of an image button). Take these extra steps to make sure that your form gets submitted properly:

1. **Select the image button and the Form element in the basement. Right-click and choose Possible Interactions.**

2. **Find and apply the interaction** `Submit [Form] when [ImageButton] is clicked`.

Specifying the execution order (don't worry — you won't be shot at dawn)

Frustration may be your fate if you publish Drumbeat sites without understanding the importance of execution order, and the CookieKing site that's the subject of most of this chapter is no exception.

Execution order simply means the order in which the list of activations and interactions is carried out. Many times, the exact order is irrelevant — indeed, the order in which you set up the validation array doesn't matter. What *does* matter is that any form-submit action comes last in line. Other actions, such as validations, must come earlier in the list; otherwise, the form is submitted and gone before those actions are implemented.

That's the point of the special option Assigned Interactions (Ordered) option that appears on the pop-up menu when you right-click empty page-space.

Using Hidden Form Elements

A *hidden form element* has a name and a value that are important to the flow of data but unknown to users of a form. In e-commerce, hidden form elements are often used to convey stuff like customer IDs and shopping cart content.

In Drumbeat, a hidden form element is represented by a thing skulking in the basement whose only attributes are Content and Name.

The Drumbeat Quick Start tutorial has a clever use of hidden form elements in Lesson 4 (create a new site based on the Quick Start Lesson 4 StartingPoint to check this out). The idea is to make the selection of a geographical area a bit more exciting than a verbal list of regions. A world map is made from five separate images, and the task is to filter a database of job vacancies according to which image is clicked. Because clicking an image cannot send data to a recordset *per se,* a hidden form element has to be associated with each of the region images so as to transmit a region ID without the user's being aware that this is what is going on.

Remember the Drumbeat Action Auction from Chapter 4? No? Well, never mind — here's another example of the usefulness of hidden form elements that relates to the auction, and may have many uses in your design of interactive forms.

A database of ongoing auctions obviously exists in the engine room of any auction site, and when users create fresh auctions, they're just adding records — exactly the process facilitated by the Insert page of a DataForm. Figure 13-11 shows what the DataForm Wizard set up for us by way of a form to enter new auctions.

Edit box name is Recordset1_nickname

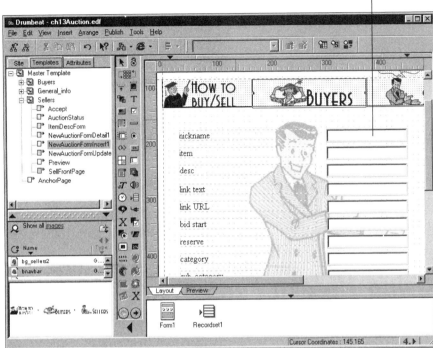

Figure 13-11:
An auction
insert page.

We want to be a bit more clever, however. Instead of the data entered here inserting straight into the recordset, we want to give the user both a preview of the auction page as it will actually look and a chance to come back and edit if something looks awry.

Great idea, but it turns out to create a ton of work. If you want to do it, follow these steps:

1. **Create a fresh page on the site, named Preview (refer to the section in Chapter 2 about creating a site structure with pages).**

   The preview page needs to have access to the same recordset as was placed on the insert page.

2. **Click the Add Assets button and choose Site Elements⊅Show All Site-Level Elements. Select the recordset that was used on the insert page and drag it into the basement.**

3. **Return to the insert page and display all interactions on the page, as shown in Figure 13-12.**

Figure 13-12:
Database
interactions.

4. **Remove all Database Edit interactions, including the one beginning with** `Insert record into`. **(It may be the only one in that category). To remove an interaction, select it in the Interactions Center, right-click, and choose Remove.**

5. **Change the names of any edit boxes that relate to the recordset to a simpler name. Names allocated by the Data Form Wizard are not very agile. Change** `Recordset1_nickname` **to** `nickname`, **for example.**

6. **Relabel the Insert button** Preview.

7. **Click the form element in the basement to display its Attributes Sheet, then click the Action Assign button on the Attributes Sheet. In the Link dialog box, choose the newly created preview page as the target of the form action.**

8. **Target the form to the newly created preview page.**

Now you have to do a complete design of the preview page, using imaginary data in all the text boxes. When those text boxes are published, they get their texts from the ASP Request object. Because a text box cannot be the source of data inserted into the recordset, however, a hidden form field has to be set on the preview page for each text box, arranged to get the same text from the Request object. The sidebar "Passing form data from page to page" in Chapter 12 explains how it works. The page also needs a Submit button for OK and a button-type button to enable users to go back to edit.

For *each and every* text field:

1. **From the Content drop-down list on the Attributes Sheet, select Server Expression and bring in the appropriate text from the request object.**

   Figure 13-13 shows the server expression to enter to bring in the text for the item description. The design text is what you get to see in the Drumbeat layout area as a stand-in.

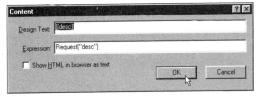

Figure 13-13: Transfer description info via a server expression.

2. **Haul a hidden form element into the basement, name it appropriately, and make its content the same server expression as for the text field.**

3. **Set up an interaction between the hidden form field, the OK button, and the recordset.**

   The interaction is `Use [hidden field] data to update/insert in Recordset1 when [approve button] is clicked`. Figure 13-14 shows the Parameters dialog box for one of these interactions, showing that you can direct the data to whatever database field you want.

Now set up the interaction between the OK button and the recordset, inserting the record when the button is clicked. Make sure that this interaction is last in the execution order.

Finally, arrange for the Back button to return to the Insert page. Although users would achieve the same effect by clicking their browser's Back button, providing all necessary navigation right there on the page is a good principle of Web design.

Ready-made contracts are available for making Back buttons, but because the whole point of this exercise is to be sure that the form data is still there in the form, ready to be edited, the best plan is to turn the button into a literal Back button. Right-click it and choose Edit Script⊃onClick from the pop-up menu cascade.

In the script tree, open the history object and drag the `history.back()` method into the scripting window. That's all there is to it. The button must not be a submit-type button, just a regular button type. Figure 13-15 shows the preview page actually working (well, almost).

This interaction...

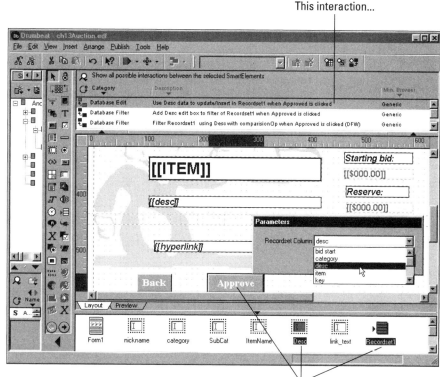

Figure 13-14:
How the
data gets to
the right
place.

... is applied between these three elements

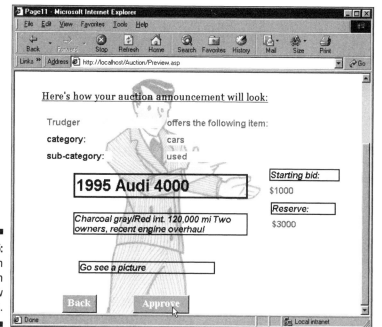

Figure 13-15:
The auction
item
preview
page.

Part IV
It's Not a Web Site — It's a Web App

The 5th Wave   By Rich Tennant

©RICHTENNANT

BUNGCO
BUNGEE CABLE
COMPANY

"Come on Walt—time to freshen the company
Web page."

In this part . . .

As you'll see in this part of the book, a database-driven web site can be more than just a series of forms: It can be a sophisticated search engine with a slick front end or a web application that offers customized features personally tailored for each site visitor. And you'll see how you can use the quick and powerful Drumbeat scripting features to customize the interactions in your site.

Chapter 14

Searching and Filtering the Database: A Traveller's Tale

Sitting around a café in the Casbah one day, waiting for a connection to help us get some black-market exit papers so that we could finally get out of this out-of-the-way traveller's dead end, we overheard someone at another table say, "Have you tried Rick's? Sooner or later, *everybody* comes to Rick's."

That's how we first found the place. Rick's Café Americain, where the drinks are on the house and the deals are all under the table.

Well, it turns out that those papers came with a price. We had to build a little web site that Rick wanted. You see, having a great deal of time to kill, and a captive audience of exiles, he was thinking of starting a little movie-distribution business to capitalize on his collection of black-market film classics. To promote it, he wanted to get the information out to all those exiles sitting around the café with their laptops with nothing better to do.

The Setup

The focus of the little web site that Rick wanted was the ability to search for movies and cinemas anywhere in town and get their screening schedules. He had heard about something like it from someone passing through, but there was nothing like it in Morocco, so he thought that he would be the first.

The site structure

We created the site structure first, and we won't bother you with the details (suffice it to say that it's much simpler than finding your way through the Casbah). What we want to focus on in this little story are the search operations. To see how we accomplished the task (and found our way out of Casablanca), you can use the pages that are already set up and follow along. The beginning site structure is shown in Figure 14-1.

Everything you need to follow along with the examples in this chapter is on the CD in the back of this book, including the database and a starter file with the basic page setup and all the queries defined. Just copy the MovieMaven folder over to your machine, and set up the DSN name MovieMaven pointing to the database file (moviemaven.mdb). Set up a publish directory for the site named movies in your C:\Inetpub\wwwroot directory. (For info about how to set up a DSN, refer to Chapter 11.)

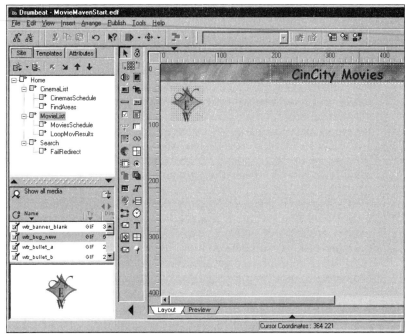

Figure 14-1:
The movie web site's site structure is laid out in the Site Manager.

The database setup

We started with the database. We found a black-market copy of Microsoft Access, circa 1992, in a dusty stall in the souk and bargained the shopowner down to a few hundred dirham. We didn't need anything elaborate because the database we were constructing was fairly simple.

It's composed of three primary tables and a couple of little guys that are useful for creating dropdown lists:

- ✔ **Movies:** Contains all the information about the movies
- ✔ **Cinemas:** Contains the information about the cinemas in town
- ✔ **Schedule:** Combines information from the other two tables and adds the screening times for each movie at each cinema

You can see the way the tables are related in Figure 14-2.

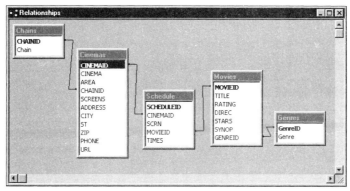

Figure 14-2:
The basic structure of the data-base, shown in Microsoft Access.

The queries you need to build the pages are already created too. You can see the content if you look at the ODBC Content Tables in the Content Center. Four primary queries and, again, a few little guys for dropdown list use, make up the lot. The primary queries are shown in this list:

- ✔ **Cinemas:** Gets all the info from the Cinemas table with a simple SELECT ALL statement
- ✔ **Movies:** Gets all the info from the Movies table with a simple SELECT ALL statement
- ✔ **MovieSched:** Gets the movie title from the Movies table and the schedule info from the Schedule table
- ✔ **CinSched:** Gets the cinema name from the Cinemas table and the schedule info from the Schedule table

The site structure consists of two sets of pages:

- ✔ The first set lets you get a list of all the cinemas in town and then select to get the schedule of movies playing at a cinema.

✔ The second set lets you get a list of all the movies playing and then select to get the schedule of cinemas where they're playing.

We show you how to create the database content for the pages using the DataForm Wizard and then applying a little magic to make them work together. Then we show you how to build the same information into the second set of pages manually, using recordsets and AutoTables.

If you want to use queries you create in one site in another site, you can set up your queries with the export-and-import feature in Query Manager. Just save a query as a .dql file and import it into the new site. We've included all the queries for the MovieMaven site in .dql files in the MovieMaven folder on the CD, so that you can try out importing queries and setting up your own site from scratch. Before importing the queries, be sure that you set up the DSN to the database.

Getting the Cinema List and Cinema Pages

The first thing you do is create the list of cinemas and the pages for each cinema. Use the DataForm Wizard to do it. The Result List page makes up the list of cinemas, and the Detail page is the individual page for each cinema:

1. **On the Site tab, click the New DataForm button to run the DataForm Wizard.**

2. **For the Data Source, choose the ODBC table Cinemas1 and name the DataForm** Cinemas.

3. **Because you're creating just Detail and Result List pages, deselect all the other options. Leave the Messages at the default values (you won't need to bother with them), and go on to the next dialog box.**

4. **For the Detail page, choose these columns: CINEMA, AREA, ADDRESS, CITY, ST, ZIP, and PHONE (click to remove the check mark from the other columns).**

5. **Using one of the pages already in the site structure, click to select the Existing Page option, click Select Page and choose the CinemasSchedule page.**

6. **In the next dialog box, uncheck the Navigation Buttons option, and then click Next. You don't need those because your site navigation will all be created by links.**

7. **For the Results List, choose just three columns: CINEMA, AREA, and Chain.**

8. **Again, select the Existing Page option, click Select Page, and select the CinemaList page.**

9. **Skip the next dialog box that has Sorting and Records/Page options and click Next.**

10. **For the column to link to the detail page, choose CINEMA and click Next.**

11. **For the unique key columns, choose** `CINEMAID` **and** `Chains.CHAINID`, **and then click Finish.**

The two pages are shown in Figures 14-3 and 14-4.

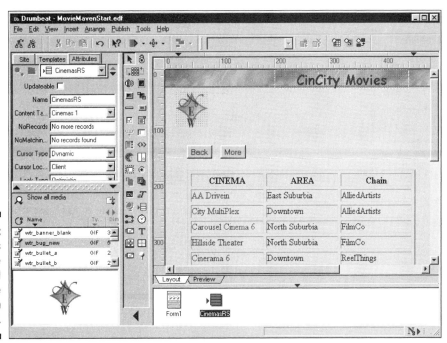

Figure 14-3: The results list page created by the DataForm Wizard.

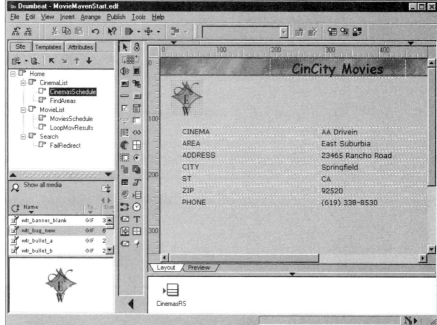

Figure 14-4:
The detail
page
created by
the
DataForm
Wizard.

Before you start adding more elements to the page and getting confused, you should rename the recordset used in this DataForm. Select the recordset, click the Attributes tab, and give the recordset the name **CinemasRS** in the Name box.

Getting the schedule info

In this section, you add the schedule information for the cinemas to the detail pages you put on the CinemasSchedules page. The information you want is the title of each movie and the times it's playing. That information is just what the MovieSched query was set up to glean from the database. If you create a result list from this query and put it on the cinema detail pages, you'll have it — almost.

Rick thought that sounded complicated, mixing DataForms, but I assured him that it wasn't. "I don't know what's what anymore," he said. "You'll have to do the thinking for the both of us."

This is what you do:

   1. **Run the DataForm Wizard again. For the Data Source option, select MovieSched.**

2. **Name the DataForm** MovieSched, **and deselect all except the Detail and Result List pages.**

3. **In the next three dialog boxes for the Detail page, leave all the selections set to their defaults and skip through, clicking Next.**

   You have no further use for this page and won't be using it, but the Wizard creates it anyway.

   "How extravagant you are, throwing away forms like that," Rick commented. "Someday, they may be scarce." But he was beginning to admire our daring.

4. **For the Results List, choose TITLE and TIMES. Select the Existing Page option and select the CinemasSchedule page.**

   It's the same page used for the Cinema Detail page.

Skip the rest of the options and click Finish to create the pages. The new CinemasSchedule page is shown in Figure 14-5.

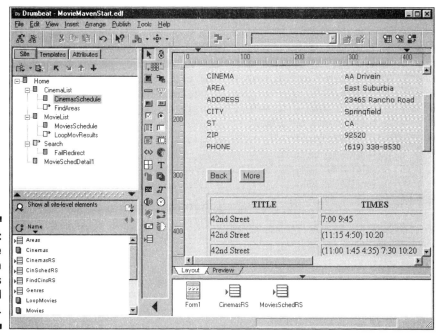

Figure 14-5: Add the cinema schedules to the detail page.

Rename the new recordset **MovieSchedRS** so that the interaction you apply next will make sense.

Filtering the schedule by cinema

So now you have the list of movies and times displayed on the cinema pages. However, there's just one problem: The list is showing *all* the movies at *all* the cinemas and not just the ones playing at *this* cinema.

Rick was philosophical about it, looking over our shoulder at this point: "Well," he said, "It doesn't take much to see that the problems of two little recordsets don't amount to a hill of beans in this crazy world."

"Just watch — we can fix that in a jiffy," we said:

1. **Select the two recordsets in the basement, right-click, and choose Possible Interactions from the pop-up menu.**

2. **In the Interactions Center, find and apply the interaction** Filter MovieSchedRS with related field from CinemasRS.

3. **In the Parameters dialog box, choose the related fields CINEMAID from the two recordsets on the FilterColumn and FilterBy dropdown lists.**

Publish the pages and give the site a browse, and you may get a polite message asking you to switch the order of the recordsets in the basement of the page. That's because the page needs to load the filter criteria before the data it's going to filter. If you want to go directly to the pages, change the default page for the site in your Publish settings (choose Publish⇨Publish Settings on the ASP or WebSphere tab) to CinemaList. (Some appropriate links are on the Home page if you leave the default page set to Home.)

Just select CinemasRS and drag it to the left of MovieSchedRS. Publish again, and the new filter works like a charm. Now a user could click a cinema name on the CinemaList page and go straight to the CinemasSchedule page and see just the movies playing at that cinema.

Getting the Movie List

We wanted to get a list of all the movies playing and a page for each movie that tells at which cinemas it's playing and when. To do it, we needed to do essentially the same thing all over again with different queries. Again, the Result List and Detail pages that DataForm Wizard generates are perfect for this task.

Follow these steps:

1. **Run the DataForm Wizard again. For the Data Source option, select the Movies1 ODBC Content Table. Name the form** Movies, **and deselect all except the Detail and Result List options.**

2. **Skip over the Messages dialog box by clicking Next.**

3. **For the Detail page, select these columns: TITLE, RATING, DIREC, STARS, and SYNOP (deselect MOVIEID and GENREID).**

4. **Choose the Existing Page option, click Select Page, and select the MoviesSchedule page.**

5. **In the next dialog box, uncheck the Navigation Buttons option again.**

6. **For the Results List, choose only the TITLE and RATING columns. Select the Existing Page option and select the MovieList page.**

7. **Skip over the next dialog box for Sorting and Records/Page options and click Next.**

8. **For Column to Link to Detail, choose TITLE.**

9. **For the unique key column, select** MOVIEID **and click Finish.**

After generating the pages, select either the MovieList page or the MoviesSchedule page and rename the recordset to **MoviesRS**.

Creating an AutoTable manually

What you want on this page is a list of cinemas that are playing each movie with the times the movie is playing. You could run the DataForm Wizard one more time to get the schedule info for each movie. Because that makes an extra page you don't want (the Detail page), however, it's just as easy (easier, really) to add the recordset and an AutoTable with the information you want to the page yourself:

1. **Select the MoviesSchedule page. Drag a Recordset element from the SmartElements toolbar to the basement of the page. On the Attributes Sheet, rename the recordset** CinSchedRS **and for Content Table, choose the CinSched Content Table for its source.**

2. **Drag an AutoTable from the SmartElements toolbar to the page. On the Attributes Sheet, assign the Content to Recordset.**

3. **In the Content dialog box, choose CinSchedRS as the Recordset element. You want to show the columns CINEMA and TIMES.**

4. **Select the rest of the columns, one by one, and click Remove to put them on the Don't Show side of the screen. (You can also double-click the column name to move it to the other window.) Then click OK.**

Now you have the list of cinemas and screening times showing on the page, just as you had when you put the Result List from the DataForm Wizard on the CinemasSchedule page.

Filtering the schedule by movie

Again, the MoviesSchedule page is not very intelligent yet. It's simply showing the screening times for every movie at every cinema. To filter the list to show only the cinemas and times for *this* movie, you have to apply the same interaction as before:

1. **Select the two recordsets in the basement, right-click, and choose Possible Interactions from the pop-up menu.**

2. **In the Interaction Center, find and apply the interaction** Filter CinSchedRS with related field from MoviesRS.

3. **In the Parameters dialog box, choose the related fields** MOVIEID **in the FilterColumn and FilterBy dropdown lists, as shown in Figure 14-6.**

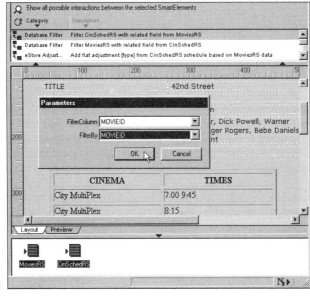

Figure 14-6:
Apply the filter inter-action and choose the related columns in the recordset.

Drumbeat wanted to see the MoviesRS on the left in the basement (so the filter criteria would load before the data it was supposed to filter), so we checked to make sure that it was in the right place before publishing, which it was.

"Publish it again, Sam," Rick said. We did. When we browsed the site, we saw the filter action on the page, as shown in Figure 14-7.

Rick was beginning to get the idea. "What brought you to Casablanca in the first place?" I asked.

"The ISPs," he said.

"The ISPs? What ISPs? We're in Morocco."

"I was misinformed," he replied.

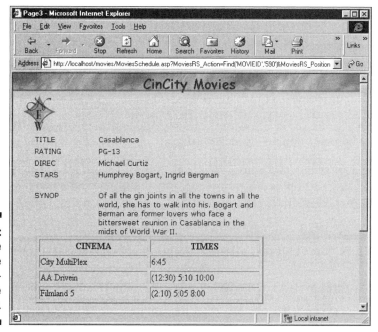

Figure 14-7:
The movie schedule page is filtered in the browser.

Doing Away with the Military Look: DataForms in Disguise

One thing is probably bothering you about these pages, and that's the rather straight, military look of it. All those boxes all lined up wearing the same starched uniform, like the Gestapo. It was bothering Rick. Reminded him of Paris during the war.

"I remember it well. The Germans wore gray. She wore blue," he said. We wanted to cheer him up, so we decided to make the DataForms look much sleeker. By using a few tricks to disguise them, we figured that we could make them not look like DataForms — more like underground members of the Resistance, maybe.

We made some styles in the sample file so that you can try out this underground operation. Taking the MoviesSchedule page as an example, first, you can delete the labels for the fields and rearrange them a bit. Then assign these styles from the Attributes Sheet:

✔ For the movie title, select Verdana12Bld.

✔ For the rest of the text, select Verdana10.

Put a SmartSpacer below the synopsis field and above the AutoTable so that the contents don't overrun the table on longer descriptions.

Next, give the AutoTable a makeover. When you select the AutoTable and click the Attributes tab, you see several things you can do on the Attributes Sheet. Follow these steps:

1. **Set the Border option to 0 to get rid of the table borders.**

2. **Set the Cell Gap option to 0 to get rid of unnecessary space between cells.**

3. **Click to remove the check mark from the Headings option.**

    It seems fairly obvious what the columns are presenting, so you don't have to take up useless space there.

4. **Set the Page Size option (the number of records showing at one time) to a sufficiently large number that all records will be displayed.**

5. **Now you can assign some styles to the table. Give the overall table a style of Verdana10. Then you can create a new style based on that one with a background color and a second one with a different background color. Assign one style to the even rows and the other to the**

odd rows, creating a color-banded schedule that's easy to read. (If you want to use the styles we created rather than create your own, use Verdana10Bg1 and Verdana10Bg2.)

The table settings are shown in Figure 14-8.

For more information about creating styles with background colors, see the section in Chapter 5 about using background and box properties.

If you repeat these steps on the CinemaList page, you don't need the navigation buttons for Back and More that the wizard generated, so you can just delete them. ("Away, you ugly jackboots!")

The new look in the browser is shown in Figure 14-9. Who could tell that this was a lowly DataForm?

"Here's looking at you, kid," Rick said appreciatively.

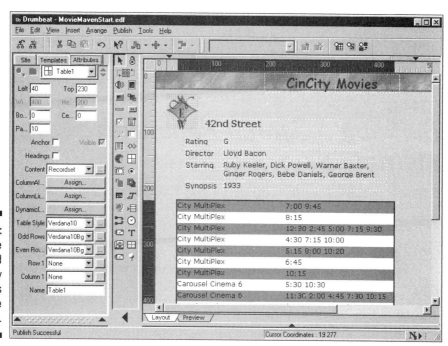

Figure 14-8: Set the styles and display options on the AutoTable.

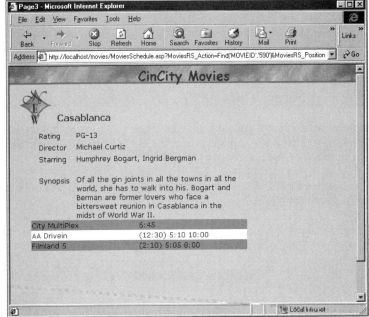

Figure 14-9:
The
DataForm
page looks
like this
after its
makeover.

Building a Search Page with Multiple Search Criteria

Now that you have the basic pages set up, you can probably think of lots of ways you may want to search the database. You have plenty of fields available in the database to set up a variety of searches. For example, you can search for cinemas by name or area or chain. You can search for movies by title (keyword), genre or ratings. You can put all these search options on a master search page we've already set up.

"Considering the importance of the case," Rick advised, "We should round up twice the usual suspects."

Searching for movies

Rick wanted to set up a search operation so that people could search for movies by three criteria:

✔ **Title:** By entering a keyword

✔ **Genre:** By choosing from a dropdown list

✔ **Rating:** By choosing from a dropdown list

We set off two sections on the Search page: one for Search Movies and one for Search Cinemas. Here's how to set up the Movie search section (we'll leave the rest to your imagination):

1. **Place three text boxes on the layout in the Movie Search part of the page. In the text boxes, enter the search labels for users:**

   Search titles by keyword:

   Search for genre:

   Search by rating:

2. **Add one edit box and two dropdown list boxes next to them.**

   You want to get the content of the two dropdown list boxes from a couple of those little queries mentioned earlier, so you have to add two recordsets to the page and bind them to those queries.

3. **Drag a recordset SmartElement from the SmartElements toolbar to the basement. On the Attributes Sheet, give it the name Genres and choose the Content Table Genres from the dropdown list.**

4. **Drag another recordset element into the basement and give it the name Ratings, and then assign its content to the Ratings table.**

5. **Add the recordset you want to search. From the Asset Center (filtered for site-level elements), drag the MoviesRS recordset into the basement.**

6. **On the Attributes Sheet for the edit box, enter Keyword for the Name option and select Text for the Content option.**

7. **Select the first dropdown list, and set these attributes on the Attributes Sheet:**

   • **Name:** GenreList

   • **Content:** Select Recordset. In the Content dialog box, select Genres for the recordset and Genres for the column.

   • **Value:** Select Recordset. In the Content dialog box, select Genres for the recordset and Genre ID for the column.

   • **Selection:** Select Recordset. In the Content dialog box, select MoviesRS for the recordset and GenreID for the column.

8. **Select the second dropdown list, and set these values on the Attributes Sheet:**

- **Name:** RatingList

- **Content:** Select Recordset. In the Content dialog box, select Ratings for the recordset and Ratings for the column.

- **Value:** Select Recordset. In the Content dialog box, select Ratings for the recordset and Rating for the column.

- **Selection:** Select Recordset In the Content dialog box, and select MoviesRS for the recordset and Rating for the column.

9. **Add a form button for submitting the search. Name this button** Find1 **on the Attributes Sheet and give it the label** Find Movies.

The page so far is shown in Figure 14-10. Now that you have all the pieces you need on the page, you're ready to set up the interactions.

Adding the edit box to the filter

After you have the form elements set up, you need to add them, one by one, to the search action on the page. Start with the edit box:

1. **Select the Keyword edit box, the Find1 button, and MoviesRS in the basement, and then right-click and choose Possible Interactions.**

2. **Find and apply the interaction** Add Keyword edit box to filter of MoviesRS when Find1 is clicked.

3. **In the Parameters dialog box, select TITLE for Recordset Field. (That's the field you want to search.)**

4. **For the Connector option, choose OR. (That's the criteria you want to search by.)**

5. **For the Operator option, select Includes so that if the string that's entered occurs anywhere within the title, the match will be made (see Figure 14-11).**

Adding the list box to the filter

Next, add the list box to the filter action on the page:

1. **Select the GenreList list box, the Find1 button, and the MoviesRS in the basement, right-click, and choose Possible Interactions.**

2. **Find and apply the interaction** Add GenreList dropdown list value to filter of MoviesRS when Find1 is clicked.

3. **In the Parameters dialog box, select GENREID for the Recordset field. (That's the field in the MoviesRS we want to search.)**

4. **For the Connector, choose OR.**

5. **For the Operator, choose =. This symbol means that it must match the numerical value exactly because it's a numerical field in the database table. See Figure 14-12.**

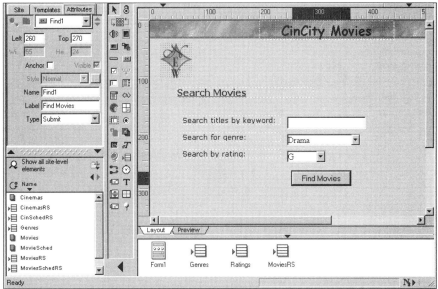

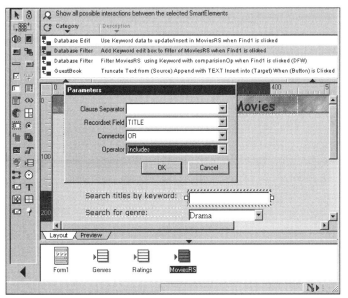

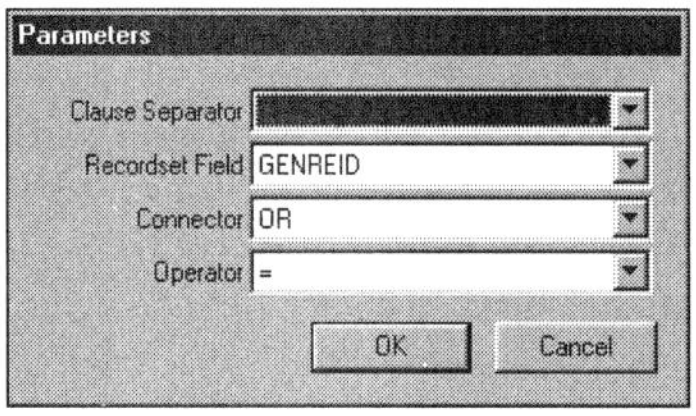

Figure 14-12:
Set up the
action on
the Genre
dropdown
list.

Adding the second list box to the filter

By now, you should be getting the idea. To set up each search operation, you just round up the usual suspects and then find the Database Filter action that applies to each one. Set the parameters and — bam. You have one more to go:

1. **Select the RatingList list box, the Find1 button, and the MoviesRS in the basement, right-click, and choose Possible Interactions.**

2. **Find and apply the interaction** Add RatingList dropdown list value to filter of MoviesRS when Find1 is clicked.

3. **In the Parameters dialog box, choose RATING for the Recordset field. (That's the field in the MoviesRS we want to search.)**

4. **For the Connector, choose OR.**

5. **For the Operator, choose =. (This field is a text field in the database, rather than a numerical field, but the choice is the same for matching the text string exactly.) See Figure 14-13.**

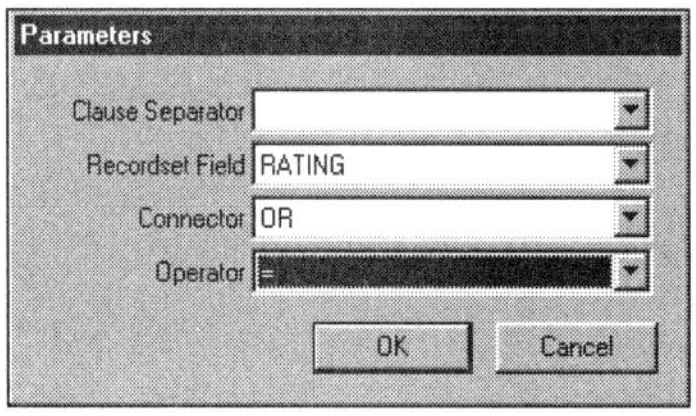

Figure 14-13:
Set up the
action on
the Ratings
dropdown
list.

Adding static options to the lists

Oops, wait a minute, you forgot something. What if someone wants to search by Genre, say for thrillers, but doesn't want to have the default Rating selection added to the search? If the default option is set to G, they get not only all the thrillers but also all the G-rated movies in the search results.

You can take care of that by adding static options to the lists so that the initial, default choice would be None:

1. **Select one of the dropdown lists, right-click, and choose Possible Activations.**

2. **In the Database Miscellaneous category, find the interaction** Add static option to list populated by a recordset **and double-click to apply it.**

3. **In the Parameters dialog box, choose a text string to display in the Option String box. Leave the Option Value at 0 so that no value will be passed to the database search if this is selected. Leave the Selected box checked so that this will be the default selection.**

4. **On the Attributes Sheet for the dropdown list, change the Selection option to None.**

   This step ensures that the default option when the page loads will be the static option. If you didn't do this step, the default option would be whatever the value is for the field in the first record of the database.

Then we did the exact same thing for the other list box.

Creating a looped results page

Trying out the search operation so far, you can see that a search produces a result list on the MovieList page, and from there you can click a link to get the movie schedule. Works, but could be better.

What if you want more information in the result list? Something like you get on the Detail page, so if you're searching for thrillers or G-rated movies, you get not only a list but also synopses and the like. No law says that a search must always go to a Result List page, as the DataForm Wizard thinks of it. We could make the search page go to the Detail page. The Detail page we created for the Movies has only one record per page, however, and the search may return several records.

We decided to create a new detail page with a data loop on it to do what we want. For this to work, you need to use the same recordset, so that you can maintain the state of the recordset as you go from page to page. You can make this easy by letting DataForm Wizard create the page from the right recordset.

1. **Run DataForm Wizard. For the Data Source, instead of selecting a Content Table, select the MoviesRS recordset.**

2. **Name the DataForm** LoopMovies, **and uncheck all the page options because you want to create only the Detail page.**

3. **Select these columns: TITLE, RATING, DIREC, STARS, SYNOP (uncheck MOVIEID and GENREID)**

4. **Select the Existing Page option and choose the page LoopMovResults.**

5. **For Records/Page enter 10. (The database has only 20 records, so this will probably give you all the results you want, but you can leave the Navigation buttons on the page so that users can click to see more if necessary.)**

Let the Wizard create the page.

Next, you want to create a link so that after looking over the search matches, you can click the one for which you want to get the schedule.

1. **Select the text element that contains the movie title and the MoviesRS in the basement, right-click, and choose Possible Interactions.**

2. **Find and apply the interaction** `Go to pagename when MoviesRS_Title is clicked and show cur rec of MoveisRS.`

3. **In the Parameters dialog box, click the assign page button and select the page MoviesSchedule.**

Now go back to the Search page and change the destination of the search. Right-click the Find button and chose Assigned Interactions (ordered). Double-click the Filter interaction (`Filter MoviesRs when Find1 button is clicked`) to bring up the Parameters dialog box again. Click the Assign button and reassign the page to LoopMovResults.

When you're setting up a page with a large number of interactions, it's important that you check the order of the interactions on the page before publishing. This is especially true if you're mucking about adding and deleting and changing things. There are two types of order that are important: the order of events on a particular element (like the all-important button) and the order of events on the page itself. Be sure to check both.

Redirecting for a Failed Search

Nobody likes to get nothing for their effort. When a search operation does not find any matches, you're confronted with just that — nothing. If you've used the DataForm Wizard to create an AutoTable, you may see an empty table with only headers. We hate when that happens.

To fix it, all you have to do is provide an alternate page for users to go to when the search returns zero results. The MovieMaven site has a page named FailRedirect for that purpose. To apply the redirection, this is what you do:

1. **Select the LoopMovResults page (the one you chose as the** *Go to Page* **in the Parameters dialog box in the last Filter action on the button).**

2. **Select the recordset in the basement that delivers the results of the search (MoviesRS).**

3. **Right-click and choose Possible Interactions. In the Interactions Center, find and apply the interaction** `Redirect if Recordset is empty`**.**

4. **In the Parameters dialog box, click the Assign button and select the FailRedirect page.**

If you publish and browse the site now, you can test the redirect by entering your own name in the keyword field and conducting a search. Unless your name happens to be Tokyo Joe, you'll be sent to Search Siberia.

Using Dynamic SQL Queries

There's one more trick we have up our sleeve for searching the movie database. Rick had heard something about dynamic SQL queries and he wanted us to show him how to use one of those on his site. Here's what you do:

Open the Query Manager (click Locate Assets⇨Queries) and click New to create a new query. Select the MovieMaven data source. The tables in the database will come into view.

You can create a dynamic SQL query based on the `Cinemas` table so that you can set up a new search for cinemas by area of town:

1. **In the SQL statement window, enter:**

```
SELECT * FROM CINEMAS WHERE AREA = @area
```

2. **In the lower window, right-click the Parameter Name header and select Append Parameter.**

   An annoying little *What's This?* box sometimes pop up — just click outside the box to get rid of it — it's a harmless little program bug. We suppose that's what you get for buying your software in the souk.

3. **Click the first row of the Parameter Name box and enter** @area**.**

4. **Click the Test Value box and enter** 'Downtown' **— in single quotes just like that, as shown in Figure 14-14.**

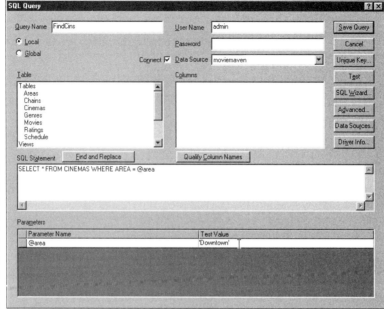

Figure 14-14:
Enter a test value for the parameter that will become the default value.

5. **Click the Test button. The SQL Query Result dialog box shows the cinema table filtered for those whose** Area **matches** Downtown. **This will be the default value for the parameter, which you can change dynamically on the page.**

6. **Close the Test dialog box, name the query** FindCins, **and click Save Query. In Query Manager, click Create Table, and then click Done.**

Now you're ready to set up a page that uses this parameter to dynamically sort the results of a recordset. In the site tree, select the page FindAreas in the CinemaList section:

1. **Drag a recordset element from the SmartElements toolbar to the basement of the FindAreas page. On the Attributes Sheet, name it** FindCinsRS. **For Content, choose the FindCins Content Table.**

2. **Place an AutoTable SmartElement on the page. On the Attributes Sheet, for Content choose Recordset, and select FindCinsRS. Choose the columns to display: CINEMA and AREA. (Double-click the other columns in the "Show" window to move them to the "Don't show" window.)**

   Notice that the default selections displayed on the page match what's in the Test dialog box.

3. **Place a new recordset element on the page. On the Attributes Sheet, name it** Area **and assign its content to the Areas Content Table.**

4. **Place a dropdown list box on the page. On the Attributes Sheet, for the Content option, select Recordset. In the Content dialog box for Recordset, select Areas and select Area for Column. For Value, select Recordset and repeat the selections you made for Content.**

5. **Select the dropdown list box and FindCinsRS, right-click, and choose Possible Interactions. Find and apply the interaction** `Pass List1 to FindCinsRS using [SQLParameter]`.

6. **In the Parameters dialog box, for the Enclosing Token option, choose '** **(the single quote). For the SQL Parameter option, select the @area parameter from the dropdown list, as shown in Figure 14-15.**

Figure 14-15:
Setting
up the
interaction.

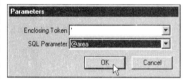

"This is the tricky part," we told Rick. "Watch carefully. We're going to do a little drag-and-drop scripting to make the table contents change."

1. **Right-click FindCinsRS in the basement and select Edit Script⇨Server. The Script Center opens.**

2. **In the Script Center, click the plus sign next to the ASP node to open it. Then open the FindCinsRS node.**

3. **Scroll to the bottom of the list of methods and select** `MoveFirst()`. **Drag it to the scripting pane on the left and close the Script Center.**

4. **Select the dropdown list box, right-click, and choose Attributes. On the Attributes Sheet, change the Selection to Server Expression.**

5. **In the Content dialog box, for the Expression, enter** Request("List1"). **Leave the other options blank.**

   This step keeps the selection made in the dropdown list selected so that the selection matches the filter applied to the table.

6. **Select the dropdown list box and the Form element in the basement, right-click, and choose Possible Interactions. Find and apply the interaction** `Submit Form1 when List1 changes`. **In the Parameters dialog box, leave the edit box blank and click OK.**

"Publish it again, Sam," Rick said.

Browse the page and try selecting an option from the dropdown list. The AutoTable remakes itself instantly with the new filter. (You can see the final file on the CD in the MovieMaven folder of the sample files.)

Rick was impressed. "This could be the beginning of a beautiful relationship," he said. We gave him a stack of business cards, and he promised to distribute them to customers at the café.

The End of the Story

We got our exit papers. Rick got his web site. Worked out well for him, too. Last we heard from him (by e-mail), he had been reunited with someone he knew from Paris years ago. "Of all the web sites on all the servers in all the world, she had to download mine," he said wonderingly.

Chapter 15

Writing Contracts and Scripts

* *

In This Chapter

▶ The Contract Manager

▶ An in-depth look at contracts

▶ Participants and parameters

▶ Support scripts

▶ A couple of ad rotators

▶ The Script Center

▶ A couple of stupid scripts

▶ The sliding tiles game

▶ Global procedures and variables

* *

*I*f you really hate computer languages and reckon that the whole point of applications like Drumbeat is that they let you avoid those languages, you can skip this chapter without losing any grade points. Although it's true in a way that Drumbeat protects you from the dark incantations of JavaScript and VBScript, it doesn't hide them behind a locked door.

If you're comfortable with JavaScript, you'll find that Drumbeat lets you see the details in two ways: first, by examining *contracts* — which are basically canned JavaScript packages — and second, by allowing free-form scripting in the Script Center. Even then, labor-saving gizmos are on hand to help out.

So farewell, JavaScript-ophobes! Join us again in Chapter 16.

What Are Contracts?

Throughout this book, we use examples of activations of single SmartElements and interactions between two or more SmartElements. Those activations and interactions are the labels given when JavaScript code is actually applied to the SmartElements. The JavaScripts themselves are *contracts,* fully exposed for inspection and editing in the Drumbeat Contract Manager. They may or may not have changeable *parameters* (the speed of a dynamic movement, for example).

The *Contract Manager* is a complex, seven-tab dialog box containing every detail of every contract your system knows about. You can edit practically everything — unless you know what you're doing, though, you're well advised to keep your sticky fingers off it! A bit later in this chapter, however, we show how some edits can be very simple after all and hopefully qualify you for sticky-fingers-on status, if you feel like it.

Figure 15-1 shows the Contracts tab in the Contract Manager. The main thing to notice is that, in routine use, you can sort the list of contracts by category and by browser compatibility. The sort criterion for browser compatibility defaults to <all>, and the contract category "remembers" which category you were last using. There are two ways to display the Contract Manager. You can either choose the menu option Tools⇨Contracts, or, in the Asset Center, click the Add Assets button and choose Contracts from the pop-up menu.

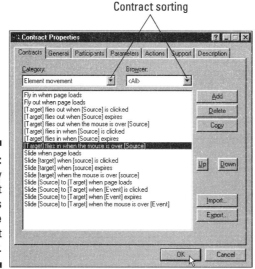

Figure 15-1:
One of many contract categories in the Contract Manager.

Because you're looking at the element movement contracts here, if you switch the browser compatibility setting criterion to Generic, the list simply disappears because HTML level 2 can't make things move. If you're a more advanced user, you may be interested in the buttons on this tab that enable you to add, delete, copy, import, and export contracts. All in due time.

Unlike many — most — Drumbeat pop-up doodads, the Contract Manager is what the programmers call *modeless*. To the rest of us, it means that you don't have to close it down to continue working on the main Drumbeat screen. You can push it aside or minimize it.

Anatomy of a Contract

Taking an example not quite at random, this section explains what you see when you pull a contract apart and look at its stuffing in some detail. The contract this section examines is

```
Element movement: [Target] flies in when the mouse is over
                  [source]
```

Participants

Drumbeat offers the element movement contract as a possible interaction between two SmartElements on a page, so long as the SmartElements — the contract *participants* — satisfy certain conditions that you find out about shortly. Check the Description tab and you find this text:

```
The element will move from the specified offscreen position
              to the position it occupies in the Drumbeat layout
              view when the mouse moves over an element.
```

Figure 15-2 shows the General tab for this contract. The tab is primarily of interest to programmers writing new contracts — the only new information is the lowest-level browser that would support the contract.

The Participants tab, as shown in Figure 15-3, reveals everything about which SmartElements qualify to participate in this contract, if you know how to read it.

Here's the deal. The contract defines what type of participants it needs by placing restrictions, or *requirements,* on them. Each participant may be required to have certain events, properties, or methods — and it's that list of requirements that determines what combination of SmartElements qualifies as appropriate for the contract. Contracts can have many participants or seem to have none (however, that's an illusion).

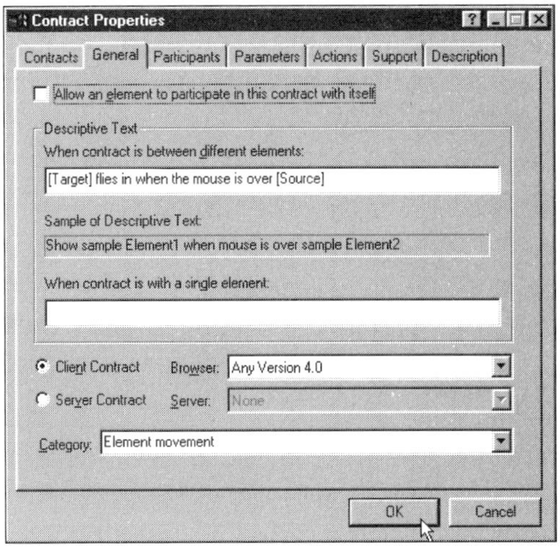

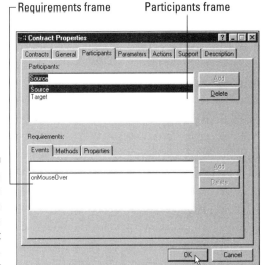

Figure 15-2:
The General
tab in the
Contract
Manager.

Requirements frame   Participants frame

Figure 15-3:
The
Participants
tab in the
Contract
Manager.

In Figure 15-3, you can see that the source object needs to be able to capture an `onMouseOver` event — naturally, because the contract is all about what happens when a user of a page mouses over something. That eliminates many SmartElements from consideration right away. Form elements generally don't capture mouseovers. Text objects and images are the most likely contenders to be the source of this contract.

Figure 15-4 shows the only requirement for the target object: It must have a property named `Style`.

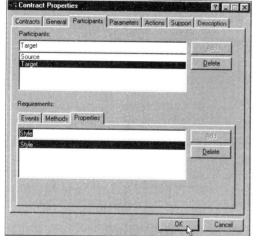

Figure 15-4:
Require-
ments for
the target
of this
contract.

So what has style? Most objects that appear on the page, it turns out. Images have `Style` and also have `imageStyle`. Text has `Style` and also `textStyle`. All the visible form elements have `Style`. Even a media controller has `Style`. About the only standard, visible, SmartElement that does *not* have `Style` is an AutoTable. All these things can qualify to fly on and off the page in dynamic (we nearly said "stylish") fashion. If you're adept with HTML, you understand why — HTML novices wouldn't want to know anyway.

To sum up what the Participants tab tells you about this particular contract, it's valid when the source is sensitive to a `MouseOver` event and the target is some visible element that can be made to move. It's all perfectly logical.

Parameters

We use many examples of contract parameters during the course of this book. Practically all the token substitution and form validation examples in Chapter 13 have parameters. Parameters are properties of the *contract itself* rather than of its participants. The user of the contract (that's you) can give the parameters values at the time it's applied as an activation or interaction.

The parameters of this particular contract are "Where do you want this thingamajig to fly in from?" and "How fast do you want it to fly?" To get a bit more technical, the user of the contract is forced to choose from a range of values for the two JavaScript variables *From* and *Speed.*

Figure 15-5 shows what you see when you select the Speed parameter and edit it. The choices are offered from a list: Fast, Medium, and Slow. The From parameter has a longer values list — eight possible directions from which the thingamajig can fly in.

Figure 15-5:
The details of the Speed parameter.

Later in this chapter (see Figure 15-10, for example), you see other ways to prompt the contract user for a parameter value.

Actions and support

We can no longer delay the moment when we have to start talking actual JavaScript. We try to keep it simple and not explain absolutely everything.

Actions are the JavaScript functions that make the contract work. *Support* refers to the library routines that are also included.

The majority of contracts have only one JavaScript function — the element movement contract happens to have two. Take a look at Figure 15-6.

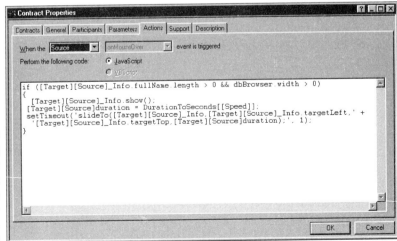

Figure 15-6:
Canned
JavaScript
for the
MouseOver
event.

This main function is performed when the source object captures an onMouseOver event. See those two dropdown lists at the top of the figure? Play with the left one, and that's when you see the surprise guest at the party: the *document,* which has a privileged status as a possible participant in every contract. (That's why some contracts can seem to have no participants.) Adjust the dropdown on the right to show the document onLoad event and — behold — you see a couple of variable definitions and another function, as shown in Figure 15-7.

So something happens when the document is loaded, and something else happens when the mouseover event occurs. This section takes a perfunctory look at the document onLoad script; as you step through this process, bear in mind that you're dealing with four separate tokens that are substituted when the contract is applied, as explained in Table 15-1.

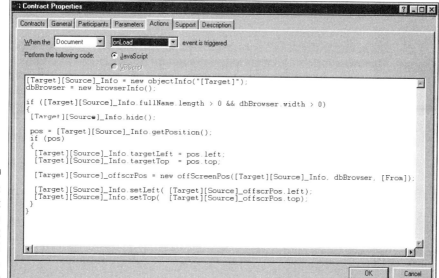

Figure 15-7:
JavaScript
for the
document
onLoad
event.

A *token* is a short word, normally enclosed in square brackets [like this], used as a temporary stand-in for some variable that's invoked when a contract is applied in a real situation.

Table 15-1 Token Substitution in The "Fly-In OnMouseOver" Contract

Token	Substituted With
[Target]	The identity of the object that flies in; the name of an image, most likely
[Source]	The identity of the object (a different image, for example) that captures the `onMouseOver` event
[From]	Parameter value (Top Left, for example) chosen at apply-time
[Speed]	Parameter value (Medium , for example) chosen at apply-time

The first line of the document `onLoad` script is

```
[Target][Source]_Info = new objectInfo("[Target]");
```

This line simply creates a JavaScript object, calling a function contained in the `getObjectInfo` support script. `getObjectInfo` is a fairly hefty piece of code — it drills down into the document object model and finds out whatever it can about the named component. In this case, `getObjectInfo` is asked to go fetch details of the target: The only information used in the contract is its width and height, which are the objects `[Target][Source]_Info.width` and `[Target][Source]_Info.height`.

The next line, a call to the `getBrowserInfo` support script, returns the browser type and also the window geometry as `dbBrowser.width` and `dbBrowser.height`:

```
dbBrowser = new browserInfo();
```

Remember the way this contract works: When you use it, you place your thingamajig on the page in the position in which you want it to *end up*. You then specify where you want it to fly in from and how fast.

Now it's easy to see that the `onLoad` script has the information it needs to do three things: Make the thingamajig invisible, store its present position, and then use the width and height information it has collected to send the thingamajig to a position offscreen from which it eventually makes its entrance. That's exactly what the rest of the script does.

What happens at mouseover time? The second script is triggered. The first thing it does is make the thingamajig visible again, and then it does this:

```
[Target][Source]duration = DurationToSeconds[[Speed]];
```

This line sets up a variable and gives it a value that's read from an array. The array converts the Speed parameter into a fly-time period in seconds: Slow=6, Medium=3, Fast=1. The `DurationToSeconds[]` array is defined in the support script `DurationArray`.

The actual fly-in action is done by the `slideTo` function, contained in *another* support script (not surprisingly because it's shared by every one of these element movement contracts).

Although `slideTo` is a neat piece of scripting, we have no need to take it apart and examine it. It cuts the flight-time into 20-millisecond legs, computes the intermediate position at each leg, and then moves the object there.

So what we're saying is. . . .

By looking at the details of this particular contract, you can tell that it's valid between two SmartElements — a target that has the property `Style` and a source that can capture a mouseover event. The contract achieves what it does with two scripts and five support scripts. Figure 15-8 shows four of the support scripts checked off on the Support tab (the fifth, not visible, is `DurationArray`).

Figure 15-8:
Four of the five support scripts used by this contract.

If you use this contract as part of a page design, make the fly-in object invisible. Yes, the `onLoad` script does that too, although it may take half a second or so to take effect. Unless your thingamajig is invisible, it flashes when the page loads before blinking out again.

Editing Contracts

Edits to all those tabs in the Contract Manager are almost too easy. Change something, switch tabs, and it's done. If your interactions later display JavaScript errors, we wish you lots of luck in debugging your edits. Our advice is to use the Copy button on the Contracts tab of the Contract Manager to make a safety copy. That way, if your new version "fubars," you can at least restore the original version.

Changing flight times

Small edits can also have far-reaching effects. For example, we mention an array earlier in this chapter, in the section "Actions and support," that converts the [Speed] token into an actual flight time in seconds. Suppose that you feel that the Slow option isn't slow enough. Figure 15-9 shows what you see when you check the DurationArray script on the Support tab and click the Edit button.

Array size declaration

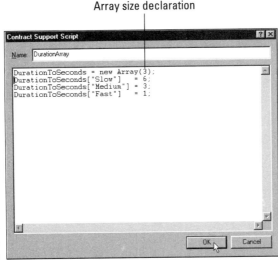

Figure 15-9:
The edit window for the Duration- Array support script.

It's this simple: Change the 6 to a **12** and close the edit window; your "slow" is then twice as slow.

Hang on, though: You could have a problem. This support script is used by not only all the element movement contracts but also by the edge transitions and quite possibly others you don't necessarily know about. Do you really want to affect all those contracts? Keep reading.

A better bet

If you don't want an edit to affect all the contracts, here's a better idea: Create your own value for the Speed parameter and call it **Snail Speed**. Add this line to the `DurationArray` support script:

```
DurationToSeconds["Snail Speed"] = 12;
```

It doesn't matter where you add it. Also change the array size declaration from 3 to **4**. You get a reminder that a change has been made that affects previously published pages. Ignore it — in this particular case, it's lying through its teeth.

Click the Parameters tab for the contract you want to slow down, and select Speed, Edit, and then Options. Figure 15-10 shows the process of adding the new parameter value to the list. Don't forget to click the Add button.

You've created more work for yourself because you now have to go around adding that option to every contract you want to have it available to — but we think that this method is safer than making the global change that affects them all at one time, plus who knows which other contracts.

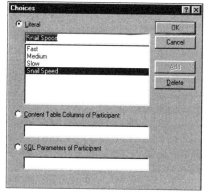

Figure 15-10:
Add a new value to a parameter list.

Copying and editing a contract for a custom requirement

Most Drumbeat users' first venture into real contract writing is likely to be a form of editing. We took our first steps along that road when we came across what we thought were limitations in the preloaded contracts, so we made copies of the originals and then set about building in new and desirable features.

We worked through the one in this section one summer afternoon (while simultaneously dealing with e-mail and ICQ messages). An existing contract creates a "drop zone" for drag-and-drop objects in environments for Internet Explorer Version 4.0 and later. We show you in Chapter 8 how to use it to play animal squares (a type of simple jigsaw puzzle). The contract lets you place an invisible zone of variable size that is the only place on-screen where a draggable image can drop. Although the contract is ingenious, it enables the wandering image to drop anywhere the two elements overlap. It would be nice to have a different contract that places the image precisely when you drop it, with the upper-left corners of the image and the drop zone aligned.

Analyze the contract

The first step in analyzing a contract is to take a look at the existing contract and get a general understanding of what goes on "under the hood." The contract in question here is

```
DragDrop: Set [target] the drop zone for [source]
```

First, check out the Participants tab. The source needs to capture the events `onMouseDown`, `onMouseUp`, and `onMouseOver` and to have the property `imageStyle`. Okay, the source has to be an image or one of the image button form elements. The target requirements are shown in Figure 15-11. Two methods that are quite specific to a drop zone are `GrabIt` and `HitTest`.

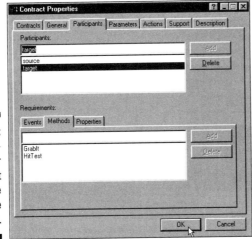

Figure 15-11: Requirements for the target of the drop zone contract.

Because this contract has no parameters, you next look at the actions and support. The three action scripts correspond to the three events the [source] image captures:

- ✔ **onMouseOver:** The script finds out where the image is and how big it is by asking the objectInfo() function, just like the Element Movement contract does. The script then sets a flag SemZ that's picked up later and clears the status window.

- ✔ **onMouseDown:** Aha! — the user has clicked the image. The script picks up the SemZ flag, stores the original Z-Order of the image, and then sets the Z-Order (position in the third dimension) very high so that it floats over everything. Then the script calls the getddParameters() routine and initiates drag, setting dragOk = true. The start position is saved as orgLeft, orgTop. We looked at getddParameters(), which is in a support script and decided that we didn't need to change any of that when we made the new precision contract.

- ✔ **onMouseUp:** The image has been released. The script decides whether the image has been captured by the drop zone. Document-level event capture uses the drop zone's HitTest method to check continually for overlap while the mouse is moving. If the variable anyhit shows an overlap, the GrabIt method is used to fix the image's position. If not, the orgLeft, orgTop position is restored, and the image springs back to where it started. Obviously, this script is the one you need to tamper with to get the change you're after.

Last, make sure that you understand (more or less) what's in the three support scripts that are used and hope that you don't have to mess with them. Playing the same editing game with support scripts, if necessary, is perfectly possible — by creating a new one based on a copy of an existing one.

Make a copy of the contract

Switch back to the Contracts tab in the Contract Manager, and make sure that the correct contract is still selected. Then click the Copy button, over to the right. Select the General tab and edit the name of the contract to Set [target] the precision drop zone for [source].

Switch back to the Contracts tab, and you see a warning box. That's how you know that you've successfully copied the old contract under a new name.

Find the bits that need changing and change them

It doesn't take long to inspect the `mouseUp` script and see the line that sets the drop position of the thingamajig:

```
eval(activeEl.fullName + ".DDarr[i].GrabIt(activeEl, topX,
        topY)");
```

Without even knowing any details of the `GrabIt` method, it obviously takes three arguments: the object to be grabbed and the *x,y* coordinates of the drop point.

Having made our afternoon tea, we peered at the `trackdragdrop()` function to see where `topX` and `topY` got their values. (It's in `DragDropSupportScript`.) Logically enough, they're simply the position of the object at drop time, so we decided that we probably needed to substitute them with the coordinates of the upper-left corner of the *drop zone.*

Wishing that we had another of those delicious raisin scones, we poked about to see whether the script knew the position of the drop zone and decided that it didn't. Logically, we need to place a call to the `getPosition()` routine to find out. Cribbing from what's already there in relation to the `[source]` object, we figured that the following is what it would take:

```
DropZone_Info = new objectInfo("[target]");
dzpos = DropZone_Info.getPosition();
```

Then the coordinates we craved would be `dzpos.left` and `dzpos.top`.

Where does this code belong? In the original contract, the position of the source object has to be computed every time a user picks it up because who knows where it may be? The drop zone is fixed, though — you have to find out its position only once. We put those two lines of code in the document `onLoad` window and tested to see whether we picked up the correct numbers. Yes. Oh, good — we had one more raisin scone, after all.

It wasn't quite plain sailing from then on because the coordinate substitution we had in mind didn't work. Something about the `GrabIt` method isn't quite straightforward. As more ICQ messages demanded our attention, we felt that it was time for a bold move. We commented out the `GrabIt` line and used a more straightforward way of setting the position. Figure 15-12 shows the successful code.

These lines commented out

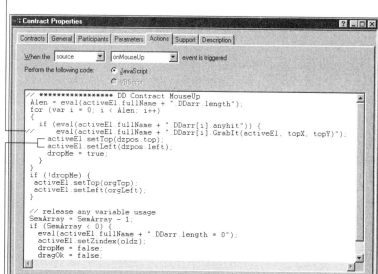

Figure 15-12:
The original
JavaScript,
successfully
modified.

These lines added

Writing a New Contract (An Ad Rotator)

Whereas you may have been able to cope with earlier sections of this chapter with only a vague grasp of JavaScript, it starts getting tougher soon if you're JavaScript-challenged.

We make no claim whatsoever to be providing a JavaScript tutorial in this section. If you feel the need to take a time-out and brush up on your JavaScript, go ahead. We'll still be here when you get back. Try either of Emily A. Vander Veer's books: *JavaScript For Dummies,* 2nd Edition, or *JavaScript For Dummies Quick Reference* (IDG Books Worldwide, Inc.).

Perhaps, like us, you've written banner ad rotator scripts using just your JavaScript skills, but the old steam-driven scripts don't transfer well into Drumbeat, and we all need a fresh start.

In case you've been (mercifully) protected from these types of scripts, an ad rotator reserves some space on a Web page for advertising and rotates several possible ads through the same space. The owners of the site may sell that same space to 20 advertisers, and as long as the owners can guarantee to all individual advertisers that their products will be seen $\frac{1}{20}$ of the time, all's fair.

The effect from your point of view as the user is that the first time you load the page, it yells "Buy Boffo!" The next time, it says "Buy Biffo!" and so on until it's Boffo's turn again.

Setting up

 It so happens that the Drumbeat DynaImage is extremely well suited to the task of rotating ads. A *DynaImage* is a SmartElement, normally used for animations, that can contain a stack of images. It has a built-in method, getImageCount(), for finding out how many images are on the stack, and another method, setIndex(n), for forcing the *n*th image to the top, where it becomes the visible image.

All you need is a simple contract that's made available as an activation to DynaImages — a contract that loads a random number into the setIndex(n) method. The trick is to make sure that the random number gives everyone the same chance and never goes out of range.

The test bed is a page containing a DynaImage with a handful of easily distinguished images loaded into it. Get the DynaImage from your SmartElement toolbar, and give this one the name **AdRotator**.

Making the basic contract

Here are the steps we suggest for setting up the ad rotator:

1. **Bring up the Contract Manager, and click the Add button. You see a** New contract **line at the bottom of whatever list you happen to have displayed.**

2. **Click to switch to the General tab. Check the check box for the option Allow an Element to Participate in This Contract with Itself (that's what allows the contract to be applied as an activation).**

3. **In the Descriptive text frame, in the single element window, type** Rotate image in [source].

4. **Select Any Version 4.0 from the Browser dropdown list.**

5. **Select Image from the Category dropdown list.**

6. **Return to the Contracts tab and verify that the new contract exists in the Image category. An Edit warning appears. Click Yes.**

7. **Click the Participants tab. In the Participants edit box in the upper frame, enter source and click Add.**

8. **In the lower frame, click to select the Methods tab, and add the two methods** setIndex(index) **and** getImageCount(). **They're case sensitive.**

Writing the code

You need this contract to do something immediately when the page loads and not wait for anything to be clicked or moused over. Therefore, the event you need to write code for is document.onLoad:

1. **Click the Actions tab. Because you didn't enter any events for the source object on the Participants tab, the upper-left dropdown is already set for Document. Set the upper-right dropdown to** onLoad.

2. **As a first test, write the following code in the scripting pane. In case you don't get the point, the idea is to test the general setup by reporting onscreen the number of images loaded into the AdRotator:**

```
var totads = [source].getImageCount();
alert(totads);
```

3. **Click to switch to the Contracts tab, say Yes to the two alert messages, and minimize the Contract Manager. Then right-click your test DynaImage and choose Possible Activations from the pop-up menu.**

4. **In the Interactions Center, scroll the list until you see the line** Image AdRotator: Rotate image in AdRotator, **and double-click to apply it.**

5. **Publish and browse the page. You should see a JavaScript alert message with the correct figure for the number of images you loaded into the AdRotator.**

If you never see that activation offered: The reason is almost certainly that you made some error in entering the methods for the source object. Return to the Participants tab and gaze long and hard at what you entered there. If it doesn't look exactly like the one shown in Figure 15-13, that's your problem.

If you activated the AdRotator but you see nothing or some nonsense when you publish: Something's wrong with what you put on your Actions tab. You may have entered the code wrong or put it in the wrong event. To check, right-click a vacant spot in the layout area and choose Edit Script⇨onLoad. The scripting window should look like the one shown in Figure 15-14.

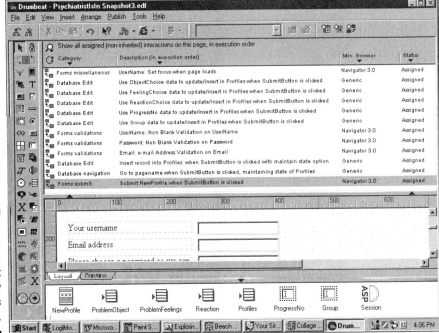

Figure 15-13:
Source require-
ments must
be exactly
like what's
shown here.

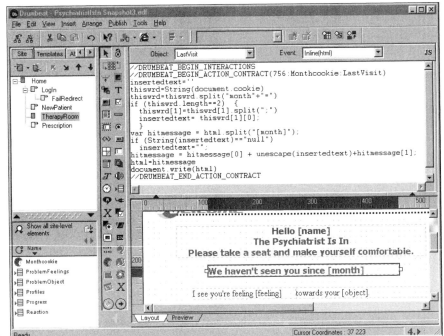

Figure 15-14:
The scripting
window looks
like this
during your
testing of Ad
Rotator.

All on the same page now? Time to move on. The basis for generating a random number is the JavaScript function `Math.random()`. It evaluates to a pseudorandom number between 0 and 1. Multiply it by the number of images in the AdRotator and convert to the next lowest integer, and you should have a good first shot at achieving what you need:

```
var totads = [source].getImageCount();
thisad = Math.floor(Math.random() * totads);
[source].setIndex(thisad);
```

Wrap that up, substitute it for the test code you wrote previously, and check it out. You have to remove the old activation and reapply the modified activation again. For debugging — or to convince yourself that all your images do get shown eventually — you could temporarily add `alert(thisad)`.

It's time for a slight optional refinement. During the half-second before the `onLoad` script has its effect, you may see a variant of the "flicker" effect we mention earlier in this chapter. You can work around this slight problem in several ways. One is to load a dummy image on top of the DynaImage stack as a temporary stand-in. This image, the one that's shown during that flicker-time, can be a blank banner or transparent.

If you use that technique, you have to ensure that `Image zero` is never selected by the random-number routine, by using this amended script:

```
var totads = [source].getImageCount();
--totads;
thisad = Math.floor(Math.random() * totads);
++thisad;
[source].setIndex(thisad);
```

In your Element Library is the FrontPage (FP) Ad Rotator applet — a rotator of a different kind. This Java applet rotates ads in an image space every so many seconds, using sexy transition effects if you want. The Java class files `Fprotate.class` and `Fprotatx.class` are needed — they come with the Front Page application.

Importing and Exporting Contracts

Suppose that you go to the office party and brag about your terrific success in creating this new contract (acknowledging our help, we sincerely believe). The next day, you get e-mail from one of your bragees saying that she would love you forever if you could let her have a copy of the contract.

No problem — you can simply use the Export option, and you have a couple of options.

Take a look at what you already have in C:\Program Files\Drumbeat 2000\ Contracts\Image. Almost certainly, you have the two files ImageV10_30.ctr and ImageV10_30.doc. ImageV10_30.ctr contains details of all your contracts in the Image category. (ImageV10_30.doc is documentation you can read in Microsoft Word.)

You can do *either* of the following:

✔ Select the new contract on the Contracts tab in the Contract Manager, click the Export button, and save that one contract wherever you want with a .ctr file extension.

✔ Click+Shift+click to select all the Image contracts, click Export, and save the entire collection as ImageV10_30.ctr, replacing what you already have.

You can then transmit the (binary) file anywhere you want, and the recipient can import it by clicking the Import button on that same tab.

If the intended recipient has also made any modification to his or her Image contracts, the second method is *not* advisable. Local modifications would be overwritten.

Using the Script Center

You've already had at least a couple of foretastes of the good fun to be had romping around in the Script Center, if you've done the exercise in some other places in this book. In Chapter 7, in the section about making links do double duty in frames, we show you how to use it to make a special feature to change the content of two frames at the same time. In Chapter 13, in the section "Editing the Wizard's JavaScript," we show you how to use the Script Center to refine protection of the administrative parts of a database site.

 The Script Center is the third of the features that live in the attic, sharing living space with the Content Center and the Interactions Center. See the Script Center by clicking the Script Center icon — or you can right-click any element in the layout area and choose Edit Script from the pop-up menu.

Figure 15-15 shows the Script Center open, with just a part of the scripting tree visible. The *scripting tree* is an expandable tree listing every possible JavaScript object, property, method, and event on the current page. You can drag most of the objects, properties, and methods into the scripting window to form parts of scripts. Although you can drag and drop events in there too, a far better idea is to set up an event to script by using the Object and Event dropdown lists at the top of the scripting window.

These dropdown boxes set the event to capture

Script window   Script tree

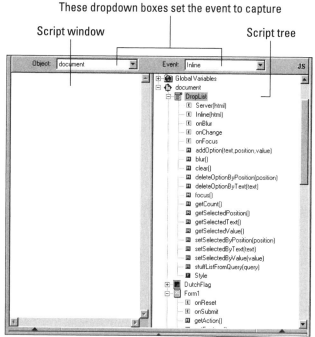

Figure 15-15:
The Script
Center.

The Script Center comes to your rescue if you need to

✔ Add your own refinement to a Drumbeat contract

✔ Debug a script you intend to make into a contract

✔ Create a completely free-form script for one-time use

Using the scripting tree

Figure 15-16 shows part of a document object model in the scripting tree, with a ColorPickerList dropdown list expanded to show its events, methods, and properties. The only property it has is Style, which, as we say earlier in this chapter, is a pseudoproperty that never has any value.

Just to see how extremely easy it is to use the scripting tree as a source of JavaScript elements, we show you how to write a complete JavaScript function by touching the keyboard only once. It's almost all mousework.

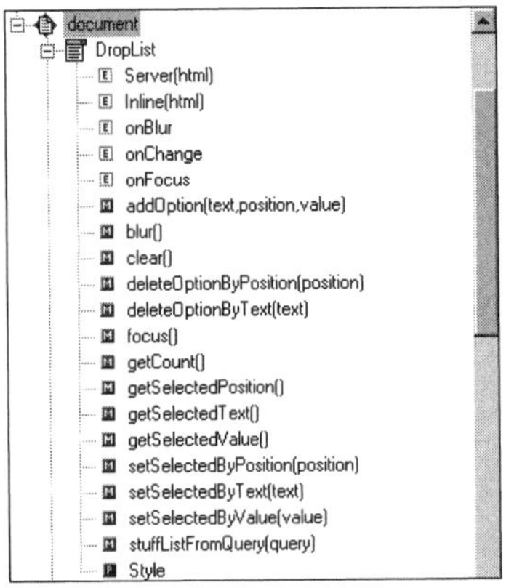

Figure 15-16:
Part of a
document
object
model
exposed in
the scripting
tree.

The ColorPickerList content is a list of colors in plain English, and its values list is the corresponding list of RGB values: Peach puff = #ffcb9f, for example. To script so that the page background color changes according to the selection made on the list, follow these steps:

1. **With the ColorPickerList object expanded in the scripting tree (refer to Figure 15-16), double-click its** onChange **event.**

   This step sets that event in the scripting window.

2. **Scroll down the scripting tree until you can see the** bgColor **property of the document, and drag that property into the scripting window.**

3. **Press the equal key (=) on your keyboard.**

   Watch out — it's a supreme effort.

4. **Scroll back up to the methods of the color picker, and drag the** getSelectedValue() **method in.**

You're done! Publish, as shown in Figure 15-17, and admire.

Puzzling over the sliding-tiles puzzle

Not long after showing you how to modify the drop zone contract successfully, we decided to see whether Drumbeat could make a sliding-tile puzzle. Why? Sorry — can't remember. We had seen a few of them done in Java, but never in DHTML. Figure 15-18 shows the easy part — making the little tile pieces and setting them by absolute positioning. The images are inventively named EIGHT, TWO, and FOUR, for example. The game is to create a script that lets a user click a tile to move it to an adjacent empty space, if there is one. If you want to make your own sliding-tiles puzzle, just make your own tiles. Ours are 30 pixels square, and the top left of the diagram is at x=100,y=100.

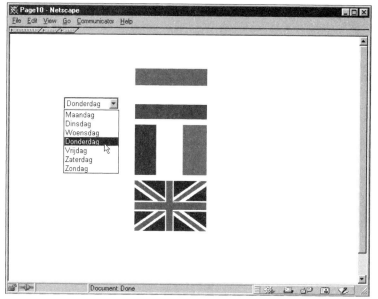

Figure 15-17:
The color
picker is
published!

The Script Center is an absolute natural for working on this problem. It's hard to imagine making a contract out of it, and, even if you did, you would probably want to develop the script here first.

Obviously an array of some kind has to represent the state of the puzzle at any moment, keeping track of where each tile is and particularly where the empty space is.

We advise putting that array into the client-side Global Variables window. *Global variables* and *global procedures* are part of the scripting tree, and their purpose in life is to stash stuff that needs to be made available to all pages in the site. In this case, however, it's just a good idea to get the array out of the way, and Figure 15-19 shows the first attempt at declaring the two-dimensional array, `tilarray`.

Because the tile positions change in random ways, the best plan is to capture a `mouseUp` event at the document level and then let the code take a look at the mouse coordinates and decide whether any action needs to be taken. What a shock — Drumbeat doesn't directly support Netscape-style document event capturing. We decided to leave that problem for another day (another section, really — see the following section, "Understanding global procedures") and concentrate for now on getting the job done à la Microsoft.

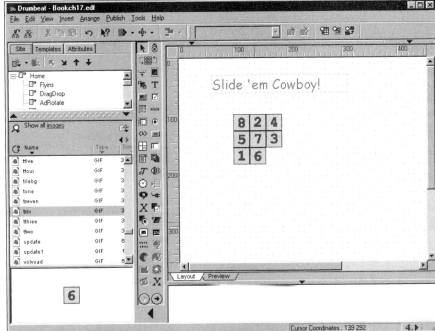

Figure 15-18:
The design
for the slid-
ing tiles.

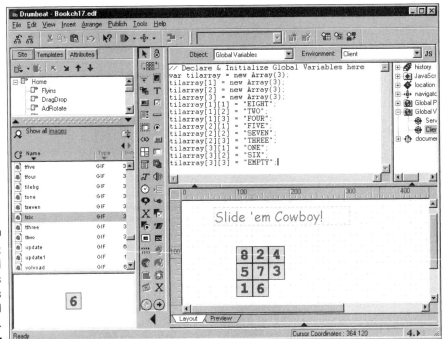

Figure 15-19:
The Global
Variables
window is
used to hold
a data array.

In Microsoft Land, the coordinates of a mouse event in relation to the upper-left corner of the screen are given by the variables `event.clientX` and `event.clientY`. Here's some preliminary code to derive the tile row and column numbers of the event, ignoring `mouseUp` events outside the puzzle and then consulting the array to find the name of the tile that has been clicked:

```
var tc = Math.floor((event.clientX - 100)/30) + 1;
var tr = Math.floor((event.clientY - 100)/30) + 1;

if (tc > 3 || tc < 1 || tr > 3 || tr < 1) {return}
thistile = tilarray[tr][tc];
```

We ran that through a test on all eight tiles plus the empty space, and it worked fine. We figured that if we could get the code right for a downward move, we could just adapt that code for up, left, and right moves. The test for whether a tile can move is whether the array term in the same column and one row down is the EMPTY term. In JavaScript terms, the test is

```
if (tilarray[tr+1][tc] == "EMPTY")
```

Microsoft has annoyingly different notation for reading the position of an object and for setting it. You read its *y* position with

```
[oldpos] = document.all.[object].offsetTop
```

You set it like this, however:

```
document.all.[object].style.top = [newpos]
```

When we first put all that together, we had one of those "Hmmm" moments you get when you're confidently programming and the code simply doesn't work. Finally we got it — in DHTML, it's not the object that moves but rather the `DIV` block containing the object. D'oh!

That's really the point of the elaborate `objectInfo()` function that Drumbeat runs through before it attempts to move anything. We thought about importing `objectInfo()` as a global procedure but rejected it in favor of a shortcut. We realized that Drumbeat has a predictable way of naming its DIV blocks — a DIV containing nothing other than an image named `EIGHT` is named `DBStyleEIGHT`. We amended the array to contain those names rather than the image names, and all went well. Figure 15-20 shows most of the final code, and we figure that you can guess the slide left script that disappeared from that figure!

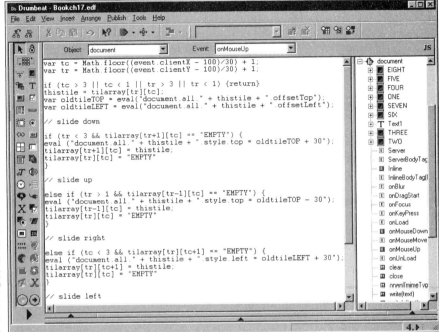

Figure 15-20:
The final
code for the
Microsoft
version of
the sliding
tiles.

```
var tc = Math.floor((event.clientX - 100)/30) + 1;
var tr = Math.floor((event.clientY - 100)/30) + 1;

if (tc > 3 || tc < 1 || tr > 3 || tr < 1) {return}
thistile = tilarray[tr][tc];
var oldtileTOP = eval("document.all." + thistile + ".offsetTop");
var oldtileLEFT = eval("document.all." + thistile + ".offsetLeft");

// slide down

if (tr < 3 && tilarray[tr+1][tc] == "EMPTY") {
eval ("document.all." + thistile + ".style.top = oldtileTOP + 30");
tilarray[tr+1][tc] = thistile;
tilarray[tr][tc] = "EMPTY"
}

// slide up

else if (tr > 1 && tilarray[tr-1][tc] == "EMPTY") {
eval ("document.all." + thistile + ".style.top = oldtileTOP - 30");
tilarray[tr-1][tc] = thistile;
tilarray[tr][tc] = "EMPTY"
}

// slide right

else if (tc < 3 && tilarray[tr][tc+1] == "EMPTY") {
eval ("document.all." + thistile + ".style.left = oldtileLEFT + 30");
tilarray[tr][tc+1] = thistile;
tilarray[tr][tc] = "EMPTY"
}

// slide left
```

Understanding global procedures

Global procedures are JavaScript functions that are accessible from every
page in the site. If you make a site for a used-car dealership, for example, you
probably would create a global procedure to compute the exorbitant payment schedules on car loans.

Unlike run-of-the-mill JavaScript functions in Drumbeat, global procedures
are given actual names, and they appear in the scripting tree so that you can
double-click them to bring them into the scripting window for editing or
right-click to rename or delete them. You can also access them by manipulat-
ing the dropdown menus at the top of the scripting window.

In the preceding section, we said that we would put off showing you how to
do a Netscape version of the sliding-tiles puzzle until "another day"? Well,
that 'nother day is here — and it's a global procedure that can save your
bacon (it saved ours!). Not that the procedure has to be globally accessible,
although you do want it to have a name of your choosing.

Here's the problem: If you want Netscape to capture document-level events
(such as a mouse click at some random point in the window), you have to
specifically tell it which events to capture and which functions you claim to
have provided to handle those events. To get it right for Netscape, write this
code in the `document.inline` scripting pane:

```
if (document.layers) { // so MSIE will ignore this
  document.captureEvents(Event.MOUSEUP);
  document.onMouseUp = goTiles;
}
```

Then, right-click Global Procedures in the scripting tree and enter the name of the event handler (goTiles) in the dialog box.

The scripting window pops up with the function name and open and close braces already written in. Slip in a quick test alert, publish the page, and check to ensure that mouseUp is correctly captured. So far, so good.

In Netscapelandia, you have to pass the *event itself* as an argument to a document-level event-handler. If the argument is given the name ev, the coordinates of a mouse-click are ev.pageX and ev.pageY. This code successfully tests the capture:

```
function goTiles(ev) {
  alert("MouseUp at " + ev.pageX + "," + ev.pageY);
}
```

Now you have to confront the peculiarities of the way Drumbeat sets things up for Netscape. Even though each positioned element is already in a DIV, Drumbeat keeps Netscape ignorant of that fact and wraps a Netscape LAYER around the DIV, even nesting that LAYER inside one of several section LAYERs. Again, all this complexity is normally taken care of by the getObjectInfo support script, and again, we think that it's more fun (although admittedly more dangerous) to shortcut it.

Just as an image named TWO is contained in a DIV named DBStyleTWO, you can bet that its LAYER ID is LyrDBStyleTWO. You have to be careful to stick **Lyr** on the front of what you retrieve from the tile array. Unless the page is quite complex, the outer wrapper is named LyrSection0, so the complete expression for the X coordinate of the TWO tile is

```
document.layers.LyrSection0.document.layers.LyrDBStyleTWO.left
```

After you have all that figured out, the rest is relatively plain sailing. Figure 15-21 shows the code.

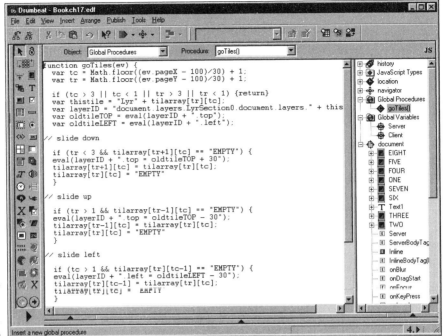

```
Drumbeat - Bookch17.edf
File  Edit  View  Insert  Arrange  Publish  Tools  Help

Object: Global Procedures        Procedure: goTiles()                    JS

function goTiles(ev) {
  var tc = Math.floor((ev.pageX - 100)/30) + 1;
  var tr = Math.floor((ev.pageY - 100)/30) + 1;

  if (tc > 3 || tc < 1 || tr > 3 || tr < 1) {return}
  var thistile = "Lyr" + tilarray[tr][tc];
  var layerID = "document.layers.LyrSection0.document.layers." + this
  var oldtileTOP = eval(layerID + ".top");
  var oldtileLEFT = eval(layerID + ".left");

// slide down

  if (tr < 3 && tilarray[tr+1][tc] == "EMPTY") {
  eval(layerID + ".top = oldtileTOP + 30");
  tilarray[tr+1][tc] = tilarray[tr][tc];
  tilarray[tr][tc] = "EMPTY"
  }

// slide up

  if (tr > 1 && tilarray[tr-1][tc] == "EMPTY") {
  eval(layerID + ".top = oldtileTOP - 30");
  tilarray[tr-1][tc] = tilarray[tr][tc];
  tilarray[tr][tc] = "EMPTY"
  }

// slide left

  if (tc > 1 && tilarray[tr][tc-1] == "EMPTY") {
  eval(layerID + ".left = oldtileLEFT - 30");
  tilarray[tr][tc-1] = tilarray[tr][tc];
  tilarray[tr][tc] = EMPTY
  }

Insert a new global procedure                                  4.
```

Chapter 16

The_Psychiatrist_Is_IN.com: A Web Site in a Day

What's a Web Application? (We Just Built One)

*E*ver heard of something called a Turing test? Passing this type of test is the supreme goal of all researchers in the artificial intelligence (AI) business. The English mathematician Alan Turing suggested, you see, that AI research couldn't be deemed a success until you could have a conversation with a robot and not be able to tell that it wasn't human.

Some of the earliest attempts at Turing-bots were computer programs designed to mimic psychotherapy sessions — the thought was that psychoanalysts are barely distinguishable from robots anyway. They just repeat what you tell them, nod, steeple their hands, say "I see," and take a whole heap of money from you.

The setup

This chapter shows how adept Drumbeat is at making a robot psychotherapist. (We gave ourselves just one day to implement it.) It's a five-page site, backed up by five related data tables, with these features:

- ✔ **Login page:** Includes form validation, user identity check, and ASP session object.
- ✔ **Login fail page:** For users who fail login because they've forgotten their passwords.
- ✔ **Registration page for new patients:** Has a few of the usual edit boxes to accept data.
- ✔ **Therapy room:** Features complex recall from the database to fool users into thinking that this page really does understand them and to allow them to report any progress in their therapy. Also features a cookie to keep tabs on patients.
- ✔ **Prescription page:** Matches suggested treatments to users' reports of progress.

It's this feature set that enables you to give this site the highfalutin title Web *application*. Hmmm, anyone can tell that this isn't a *real* psychiatric practice: No cashier. Well, never mind.

An *ASP Session Object* is a site element you can use to store small amounts of data. The data is still available when a user moves to a different page in the same site. It disappears, however, when the user leaves your site, ending his *sessions*. A *cookie* usually goes one better by maintaining the data beyond a single session, enabling you to keep track of specific users as they return to your site some time later.

The data tables

Patient data for the robot psychiatrist is contained in a Microsoft Access relational database. Although you can bring it all out into one big recordset, using a complex SQL statement with inner joins, that's a bad habit to get into because although an Access database may allow data entry to multiple tables through ODBC, other database types do not. Keep your data tables separate and do your joins (the relationships between tables) with Drumbeat interactions. It's more instructive, anyway.

These tables are in the PatientRecords.mdb file on the CD in the back of this book:

✔ **Profiles:** Has one record per patient. The key field is a unique `UserID` for each patient, defined as an autonumber field. This table has, in addition to fields for patient information, coded fields relating to the other four tables, as shown in Figure 16-1. The UserGroup is 2 for all patients.

✔ **Feelings:** Describes ten feelings patients may report, such as inadequacy, superiority, or fear. The key field is numeric, relating to the `FeelingID` field of Profiles.

✔ **Objects:** Contains five objects of the feelings: mother, boss, or alien spaceships, for example.

✔ **Reactions:** Lists eight reactions to these feelings that patients may report.

✔ **Progress:** The heart of the "artificial intelligence" here — reflects seven levels of progress a patient may report in answer to the question "How are you coping with these feelings?" The levels range from "Much better" to "Crisis," and suggested "therapies" are associated with each level.

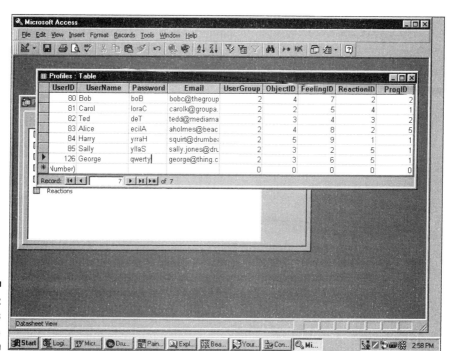

Figure 16-1:
The Profiles data table.

A starting point site for The_Psychiatrist_Is_IN is on the CD. The .edf file is PsychiatristIsIn_ASP_Start.edf for ASP or PsychiatristIsIn_JSP_Start.edf for JSP. Follow the instructions on the CD to copy the files to your Drumbeat program files directory.

To follow along as we show you how to build the application in this chapter, follow these setup steps:

1. **Make a Data Source Name (DSN) named** Patients **for the database. (To find out how to set up a DSN, refer to Chapter 10.) Create a publish directory named** therapist **in your Inetpub\wwwroot directory.**

   If you prefer to go it alone without the starting point, follow these steps:

2. **Open a new site targeted at Any Version 4.0 browser, with ASP server application support (or WebSphere server support for JSP). (To find out how to set up server application support, see the section "Are you being served?" in Chapter 2.)**

3. **Make queries and ODBC Content Tables for all five data tables. In each case, the SQL statement is simply** SELECT * FROM [whatever]. **Figure 16-2 shows the SQL Query Manager for the** Progress **query. (To find out how to create queries, see the section "Creating a query," in Chapter 10.)**

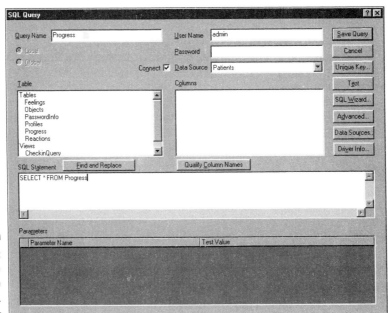

Figure 16-2: Making one of the five queries.

When you open the site, if the images aren't showing on the pages, you should update the media paths. Choose Tools⇨Media File Paths. Click Browse and browse to the Media folder of the Pyschiatrist folder, which should be in your Drumbeat program files directory, in the ASP Samples folder. Select the folder, click OK, and then click Update Path to change the path.

Logging In

Figure 16-3 shows the site tree to set up, with the five pages we describe earlier in this chapter.

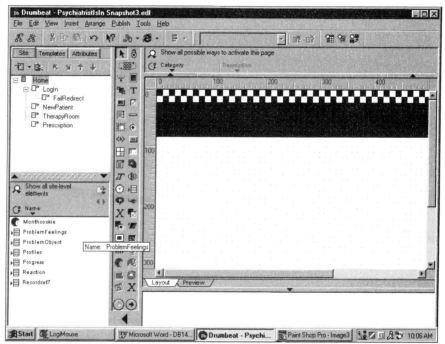

Figure 16-3:
The site tree
for the
Psychia-
trist_Is_IN
application.

Because you have ASP support, you can make use of a special interaction, designed for site security, on the login page: Security: Verify username from [userbox] and password from [passbox] and redirect (store additional variable in Session).

This extremely complex interaction is also very useful. It's an interaction between two edit boxes, a recordset, a form, and a Submit button. An ASP Session Object is also assumed to be present. The interaction also has no fewer than six parameters — we get to them in a minute.

To activate the Login page, follow these steps:

1. **Click the Locate Assets button and choose Site Elements⇨Show All Site Elements. Select the Profiles Recordset and drag it into the basement.**

   This element is your gateway to the Profiles data table containing all patient info, including their logins and passwords.

2. **Drag an ASP Session Object into the basement.**

You may not have an ASP Session Object on your SmartElements toolbar, but you can easily make one available by opening the Element Library, selecting the ASP tab, and checking the Session box. Figure 16-4 shows the complete layout. Note that the page has already been set up with two edit boxes with the prompts Patient Name and Password. On the Attributes Sheet, the edit boxes have the names UserName and Password. The form element is named LoginForm. The Submit button uses a rollover button and is named LoginButton.

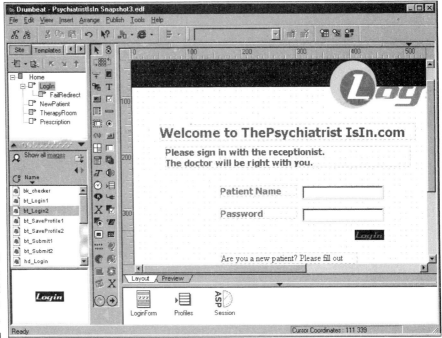

Figure 16-4: The layout of the Login page.

For new patients who don't yet have usernames and passwords, there is also a text link to the NewPatient page so that they can check in and get their usernames and passwords.

The security-redirect interaction normally expects to have a form Submit button as one of its participants. The Image button works, although it has to be made to behave as though it's a Submit button. It has already been set up for you in the starter site, but if you're building the site yourself, you need to follow these steps:

1. **Ctrl+click both the submit button and the LoginForm element to select them. Right-click and choose Possible Interactions.**

2. **In the Interactions Center, find the interaction** `Submit LoginForm when LoginButton is clicked` **and double-click to apply it.**

3. **In the Parameters dialog box, leave the check in the box for the Validate Form option. Leave the Replace Action box blank.**

Now you've assembled all the necessary actors to put on the security login show:

1. **Select both edit boxes, the Profiles recordset, the form element in the basement, and the login button. Right-click one of the selected elements and choose Possible Interactions.**

   All 12 of the security interactions pop up, as shown in Figure 16-5.

2. **In the Interactions Center, apply the interaction** Verify username from UserName and Password from Password and redirect (store additional variable in Session).

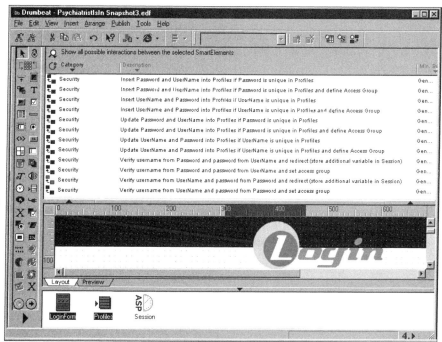

Figure 16-5:
All 12 security contracts are available with ASP support.

The Parameters dialog box pops up. What this Parameters dialog box is saying, in plain English, is "Tell me which columns of the recordset to look in to check the username and password. Tell me which page to go to if they check out okay, and, if not, which page to go to then. Then, if you want, I'll take the value of a *different* column from the recordset and stick it in the ASP Session Object so that you have it available throughout the site. I'll also offer to assign the user to a security access group, to control access to other pages in the site." Whew.

To set all these options in the Parameters dialog box:

1. **For SuccessRedirect, click the Assign button and select the TherapyRoom page.**

2. **For FailedRedirect, click the Assign button and select the FailRedirect page (under the Login page).**

3. **Leave the Access Group option blank.**

4. **For Additional Variable to Forward, select UserID.**

   You need a label guaranteed to be a unique identifier of the patient who logged in. Because neither the username nor the password is guaranteed to be unique, using them is way too dangerous. The records for two patients named George, for example, would become hopelessly muddled. The only unique identifier is UserID. Selecting it from the dropdown menu says, "Put that in the Session Object, please."

5. **For PasswordColumn, select Password from the dropdown list. For UserNameColumn, select UserName from the dropdown list.**

Now it's just a matter of putting a little icing on the cake:

1. **Set an activation in the UserName edit box so that the focus is on it (the cursor blinks in there) when the page finishes loading. Select the edit box, right-click, and choose Possible Activations. Find and apply the activation** UserName: Set focus when page loads. **(It's in the Forms Miscellaneous category.)**

   Because you also want to make sure that both the username and password fields are filled out, put form validations on both edit boxes.

2. **Select the UserName edit box, and, in the Forms Validation category, select the activation that says** Non Blank Validation on UserName. **In the Parameters dialog box for Error Msg, enter** Please enter a password.

3. **Apply the same activation to the Password edit box. In the Parameters dialog box, for Error Msg, enter** Please enter a username.

   Because you checked Validate Form on the submit interaction, an error message box pops up if a user clicks the Login button without having entered anything in one of the validated edit boxes.

Notice how the names assigned to the form elements are used in the activations. Naming the form elements appropriately helps a great deal when you apply interactions, especially the more complex ones, like the security login.

Before publishing, check all the assigned interactions on the page by right-clicking an empty space in the layout area and choosing Assigned Interactions (Ordered). You must make sure that the form submit action is the last one on the page. Select the submit action and drag it to the bottom of the list, as shown in Figure 16-6.

We won't say how many false starts we went through before we got this page behaving perfectly. Suffice it to say that it eventually did.

Publish the site and browse the Login page. To test the page, try logging in without entering anything and see that you get the alert message asking you to enter the username and password. Then log in using the username Bob and password bob. You should be sent straight to the Therapy Room. Try logging in again as Bob, and use a different password, which will be invalid. You should be redirected to the FailRedirect page.

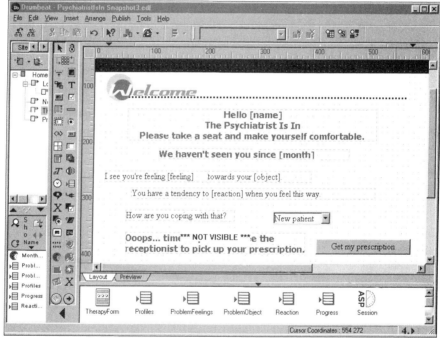

Figure 16-6:
A complete set of inter-actions on the Login page — not as simple as it looks!

The Therapy Room

Figure 16-7 shows the basic design of the therapy page. It has tokens all over the place to be substituted with actual data from the patient files, and it has a list box that needs to be populated from the database. If you're using the starter file, you also see a mysterious text box marked NOT VISIBLE, which we explain in the "Time's up!" section, later in this chapter.

Quite a bit of work goes into making all this happen, and we don't pretend that we got it right the first time. This section shows how to do it if you're *perfect*.

Using the data from the ASP Session Object

Your first setup task, other than tending to the design aspects of the page, is to interrogate the ASP Session Object, retrieve that user ID, and set up the Profiles recordset correctly:

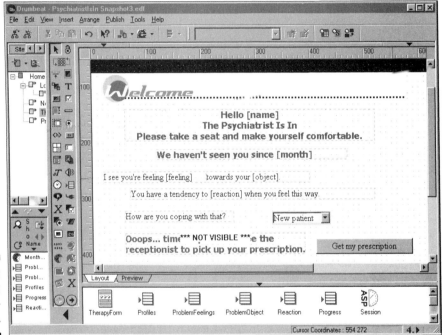

Figure 16-7:
The design of the therapy page.

1. **Drag the ASP Session Object into the basement of this page.**

2. **In the Asset Center, query for site-level elements and retrieve all five recordsets. You'll need all of them eventually, so pop them all into the basement too.**

3. **Using the session object to set up the Profiles recordset is simple: Select the Session Object and the Profiles recordset, right-click, and select Possible Interactions. Find and apply the interaction** Filter Profiles with Session variable before page loads. **(It's in the Database Miscellaneous category.)**

4. **In the Parameters dialog box, enter** UserID **for Variable Name, and, for IDColumn, select UserID from the dropdown list.**

   These parameters just ensure that you retrieve the correct variable and filter on the correct data column.

5. **Put in the first of the token substitutions. Select the Profiles recordset and the Hello text, and, on the list of possible interactions, find and apply this one in the Database Miscellaneous category:** `Replace [token] in Text2 with value of [Field] from Profiles.`

6. **In the Parameters dialog box, enter** [name] **for the token and select UserName for the field.**

Verify that everything is working by publishing and logging in as George. You need to take a look at the data tables to find George's password. We could tell you, but then we'd have to reformat your hard drive. (***Hint:*** Look in the Profiles content table in the Content Center to see what George's password is.) This time, when you log in correctly, you're sent to the Therapy Room and receive the greeting `Hello George`.

Getting all the recordsets in sync

Now you have to set up the ProblemFeelings, ProblemObjects, and Reaction recordsets for George (or whomever). In each case, apply an interaction between the recordset and the Profiles recordset:

1. **Select the Profiles recordset and the ProblemFeelings recordset. Apply the interaction** `Filter [ProblemFeelings] with related field from Profiles.` **In the Parameters dialog box, choose FeelingID for the FilterColumn and FilterBy columns.**

2. **Select the Profiles recordset and the ProblemObjects recordset. Apply the interaction** `Filter [ProblemObjects] with related field from Profiles.` **In the Parameters dialog box, for the FilterColumn and FilterBy columns, select ObjectID.**

3. **Select the Profiles recordset and the Reaction recordset. Apply the interaction** `Filter [Reaction] with related field from Profiles.` **In the Parameters dialog box, choose ReactionID for the FilterColumn and FilterBy columns.**

This is what we mean earlier in this chapter when we say "doing your data joins within Drumbeat," and it works reliably.

Now you need to make three more token substitutions:

1. **Rename the rest of the text boxes on the page to make assigning interactions easier. Name the first** FeelText; **the second,** ObjectText; **and the third,** ReactText. **While you're at it, rename as** LastVisit **the text box that says** `We haven't seen you since.` **(You'll use this one later.)**

2. **Select the FeelText and the ProblemFeelings recordsets. Apply the interaction** `Replace [token] in FeelText with value of [Field] from ProblemFeelings.` **In the Parameters dialog box, enter** [feeling] **for the token and enter** Feelings **for the field.**

3. **Select the ObjectText and the ProblemObject recordsets. Apply the interaction** `Replace [token] in ObjectText with value of [Field] from ProblemObject`. **In the Parameters dialog box, enter** [object] **for the token and enter** ObjectName **for the field.**

4. **Select the ReactText and the Reaction recordsets. Apply the interaction** `Replace [token] in ReactText with value of [Field] from Reaction`. **In the Parameters dialog box, enter** [reaction] **for the token and** Reaction **for the field.**

Publish again, and browse. You may get a message asking you to move the position of the recordsets. The Profiles recordset needs to be the leftmost of all the recordsets in the basement. You can select and drag it to this position. Publish again and log in as George, and you should see that the page is beginning to come alive!

A recordset-populated list box

You have to give the patient (George, in this example), some way of answering the question "How are you coping with that?" Select the dropdown list box, and rename it **ProgBox** on the Attributes Sheet. Now set about populating it (Figure 16-8 is an "exploded" rendering of how to set the ProgBox Attributes Sheet):

1. **Set the Content (the list the user sees) to Recordset. In the Content dialog box, select Progress for Recordset and select Progress for Column.**

2. **Set the Value (the data that's passed when the form is submitted) to Recordset. In the Content dialog box, select Progress for Recordset and select ProgID for Column.**

3. **Set the selection to None because you don't need any particular list item selected.**

Then assign a couple of activations to ProgBox. You need to add a prompt that says something like "Please tell the therapist." The first activation is a way of adding that prompt to the top of the list.

Because that's not an acceptable choice for poor George to make, use a second activation to ensure that George makes a proper choice. If George is so distraught that he leaves the dropdown list set at "Please tell the therapist," he gets beeped at and an alert message reminds him to select something. To ensure that the validation happens, make the Submit button a button-type button rather than a submit-type button and apply an interaction between it and the form element to submit with validation.

1. **Select the ProgBox and, on the list of possible activations, find and apply the one that says** `Add static option to list populated by`

a `Recordset` **in the Database Miscellaneous category. In the Parameters dialog box, for the Option string, enter** Please tell the therapist. **In the Parameters dialog box, leave the Selected box checked and leave the Option value set to 0.**

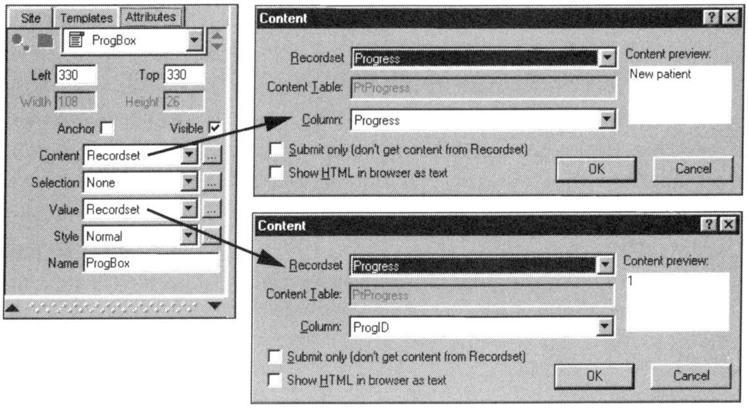

Figure 16-8: The Content and Value options for ProgBox both come from the recordset.

2. **Apply the second activation:** Validate a selection was made in ProgBox, **which is in the Forms Validation category.**

3. **To ensure that the validation happens, make the submit button a button-type button rather than a submit-type button. Select the submit button (Get my prescription), and choose Button for the Type option on the Attributes Sheet.**

4. **Select the button and the form element in the basement, and apply the interaction** Submit TherapyForm when RxButton is clicked. **In the Parameters dialog box, leave Validate Form checked and the Replace Action box blank.**

Although this page is getting full of activations and interactions, you're not done yet. You're not at the point of setting up the next page yet — and besides, you need to set a cookie.

Time for a cookie!

We wrote earlier in this chapter that an ASP Session Object can be relied on to hold data for the entire session, as a user moves around the site. A cookie goes one better than that: It holds data from session to session. That's exactly what you want: something the therapist can consult to see when George, the patient, was last in the consulting room.

Although a cookie is a standard SmartElement, again, it may not be on your SmartElements toolbar. To be able to follow along in this chapter, you have to go get a cookie. No, not *that* kind — a cookie from the Element Library. Like the ASP Session Object, the cookie goes down to the basement:

1. **Drag the Cookie SmartElement into the basement and name it** Monthcookie. **Also, on its Attributes Sheet, set the Expires option to 90 days.**

   That step is very important — a zero-expiration cookie is a nonpersistent cookie and is no different from an ASP Session Object.

   The name of the game now is to set the date in the cookie as the user exits the page, and read it when the same user reenters. Although you have no direct method of setting the date in a cookie, you can set the date in a hidden form field and then put the content of the hidden field into the cookie.

2. **Add a hidden form element to the already crowded basement, and name it** DateBus **on the Attributes Sheet because its sole function is to transport the date.**

3. **Click the ellipsis button next to Content. In the text editor that pops up, enter** [monthnumber]/[daynumber].

   Drumbeat recognizes ten standard tokens for fragments of the date/time string. You can see them by opening the Contract Manager (choose Tools⇨Contracts), selecting any of the contracts beginning with Replace tokens in in the Date category, and clicking the Description tab.

4. **With the DateBus hidden form element still selected, apply the activation** Replace tokens in DateBus with active date/time from client **in the Date category. In the Parameters dialog box, leave the check box set to the default and click OK.**

5. **Select the DateBus hidden form element, the Monthcookie, and the prescription button, and apply the interaction** Insert DateBus into Monthcookie when RxButton is clicked.

6. **In the Parameters dialog box, enter** month **for the parameter name.**

   You must put something here as a way of identifying the data when you read it back. The actual cookie content will be (e.g.) month=6 22. Now you can do your last token substitution.

7. **Select the Monthcookie and the LastVisit text, and apply the interaction** Replace [token] in LastVisit with value from Monthcookie.

8. **In the Parameters dialog box, enter the Cookie Name** month **and the token** [month].

Time's up!

To add a note of realism, it would be fun to pop up a big sign saying "Time's Up" ten seconds after the page loads. That task requires placing a timer in the basement:

1. **Select the "Times up" text box, and rename it** TimesUp **on the Attributes Sheet.**

2. **Drag the Timer SmartElement into the basement, and name it** TherapyTimer **on the Attributes Sheet. Set its Period option to** 10 **seconds.**

   To make this work as intended, the text must first be invisible and then appear on the page after the designated period. To make the text invisible, you just select the text element on the page and uncheck the Visible option on its Attributes Sheet. (It's already done for you in the starter file.)

3. **Select the TherapyTimer and the LastVisit text, and apply the interaction** Show TimesUp when TherapyTimer expires.

Interestingly, this interaction is the only one that's used in this site that won't work in Navigator 3. If you try to duplicate it on another site, be sure that your Site Preferences are set to Any 4.0 or Higher or Internet Explorer 4.0 or Higher.

Figure 16-9 shows the finished page in action.

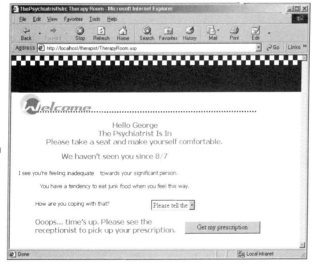

Figure 16-9:
George finally makes it to the Therapy Room.

Publish the page again. Browse the site and log in as George again. When you enter the Therapy Room this time, everything on the page should work properly.

Submitting the page

After all the shenanigans earlier in this chapter, the only thing that the patient's interaction with the page changes is his progress, measured by what he indicates in the list box, on a scale from Panic to Much Better. Your data-management task is to update his (George's) record to reflect that — you're interested in the numerical progress code `ProgID` rather than in the explanatory text.

Two separate interactions are necessary to achieve this goal, and this part causes more trouble than any other aspect of getting this site up and running. The problem is that ProgBox gets its content and values from the Progress recordset, as shown in Figure 7-9; when the page is submitted, however, you want to use the selected value to update a *different* recordset, Profiles.

In creating this example, we found what seemed like all you would need in an interaction:

1. **Select the ProgBox, the Profiles recordset, and the Submit button. Apply the interaction** `Use ProgBox data to update/insert in Profiles when RxButton is clicked` **in the Database Edit category.**

2. **In the Parameters dialog box, choose the Column** ProgID.

   That's not sufficient, however. After publishing, finding that it didn't work, and thumping our desk a few times, we actually had to RTM (read the manual). There, on the Descriptions tab in the Contract Manager, in relation to this contract, it says

   ```
   Values will not be reflected in the recordset unless an
         accompanying Insert or Update contract is applied
         between the button and recordset.
   ```

3. **The next interaction you apply on this page is between the Profiles recordset and the Submit button:** `Update active record when RxButton is clicked`.

   It turns out that it doesn't matter whether this interaction comes before or after the `Use ProgBox data to update/insert...` interaction in the execution order.

   One more interaction, and you're done. This setup doesn't work if the form is submitted conventionally.

4. **Select the prescription button and the Profiles recordset, and apply the interaction** `Go to pagename when RxButton is clicked, maintaining state of Profiles`. **(It's in the Database navigation category.)**

5. **In the Parameters dialog box, click the Assign button for pagename and select the Prescription page.**

What you just did

That really was the mother of all pages. Not that the actual layout was that complex, but rather what goes on behind the scenes: 10 hidden objects in the basement and no fewer than 17 contracts. Figure 16-10 lists the interactions in the correct order. The ten basement objects are a form, five recordsets, a session object, a cookie, a timer, and a hidden form element.

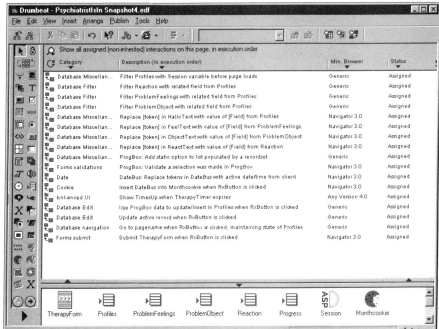

Figure 16-10: The attic and the basement are mighty full of junk on the finished therapy page.

The Prescription Page

Compared with the marathon of tasks you have to follow in the section "The Therapy Room," creating the Prescription page is a piece of cake. Everything you need is in the Progress recordset, as long as you set it up to correspond with George's (the patient's) report of his progress — or relapse.

Because you can be sure that the Profiles recordset is now updated with George's `ProgID`, you merely have to drag both the Profiles and Progress recordsets into the basement and filter Progress with the corresponding Profiles field. Then it's a matter of token substitution, as shown in Figures 16-11 and 16-12:

1. **Rename the text elements on the page on their Attributes Sheets to make assigning interactions easier. Name the first one** Thanks; **the second,** Report; **and the third,** Suggest.

2. **Select the Profiles and Progress recordsets. (Right-click and choose Possible Interactions, if the Interactions Center isn't already open.) Apply the interaction** `Filter Progress with related field from Profiles` **in the Database Filter category.**

3. **In the Parameters dialog box, for both the FilterColumn and FilterBy Columns, select ProgID.**

4. **Select the Thanks text and the Profiles recordset, and apply the interaction** `Replace [token] in Thanks with value of [Field] from Profiles.` **(It's in the Database Miscellaneous category.) In the Parameters dialog box, enter [name] for token and select UserName for Field.**

5. **Select the Report text and the Progress recordset, and apply the interaction** `Replace [token] in Report with value of [Field] from Progress.` **In the Parameters dialog box, enter [prog] for the token and select Report for the Field option.**

6. **Select the Suggest text and the Progress recordset, and apply the interaction** `Replace [token] in Suggest with value of [Field] from Progress.` **In the Parameters dialog box, enter [treat] for the token and select Treatment for the field.**

The design of the page is shown in Figure 16-11.

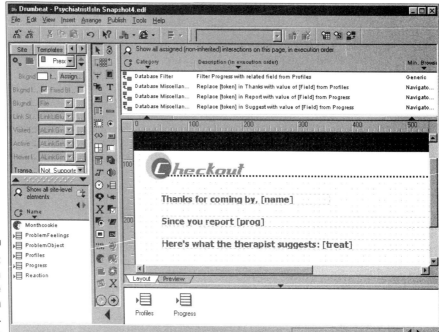

Figure 16-11: The design of the Prescription page.

Publish and browse. Log in as George, make a selection from the dropdown list on the Therapy Room page, and click the Get My Prescription button. On the Prescription page, you see the custom advice tailored to your condition handed out by the psychiatrist bot, as shown in Figure 16-12.

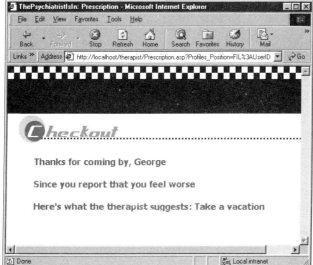

Figure 16-12:
After getting through this exercise, you may want to take the doctor's advice.

Getting a new patient's profile

You still have a major page to create. (We're watching the clock because we claim, after all, that we're showing you how to create "a Web site in a day.") The patient population doesn't remain static, of course, as new patients check in. You have to collect personal info from them and give them some sort of perfunctory advice or admonition because it's their first time.

The fields you need on the page match the columns in the main database that hold users' individual profiles. Use dropdown lists to make selections. To make the lists easy to update with any new ideas for content, arrange for the content of the dropdown lists to come directly from the data tables. First, you set up the three edit boxes:

1. **Select the NewPatient page, as shown in Figure 16-13. From the list of site-level elements in the Asset Center, select the Profiles recordset, and drag it into the basement.**

   It's the recordset you've already used on all three pages (LogIn, TherapyRoom, and Prescription). Next, assign the content of the three edit boxes that take the entries for username, e-mail address, and password.

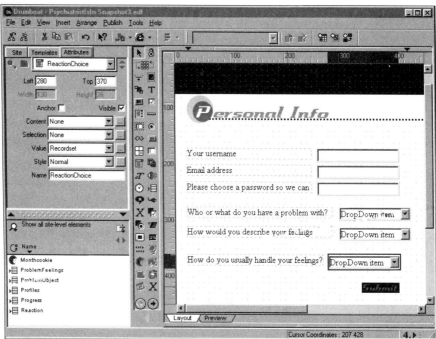

Figure 16-13:
New
patients
sign in here.

2. **Select the UserName edit box, and select Recordset for Content. In the Content dialog box, select Profiles for Recordset and select UserName for Column. Check the box for Submit Only (Don't Get Content from Recordset).**

   This action makes sense — if you don't check that box, you would find the user details from the first record of Profiles already in the edit boxes. That's not what you want.

3. **Select the Email edit box, and select Recordset for the Content option. In the Content dialog box, select Profiles for Recordset and select Email for Column. Check the box for Submit Only (Don't Get Content from Recordset).**

4. **Select the Password edit box. Select Profiles for Content and select Password for Column. Check the box for Submit Only (Don't Get Content from Recordset).**

Next, you can set up the three dropdown lists:

1. **Drag these three recordsets into the basement of the page: ProblemObject, ProblemFeelings, and Reaction.**

2. **Select the ObjectChoice dropdown list box. On the Attributes Sheet:**

   For Content, select Recordset. In the Content dialog box, select ProblemObject for Recordset and select ObjectName for Column.

For Value, select Recordset. In the Content dialog box, select ProblemObject for Recordset and select ObjectID for Column.

Set the Selection option to None.

3. **Select the FeelingChoice dropdown list box. On the Attributes Sheet:**

For Content, select Recordset. In the Content dialog box, select ProblemFeelings for Recordset and select Feeling for Column.

For Value, select Recordset. In the Content dialog box, select ProblemFeeling for Recordset and select FeelingID for Column.

Set the Selection option to None.

4. **Select the ReactionChoice dropdown list box. On the Attributes Sheet:**

For Content, select Recordset. In the Content dialog box, select Reaction for Recordset and select Reaction for Column.

For Value, select Recordset. In the Content dialog box, select Reaction for Recordset and select ReactionID for Column.

Set the Selection option to None.

Setting up the New Patient page interactions

All the elements for the new patient profile are now on the page. The next step is to set up the interactions with the recordsets. Start with an easy activation:

1. **Select the UserName edit box, and apply the activation** Set focus when page loads **in the Forms Miscellaneous category.**

   The main group of interactions says what belongs where. The edit boxes for UserName, Email, and Password take care of themselves because they're already bound to the Profiles recordset. Because the dropdown lists are getting their content from other tables, however, you have to specify where their data should be sent in the Profiles recordset. (If you open the Content Center and select the Profiles content table, you can see all the columns for this recordset that are involved.)

2. **Select the ObjectChoice dropdown list, the Profiles recordset, and the Submit button, and apply the interaction** Use ObjectChoice data to update/insert in Profiles when SubmitButton is clicked. **In the Parameters dialog box, select ObjectID for the Recordset Column.**

3. **Select the FeelingChoice dropdown list, the Profiles recordset, and the Submit button, and apply the interaction** Use FeelingChoice data to update/insert in Profiles when SubmitButton is clicked. **In the Parameters dialog box, select FeelingID for the Recordset Column.**

4. **Select the ReactionChoice dropdown list, the Profiles recordset, and the Submit button, and apply the interaction** `Use ReactionChoice data to update/insert in Profiles when SubmitButton is clicked.` **In the Parameters dialog box, select ReactionID for the Recordset Column.**

Now the `UserName`, `Email`, `Password`, `ObjectID`, `FeelingID`, and `ReactionID` fields are taken care of. The `UserID` field is given a new unique number automatically because it's designated as an autonumber field in the database. (See Appendix A if you don't know what that statement means.)

That leaves two fields you haven't fed yet: `ProgID` and `UserGroup`. The `ProgID` field needs to be set to 1, indicating a new patient. (Let's face it: A new patient can hardly be expected to indicate any progress.) The `UserGroup` field needs to be set to 2.

Because these settings can happen — *should* happen — out of sight of the user, you have to follow these steps with hidden form fields:

1. **Drag a hidden form element into the basement. On the Attributes tab, name it** ProgressNo. **Click the ellipsis button next to Content, enter** 1 **in the text editor, and then click OK.**

2. **Drag another hidden form element into the basement. On the Attributes Sheet, name it** Group. **Click the ellipsis button next to Content, enter** 2 **in the text editor, and then click OK.**

3. **Select the ProgressNo hidden form field, the Profiles recordset, and the submit button, and apply the interaction** `Use ProgressNo data to update/insert in Profiles when Submit button is clicked.` **In the Parameters dialog box, select ProgID for the Recordset column.**

4. **Select the Group hidden form field, the Profiles recordset, and the submit button, and then apply the interaction** `Use Group data to update/insert in Profiles when Submit button is clicked.` **In the Parameters dialog box, select UserGroup for the Recordset Column.**

The UserGroup is there to define a group for patients, using the arbitrary designation 2. We intended to invent another user group for staff, but we didn't get around to it. You can see the exact interactions later in this chapter, in Figure 16-14.

Remember that none of these five database edit interactions take effect unless they're followed by a data insert-update interaction.

Now you have to look ahead to think about what the receiving page, Prescription, expects. (Oh, heck — why not admit it? — we screwed up this task on our first attempt and *then* went back and thought about it.)

The only setup the Prescription page expects is that the Profiles recordset is set up for the correct patient. The *data cursor* has to be set correctly, in database parlance. Everything else follows along from that. Somehow, you have to make that happen, and at the same time get the form submitted in order for the validations to get checked. The problem is that if you apply a conventional form submit, with the form's action attribute dictating the next page, you have no way to preserve the data cursor.

The answer is two separate data Insert interactions between the submit button and the recordset, followed by a sort of fake form submit that goes nowhere:

1. **Select the submit button and the Profiles recordset, right-click, and choose Possible Interactions. In the Interactions Center, find and apply the interaction** Insert record into Profiles when SubmitButton is clicked with maintain state option **in the Database Edit category.**

2. **In the Parameters dialog box, click to uncheck the Maintain Original State check box.**

   You *must* click to uncheck that box. You see, this interaction offers to maintain the data cursor in two possible ways: the state the cursor was in *before the insert* (checked) or the cursor *at the insert point* (unchecked). Obviously, you want the second option.

3. **Next, keeping the submit button and the Profiles recordset selected, scroll to the Database Navigation category, and apply the interaction** Go to [pagename] when SubmitButton is clicked, maintaining state of Profiles.

4. **In the Parameters dialog box, click the Assign button for pagename and select the Prescription page from the site tree.**

5. **Finally, apply the submit action between the submit button and the form. Select the submit button and the NewProfile form in the basement. Apply the interaction** Submit NewProfile when SubmitButton is clicked. **In the Parameters dialog box, leave the Validate Form check box checked and the Action box blank.**

The Submit action must be the last one on the list to occur. If you set up your interactions in a different order or remove and reapply any interactions, always check to be sure that Submit comes last. Right-click an empty space in the layout area and choose Assigned Interactions (Ordered). Select the Submit interaction and drag it down to the last position.

Publish the site and browse. This time, on the Login page, click the link to go to the New Patient sign-in. Fill in the information as you please and submit it. You're sent to the Prescription page immediately to get your first prescription.

After you get everything working fine, you can place some validations on the edit boxes in the form. You want to ensure that a username and password are entered and that the e-mail address is in the proper format. The validations you apply are all in the Forms Validation category. Follow these steps:

1. **Select the UserName edit box, right-click, and choose Possible Activations. Apply the interaction** `Non Blank Validation on UserName`. **In the Parameters dialog box, enter the Error Msg Please enter a username.**

2. **Select the Email edit box. Apply the interaction** `E-mail Address Validation on Email` (check required).

3. **Select the Password edit box, right-click, and choose Possible Activations. Apply the interaction** `Non Blank Validation on Password`. **In the Parameters dialog box, enter the Error Msg** Please enter a password.

After adding the validations, reorder the assigned interactions so that the Insert and Submit actions are again last. The complete set of assigned interactions in the Interactions Center should look like the one shown in Figure 16-14.

Figure 16-14:
The complete set of interactions for the New Patient page.

Bells and Whistles

If you've followed along with all our instructions in this chapter, you can easily call it a project at this point. It's still only dinnertime for us, though, so we thought that we would suggest how you might start on a "second generation" Psychiatrist_Is_IN. We have a few ideas.

An authentic note of sarcasm

From what we hear, psychiatrists are fond of trying to read meaning into the innocent or random behavior of their clients. If you arrive early for an appointment, for example, you're "overanxious" about it. If you arrive late — "Perhaps ziss is a sign zat you vant to *avoid* ze appointment."

We can't exactly manage appointment times, but we thought that you may gain some extra realism if you arrange for the online therapist to make a sarcastic comment, on the TherapyRoom page, according to how many days have elapsed since the patient's (George's) last visit, as read from the Monthcookie cookie.

This exercise involves scripting. If the thought of writing your own script makes you break out in a sweat, go take a break (and get a candy bar as a reward for getting this far) and leave this section alone.

To provide several alternative "greetings," you have to tamper with whatever scripting Drumbeat has come up with to do the date substitution in the LastVisit text. (It was created when you applied the token replacement interaction in the "Time's up!" section, earlier in this chapter.) Right-click the LastVisit text box and choose Edit Script⇨Inline from the pop-up menus. Figure 16-15 shows what you see in the Scripting Center.

If you inspect this figure, you can see that the variable html is the content of the text box. All the script does is read the cookie, separate the text into the part before the token and the part after the token, and then set the cookie text in the middle and write the whole thing out. After a bit of poking about, you can see that the html variable contains this code (or something similar):

```
<LAYER ID="LyrLastVist" CLASS="Tahoma12Grn" LEFT=30 TOP=220
        WIDTH=560 HEIGHT=19 VISIBILITY="show" Z-INDEX=10>
<DIV ID="LastVisit" CLASS="Tahoma12Grn">
We haven't seen you since [month].
</DIV></LAYER>
```

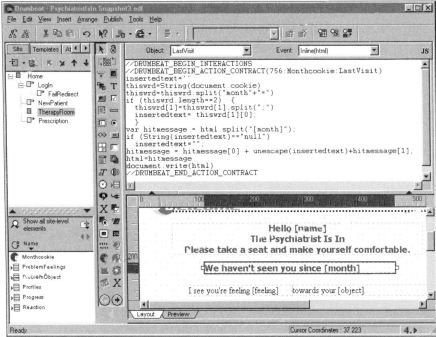

Figure 16-15:
The preset script for the cookie data substitution.

Although the Drumbeat folks make it illegal to edit JavaScript that derives from an applied interaction, they can't stop you from copying their script, removing the interaction, and then rescripting the exact same event manually — which is what we tell you how to do here. The event is the inline(html) event of Text3. The top and tail of the handmade script need to be something like this:

```
html = '<LAYER ID="LyrLastVist" CLASS="Tahoma12Grn" ';
html += 'LEFT=30 TOP=220 WIDTH=560 HEIGHT=19 ';
html += 'VISIBILITY="show" Z-INDEX=10>';
html += '<DIV ID="LastVisit" CLASS="Tahoma12Grn">'
tailtext = new String();
tailtext = '</DIV></LAYER>';
sarcasm = new String();
:
:
document.write(html);
document.write(sarcasm);
document.write(tailtext);
```

The sarcasm string has to be different according to how many days since the last visit. Change the cookie text from [monthname] [daynumber] to **[monthnumber]/[daynumber]** so that you have something more arithmetical to work with. The text is the Content attribute of the DateBus hidden form element. The complete cookie value is now something like this:

```
month=4/22;ASPSESSION=xyzzz
```

Here's how to calculate the day value represented by the cookie:

```
Thiswrd = String(document.cookie);
Thiswrd = thiswrd.split("month"+"=");
thiswrd[1] = thiswrd[1].split(";")
d = thiswrd[1][0].split("/");
yearnum = eval(d[0]*30+d[1]*1);
```

And here's the equivalent value for today's date:

```
today = new Date();
thismonth = today.getMonth()+1;
thisday = today.getDate();
todaynum = eval(thismonth*30+thisday*1);
```

After collapsing some of the variable declaration, you may come up with the following code to select the appropriate sarcastic comment:

```
Dayssince = eval(thismonth*30+thisday*1)-
            eval(d[0]*30+d[1]*1);
if (dayssince > 10) {
  sarcasm = "We haven't seen you for " + dayssince + " days.
            Are you taking this seriously enough?";
}
else if (dayssince == 0) {
  sarcasm = "I've already seen you today. I think you are
            overanxious.";
}
else {
  sarcasm = "It's only been " + dayssince + " days since your
            last visit. Do you think you may be overanxious?";
}
```

Figure 16-16 shows the new script in action. If you're a purist, you'll (justifiably) complain that this code produces an absurd result if the time between visits bridges over a new year. Yes, yes — we're running out of room in this book and your nice Web site would turn into a pumpkin if were to linger over explaining how to fix that problem. Besides, fixing it up would raise all kinds of nasty Y2K compliance questions.

If you want to take a shortcut to success, just use the CD in the back of this book to load up the completed The_Psychiatrist_Is_IN application. It represents the application you've built to this point if you're following along in this chapter, and includes the complete sequential script created for the "Authentic note of sarcasm."

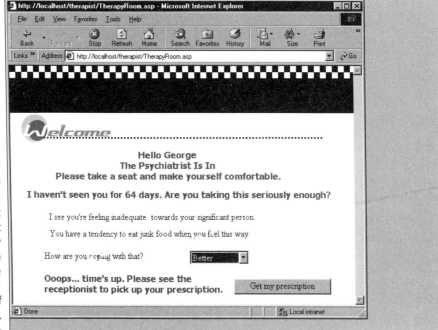

Figure 16-16:
Refinement
brought
about by
scripting the
`inline`
`(html)`
event of
`LastVisit.`

The post mortem: Better prescriptions?

Let's face it: The prescription policy in the site so far is somewhat crude. The prescription is made entirely from a patient's own report of his progress. Notice, though, what a wonderful array of data is available for improving diagnosis and prescription if the site were something more than "a web site in a day." You could read not only the progress data but also the feelings data and prescribe on the basis of a combination of those two dimensions. Six levels of progress multiplied by 10 feelings makes 60 possible prescriptions right there.

If you expand to more dimensions, the process could get quite sophisticated. In fact, if only we'd given ourselves more than a day to build this application, we could have been serious contenders for the Turing test. Then we would win prizes, become famous, and go on all the talk shows. We would be offered a chair at M.I.T., but we would gracefully turn them down as we headed for that Greek island.

Dreams, dreams, Drumbeat dreams. . . .

Part V

The Part of Tens

The 5th Wave

By Rich Tennant

"Games are an important part of my Web site. They cause eye strain."

In this part . . .

The Part of Tens lists some cool stuff you can use to accelerate your web site development or add special features. DrumNotes are minisites illustrating useful techniques you can copy — we've collected some popular ones on the CD in the back of this book to get you started, and we explain them here. The Interactions Center has more interactions in it than you can shake a stick at — you'll find some good ones that you may have overlooked. Finally, you'll discover some cool components you can add to your Drumbeat environment to do things like send e-mail from your site or add Shockwave or Director files.

Chapter 17

Rainy Day DrumNotes Nos. 12 & 34 (And Other Variations on a Theme)

- -

In This Chapter

▶ Understanding how to play a DrumNote

▶ Building and improving on database pages

▶ Using cookies and COM objects

▶ Creating better password protection

▶ Making even better form validation

▶ Using search tricks

- -

*N*othing works like a good example — except maybe a good guitar or harmonica riff. That's just what we were thinking on a rainy day while we were sitting in a conference room with sheets of rain pouring down the windowpanes and we were contributing the name DrumNotes to a newly hatched idea at Elemental Software. (If you're *not* a baby boomer, let us clue you in. *Rainy Day Women Nos. 12 & 34,* by Bob Dylan, was one of the best blues harmonica pieces to come out of the 1960s.)

What are DrumNotes? *DrumNotes* are real, live examples of popular web site features that include mini site files you can use or copy into your own application. Instructions for replicating the DrumNote technique are included in the site file, and you can examine all the components to see exactly how it works. You can even use a DrumNote as a starting point for your own site.

We list in this chapter (in order) the top ten most frequently downloaded DrumNotes from the Drumbeat web site. They're followed by recommended DrumNotes that explain processes often confusing to new users.

Lots more DrumNotes are available by download from the Drumbeat web site. Just visit `drumnotes.drumbeat.com` to browse the musical catalog. You may find a tune that strikes a chord. And they're all on the CD! (Not all the DrumNotes were available in a JSP version at the time this book was printed. If you're a JSP user, check the Drumbeat web site for updated JSP versions of the missing DrumNotes.)

How to Use DrumNotes

To begin using a DrumNote, just double-click the DrumNote.exe file (for example, DrumNote_24.exe). A pop-up message tells you that this action will install the DrumNote and asks that you please install it in your Drumbeat 2000 directory. The DrumNote makes a separate folder for itself named DrumNote_# (for example, DrumNote_24) in Drumbeat 2000/DrumNotes, where all the components you need are dumped. The Readme.txt file normally opens automatically, with any special instructions you need then displayed.

A few DrumNotes require you to create a Data Source Name (DSN) for a small database that's included. Most, however, use one of the Starting Point databases. They're installed for you with the DSNs automatically created when you install the full version of Drumbeat. Some DrumNotes also require you to import new contracts or SmartElements. Just follow the instructions in the Readme file, and you'll be okay.

To open the DrumNote example, navigate to the Drumbeat 2000/DrumNotes directory and find the .edf file in the appropriate DrumNote folder. The .edf file is located in a directory named DrumNote_# (for example, DrumNote_24). Double-click the .edf file to open it. Depending on which version of Drumbeat you're using, you may be asked to convert the site database to make it compatible with your version of Drumbeat. Just click Yes to convert the database and open the file.

No. 13: Creating Lookup Lists

Browser support: Generic

Lookup lists not only help users of your web application but also save you from many headaches caused by having to clean up your database when users enter the wrong type of date or misspelled choices, for example. Lookup lists also help users search for things without feeling like they're entering a spelling bee. This DrumNote site demonstrates how to create a lookup list for a typical database page. It shows how a dropdown list populated from one recordset can be used to interact with another recordset. You need to know how to do this task — for your own protection. (You can also read our description and follow the examples in Chapter 12, in the section about list boxes and dropdown lists.

No. 21: Updating and Inserting Records in a Database

Browser support: Generic

Want to create your own Insert and Update pages without using the DataForm Wizard? This option could be a smart one if you're a finicky designer or have a finicky database. This DrumNote shows you how to build your pages, piece by piece and interaction by interaction, without using the DataForm Wizard.

No. 19: Creating Links Using Fields in a Recordset

Browser support: Generic

Hey, who doesn't have an e-mail address or a web site these days? Whenever you're building a database for web use, you would be foolish not to provide a field or two (or more) for e-mail addresses and web site URLs. You can build links based on these fields in a database by using the Recordset link type. This DrumNote demonstrates how to create links that can change dynamically based on a database, which is a good thing, what with all the dynamic change going on all around us these days.

No. 3: Password-Protecting Pages

Browser support: Generic

Need a burly bouncer to stand at the door of your database? This DrumNote shows you how to password-protect pages and redirect users based on login ID access rights. Group 1 gets to go to the party, Group 2 has to go back and do its homework, and Group 3 gets tossed into the gutter.

The DrumNote uses the UserLogin database from the UserLogin Starting Point, which comes with Drumbeat and is preconfigured at installation so that you already have everything you need to try it. In Chapter 13, we give you a simple example of password-protecting a page, in the section "Feeling insecure?"

No. 30: Creating Search Pages

Browser support: Generic

Searching can be a complicated business, and setting up a user-friendly search takes a great deal of thought. You want people to be able to search one field on very loose criteria; another search field has to match exactly, or else it goes nowhere. Sometimes, the more search fields, the merrier. At other times, less is more. You can create exactly what you need, quickly and easily, if the DataForm

Wizard is too restrictive for you. DrumNote No. 30 demonstrates how to use those tools to create pages that search a database in a myriad of ways without using the DataForm Wizard. (To get started, you can also follow the example in Chapter 12, in the section about building a search page by hand.)

No. 24: Multi-Page Forms Using an ASP Session Object

Browser support: Navigator 3 and later

Most simple forms happily fit on one web page. What if you're building a longer form, however, that you want to break down into a couple of pages? The answer is the ASP Session Object. This DrumNote shows you how to create multipage forms by using the ASP Session Object. The example splits a form into two pages: Page1 and Page2. The third page is a "Thank You" page that shows all the data just entered.

No. 10: Using a Redirect Page If the Value Searched Is Not in the Database

Browser support: Generic

"I'm dreadfully sorry, Sir, but the filet mignon is not available this evening. Would you like to take another look at the menu? If I may, I'd like to recommend. . . ."

Who wouldn't find this approach to a dead-end database search more appealing than the terse and uninformative "No records found"? This DrumNote explains how to set up a Redirect Page to be displayed when a user searches for a value that isn't in the database. We can't help you find the perfect waiter and the perfect line to satisfy all unhappy customers, but we can help you put together your own solution.

No. 23: Validating Forms

Browser support: Navigator 3 and later

A date is a date. A phone number is a phone number. A zip code is a zip code. An integer is a whole number. All these items have their required formats. If someone visits your site and omits the area code from her phone number, you could lose a potential contact or sale. If she puts the name of the item or a fraction in the Quantity field, for example, the database could have a conniption!

The use of form validation can prevent this situation. You can use one of dozens of ways to ensure that everything has been correctly entered before the form is submitted. This DrumNote shows you how to validate a form under three different scenarios. (Refer to the section in Chapter 13 about validating form entries.)

No. 27: Displaying a Prompt or Blank Value As the Default in a Dropdown List

Browser support: Generic

What happens when you let a recordset populate a drop-down list? What's visible to the user is, inevitably, the first option on the list. A human would want to put either a blank or a prompt message, such as "Please make a selection" or "Who cares?" A recordset would never add this *static* option automatically because it doesn't correspond to any column in the parent database.

DrumNote No. 27 shows how to add static options to dropdown lists and list boxes, without fearing that the prompt message may find its way into the database if the user makes no change. (We fully describe list boxes and another example of this technique in Chapter 12, in the section about list boxes and dropdown lists.)

No. 34: Displaying the Number of Records Returned By a Search

Browser support: Generic

This DrumNote site demonstrates how to display the number of records returned by a search and how to tell users where they are when they're browsing the results list.

No. 42: Using Cookies

Browser support: Navigator 3 and later

"Oh, how lovely to SEE you, MADAM! I do hope that MADAM was completely SATISFIED with the furniture items this store had the PLEASURE of selling her last — um — February. How may we be of SERVICE to MADAM today?"

Cookies were invented in an attempt to make shopping-cart web sites almost as unctuous as that parody of an old-fashioned haberdasher. Technically, a cookie is nothing more than a little text file that infiltrates the shopper's own computer and writes some ID info. The next time the shopper walks into the store, it's a simple matter to read the cookie, consult the shopper's records, and get instant unctuousness. Although we were once all paranoid about this technique, it is now accepted as a sensible and valuable way to preserve visitor information and personalize a web site.

This DrumNote demonstrates how to use a cookie to add personalization to your web site. It's surprisingly easy. The technique is demonstrated in Chapter 16, too, in the section "Time for a cookie!"

No. 18: Sending a Form as an E-mail Message Using CDO NewMail

Browser support: Generic

This DrumNote explains how a Drumbeat form can be sent in an e-mail message by using the CDO COM object (only for ASP). The first example in the DrumNote demonstrates sending two e-mail messages in response to submitting a survey. The second example in the DrumNote demonstrates how to insert the survey data into a database before sending the messages. (See the description of the CDO Email COM object in Chapter 19.)

Chapter 18

Ten Useful Interactions You May Have Overlooked

*B*ecause those inventive Drumbeat folks are forever thinking up new activations and interactions, your kit bag of these things is almost certainly not up-to-date. Your savior is the Element Exchange, at www.drumbeat.com/ElementExchange/. At this web site, you can browse and search the contracts library, read descriptions, and download new contracts as .ctr files (contracts are what make interactions possible — refer to Chapter 15). Your C:\Program Files\Drumbeat 2000\Contracts folder contains a subfolder for each of the contract categories, containing a .ctr file and a .doc file. By the time you read this book, even more useful and cool interactions are likely to be available.

Escape From Frames

Miscellaneous: Break This Page Out of Frames

If you discover that your beautiful web page has, because of some quirk of hyperlinking, opened into some miserable, scrunched-up subframe designed for other purposes, you'll certainly be annoyed. A simple piece of JavaScript prevents this situation by detecting it and opening a full-size window:

```
if (window.parent.frames.length != 0){
    window.open(location.href)
    history.back()
}
```

To adopt this safeguard, you don't need to copy the script. Just apply this activation to the page itself.

The Day/Night SmartElement

```
DayNight: Set text in [target] object based upon DayNight
         [source]
```

Want to greet users of your site, but not sure whether to say "Good morning," "Good afternoon," or "Good evening"? What you need is the DayNight SmartElement and this interaction.

The source is a DayNight SmartElement, which sits in the basement, and an edit box in the layout area. You aren't limited to the standard phrases — you can get whimsical with phrases such as "Sleep well?" — and you can define the times when the greeting message should change. You can also specify, for Internet Explorer only, styles for displaying the messages. Here are some other fun things the DayNight fairy can do for you: Display an appropriate image for the time of day, Set a background color or image, Go to an appropriate URL.

The DayNight SmartElement isn't a standard element on the SmartElements toolbar. Find it on the JavaScript tab in the SmartElement Library.

Simple Token Replacement

```
ASP Miscellaneous: Replace [Token] with Contents of Form
                  Element
```

In Chapters 12 and 13, we write about passing form data from page to page, and we suggest using the server request object for that purpose. For what we have in mind in that chapter — a "data preview" page a user can add to a recordset after approving the layout — that's the best technique.

The interaction in this section, however, is more informal for picking up form data and displaying it by token substitution. It may be used for writing Thank you for your input, [token] in a text box, picking up the token from a name entered on the submitting page.

You even get a little bonus. One of the parameters is Substitute for null incoming data. That's where you can put a statement such as Er, sorry, have we been introduced? if no name arrives.

Complex Token Replacement

Database Miscellaneous: Replace Multiple [tokens] in
[TextElement] with values from [Recordset]

To make your database pages more informative, you can use a few of the
Database Miscellaneous interactions, some of which are covered in Chapter
13. One of them replaces text tokens with the current record and the total
records in a recordset.

This complex interaction enables you to grab the current values of as many
data fields as you want to make up a text string. Doing so makes sense only
on a detail page, which (usually) has only one current record. On any other
page, it would simply use the record at the data cursor, which may not be
relevant.

E-Mail Direct from Your Recordset

Database Miscellaneous: Link to E-mail address from [source]
when [target] is clicked

Like the interaction in the preceding section, this one makes sense only on a
one-record page. If one field of the recordset contains e-mail addresses, this
interaction enables you to bind a mailto: event to something clickable, such
as a button. From the user's point of view, it causes an e-mail form to pop up
when the button is clicked, with the destination address already present.

Get Today's Date

Forms set value: Set to today's date in different formats

This interaction is a more informal (all right, cruder) version of the date
token substitutions we describe in Chapter 8, in the section about using
token substitution. This version simply displays today's date in an edit box.
You can choose one of ten date formats, and no one can stop you, of course,
from imposing a style on the box.

Change the Cursor Shape

Miscellaneous: Set Cursor

This interaction is an activation of an image or a text box. You can specify that as long as the mouse pointer hovers over an object, the cursor becomes one of these elements: Auto, Crosshair, Default, Hand, Move, Text, or Wait.

Netscape and Internet Explorer differ (not surprisingly) in their interpretations of these variants.

Pop-Up Windows

Navigation: Open custom window when clicked

We almost included this interaction in Chapter 8 but decided that it doesn't count as design, which is the topic of that chapter.

If you want to pop up a second window whose dimensions, appearance, and content you can specify; this interaction makes it possible. (It also makes it possible for you to be pestered by pop-up ads for laundry soap when you're looking for movie screening times on the Web.)

The interaction has no fewer than 14 parameters to enable you to freely define the characteristics of the new window. The seven check boxes enable you to define the properties of the new window, or how much "chrome" it has, in the jargon.

Even more information about this interaction is available as DrumNote No. 16, on the Web at www.drumbeat.com/DrumNotes/.

File Last Modified

File Scripting: Replace [token] with file last modified date/Directory listing

This interaction is actually two separate interactions. They're activations of a text box, substituting a file-last-modified date or a complete directory listing for a token in the text. The file or the directory must be accessible at the server, obviously. The directory must also have a virtual path set up (we explain that subject in a Technical Stuff paragraph in Chapter 2).

The directory listing interaction presents something of a design problem because you have no way of predicting how long the list will turn out and, therefore, how much vertical space it needs. Try placing a SmartSpacer (refer to Chapter 3) just under the box where the listing will appear.

Appendix A

Database Basics

Databases and Relational DBMSs

A *database* is simply a collection of data (which is really just a bunch of *1*s and *0*s stored on a computer). At the most basic level, you don't really need *any* program to make a database. You can make a simple text file to serve as a database, separating each field with commas or tabs or some special character you choose. To retrieve and manipulate the data from that text file, however, you would have to either write your own programming scripts to access it or use a database management system.

A database management system (DBMS) is the front end to your database (don't confuse it with the database itself), which enables you to manipulate the data in various ways. For simplicity, we call the DBMS your *database application*. Database applications include Access, Oracle, SQL Server, FoxPro, FileMaker Pro, DB2, and a host of others.

Relational database management systems (RDBMS) are practically the only kind anybody bothers with these days — unless you just happen to be stuck in some company with a giant legacy database built in the 1950s that no one has yet figured out how to migrate to Relational Database Land. A sort of cult has developed about relational mumbo-jumbo in database techie circles, where they like to sit around and point fingers at each other and say "but such-and-such isn't a true relational model."

You don't really have to worry about it. If anybody asks you whether your database is relational, just mutter "Of course" and stuff something in your mouth so that you can't answer any more questions.

Which Databases Can I Use with Drumbeat?

You can use almost any ODBC-compliant database to create ASP applications with Drumbeat. We have built ASP applications with Drumbeat successfully with Microsoft Access and various versions of Oracle, SQL Server, and DB2. We know of Drumbeat users who also use FoxPro. The primary limitation is the ODBC drivers. You may need to get up-to-date drivers for your database application from the manufacturer. Check with the Drumbeat technical-support people (at www.drumbeat.com/TechSupport/) if you have specific questions about your database application.

If you're just starting out with databases, we suggest that you try Access, which is fairly easy to learn and integrates well with Drumbeat for small applications. The database samples in this book for ASP use are provided on the CD in Access mdb files. Access has its limitations with large databases and applications in which security is a big concern, however. If you're thinking big, you may want to switch to something with more industrial power.

The JavaServer Pages Edition of Drumbeat included on the CD in this book is set up to work with DB2 as the database application. The sample databases on the CD are also provided in DB2 for JSP users. By the time this book gets into your hands, however, later versions of Drumbeat for JSP may well be available that will work with other database systems, most likely including SQL Server and Oracle first.

Tables, Columns, and Rows

Tables are the primary building blocks of your database. A *table* is designed to hold information, all of the same type, about any number of things, such as your CD collection or your 25 cats.

Tables consist of rows (horizontal) and columns (vertical). Columns are also often referred to as *fields*. (Although *field* technically refers to the data within the column, most people don't bother to make the distinction.) Column names within a table must be unique. For your CD collection, the column names may be Title, Artist, and Genre, for example. For your cats, they may be Name, PreferredFood, SleepHours, and BirdsCaught.

Each row in a table represents one record. If you're storing a list of contacts in a database table, each row represents a person.

Whenever you want to use a piece of data in your database, the DBMS must find the correct column and row to locate the precise piece of information you want.

Primary Keys and Relationships

If each column in a database has a unique name, finding the column is easy. But how do you find the correct row? Suppose that you have a list of employees in a big company that employs six people named John Brown. Clearly, you can't use "John" or "Brown" to find the right row. Neither can you use their job title, if 3 are engineers and the company also employs 200 other engineers.

That's where primary keys come in. Each database table should have one column designated as the primary key. The only hard-and-fast rule about primary keys is that they must be unique. That's why the most common type of primary key is an automatically generated number that is guaranteed by mathematical formula to be unique. In Access, you choose the AutoNumber type, and Access makes up the numbers for you as you go. A primary key may be something else, however — such as an SKU number for merchandise inventory purposes or an ISBN number, for example, for a database table of book titles.

When you have lots of tables in your database, repeating the same information in several tables is inefficient. For one thing, the database then takes up a great deal of file space; for another, database access is slower. You have to set up a way to streamline the information using the primary keys. A primary key in one table is often a foreign key in another table.

Here's a list of columns in a database table of zoo animals, where `ANIMALID` is the primary key:

- ✔ AnimalID
- ✔ AnimalName
- ✔ Species
- ✔ Cage
- ✔ KeeperID

In a second database table of keepers in the zoo, `KEEPERID` is the primary key:

- ✔ KeeperID
- ✔ KeeperName
- ✔ Shift
- ✔ Species

In the keepers table, the KeeperID field is a foreign key for the animals table. The Species column in both tables could also be a foreign key to a third table. The fact that they have this field in common lets you create queries that join information from the two tables. This process is often referred to in database-ese as "creating a JOIN."

Talking SQL to Your Database

Whenever you want to request a set of data from your database, you use Structured Query Language (SQL). *SQL* is a kind of pidgin database language that's supposed to transcend all the proprietary coding that goes into database applications. As much as the DBMS makers slug it out in the marketplace, they all realize that they need to cooperate with each other so that users with different applications can get things done.

Although many database applications have their own variations of SQL, they all should understand the basic SQL commands. The principal commands you use repeatedly are SELECT, FROM, and WHERE. There's a slew of other commands, but it's all pretty basic, and what counts most is the *syntax,* the order in which you say things and how statements get put together. (Your seventh-grade English teacher would love it.)

To get the information you want from the two tables in the preceding section, you construct a simple, humorless SQL statement that goes like this:

```
SELECT * FROM ANIMALS, KEEPERS WHERE ANIMALS.KeeperID =
          KEEPERS.KeeperID
```

See Chapter 10 for more info about SQL and how to use it to construct queries to your database in Drumbeat. Remember this little rhyme:

> *Talk see-quel to your database*
>
> *And beat it when it chokes*
>
> *It only does it to annoy*
>
> *Because it knows no jokes.*

Appendix B

About the CD

What's On The CD

▶ Two versions of Drumbeat 2000 (choose ASP or JSP)

▶ Demo site files used in this book

▶ A selection of Drumbeat DrumNotes

▶ The latest versions of the leading web browsers: Internet Explorer 5.0 and Netscape Communicator 4.5

▶ A bunch of other useful things

System Requirements

Recommended system requirements for Drumbeat 2000:

- ✔ 200 MHz Pentium
- ✔ 60 MB free disk space
- ✔ 64 MB RAM
- ✔ Windows 95, Windows 98, or Windows NT 4.0

You may be able to get by with less computer power, if you have plenty of free disk space and RAM. At the least, you need a 166 MHz Pentium, 30MB of free disk space, and 32MB of RAM. The larger your sites, the bigger your requirements should be. If you have an older computer and you find Drumbeat operating too slowly, a cheap solution is to consider increasing your RAM and disk space.

To create, publish, and view Active Server Pages with the ASP version of Drumbeat, you also need

- ✔ Internet Information Server 3.0 or later for Windows NT or Chili!ASP or other ASP-interpretive software installed on the server to which you publish your final product.

✔ Personal Web Server (PWS) for Windows NT or Windows 95 or Windows 98 (PWS is included with Windows 98) for local ASP publishing. (If you're publishing directly to an ASP server, you don't need PWS, although it's nice to have so that you can view your site locally.)

✔ A relational database management program to create your database. Microsoft Access, SQL Server 7, FoxPro, or any ODBC-compatible database program will do.

To create, publish, and view JavaServer Pages with the JavaServer Pages edition of Drumbeat included on the CD, you need an IBM WebSphere application server and a DB2 database

Check the Drumbeat web site (www.drumbeat.com) for updates to both versions of Drumbeat. The Service Pack 2 upgrade to Drumbeat 2000 (not available at the time this book was printed) is a newer version than the one supplied on the CD. We highly recommend that you get this version because it contains some newer interactions used in some of the examples in this book. (You can install the service pack with the trial version.)

How to Use the CD

Your first task is to figure out how to get that sealed plastic package open without ripping the book apart. After you've mastered that task, put the CD in your CD drive. Navigate to that drive in Windows Explorer, and open the INDEX.HTM file. It has an explanation of everything on the CD with instructions for installing Drumbeat and all the related items.

Freebies on the Frisbee

The software on the CD-ROM includes trial versions of Drumbeat and other programs, along with examples and useful information for setting yourself up for ASP publishing.

A few words about shareware: Shareware programs are available to you for an evaluation period (typically, anywhere from 30 to 90 days). If you decide that you like a shareware program and want to keep using it, you're expected to send a registration fee to its author or publisher, which entitles you to technical support and notifications about new versions. (It also makes you feel good.)

Because most shareware operates on an honor system, the programs continue working even if you don't register them. It's a good idea, however, to support the shareware concept and encourage the continued production of quality, low-cost software by sending in your payment for the programs you use.

Drumbeat 2000

Two 30-day trial versions of Drumbeat 2000 are included on the CD. Look in the DRUMBEAT folder (ASP version) or DRUMBEATJSP folder (JSP version). You can choose whether you want to create Active Server Pages using Microsoft ASP technology or JavaServer Pages using an IBM WebSphere application server.

Read the system requirements at the beginning of this appendix, and choose your weapon carefully before installing the program. You cannot install both versions on the same machine.

Whichever version you choose, you should go to the Drumbeat web site (www.drumbeat.com) after installing the software and get the latest upgrade with Service Pack 2.

After the 30-day trial period is over, you can purchase a registered version of Drumbeat. Go to the Drumbeat web site for the latest information about how to register your product or purchase a new full version. Be assured that any sites you build with this trial version will work with a later version of the software too.

DrumNotes

DrumNotes are mini site files that demonstrate popular techniques and features you may want to add to your web site. Why wrestle with trying to figure out how to use a component you want or add a complicated new feature to your site when you can just copy the example? (Hey — we all have better things to do.) Look in the DRUMNOTES folder.

We've picked some of the most popular DrumNotes to put on the CD. Refer to Chapter 17 for a brief description of each DrumNote on the CD. Tons more are available at the Drumbeat web site, so if you don't find what you want, search at www.drumbeat.com/drumnotes.

When you attempt to open a DrumNote file for the first time, a message may tell you that the site database is out of date and ask whether you want to convert it. Just click OK. You simply have a later version of Drumbeat than the one used to create the DrumNote site.

Drumbeat For Dummies site samples

The sample sites used in portions of this book are included on the CD so that you can follow along with the examples. You can install all the sample files at one time by clicking the link to the executable file on the BookSamples.html page on the CD (you can get there by clicking on "Sample Sites" within the interface). If you use Windows Explorer, the Setup.exe file to install the samples is in the ASPSamplesInstall or JSPSamplesInstall folder on the CD.

If you prefer to copy the files directly, copy folder ASPSamples (for the ASP version) or JSPSamples (for the JavaServer Pages edition) into your Drumbeat 2000 directory. If you have installed Drumbeat in the default location, the path is C:\Program Files\Drumbeat 2000. You may have to change the properties of the Drumbeat .edf and the database files from read-only: Right-click the filename in Windows Explorer, choose Properties, and uncheck Read-Only.

After the files are installed, you see that the ASPSamples (or JSPSamples) folder contains three folders, one for each sample site, described in the following sections. Each sample site contains these components:

- ✔ **Two or more .edf files (Drumbeat site files):** Includes a "start file" you can use to build the examples in each of the affiliated chapters.

- ✔ **A site database:** For ASP, the database is supplied in Microsoft Access format. For JSP, a .sql file is supplied that you can run to create the database with DB2. The CookieKing and MovieMaven folders also include .CSV files that you can import into another database application and then set up the database yourself.

- ✔ **A folder of images used in the site (except for the MovieMaven site, which uses Drumbeat clip art).**

- ✔ **Sometimes other files that are noted in the chapter:** Contracts (.ctr files) or SQL query files (.dql).

In each case, before you can use the sample site, you have to set up a DSN for the database used in the site. The instructions for each site following tell you what DSN name you should use. Refer to Chapter 10 for instructions for setting up a DSN if you don't know how.

If you cannot open the files after you install them on your own computer, the problem is most likely related to the file permissions set up on your CD drive or computer. To fix this problem, right-click the site file in Windows Explorer and choose Properties. In the Attributes section of the Properties dialog box, make sure that both the Read-only and Archive options are unchecked. Do the same for the database file.

One more note: If you have a later version of Drumbeat than the one used to create the sample sites (for example, if you have the latest upgrade), when you attempt to open the site file the first time, you may see a message telling you that the site database is out of date and asking whether you want to convert it. Just click OK.

The CookieKing

The CookieKing site shows how to set up a basic database-driven site, using the DataForm Wizard, and then customize pages and use different form elements. The examples in Chapters 11 and 12 and part of Chapter 13 use the CookieKing site.

To set up the site:

  ✔ Set up the DSN "CookieKing" to point to the CookieKing.mdb database (if you're using Microsoft Access).

  ✔ Set up a publish folder in your C:\inetpub\wwwroot folder named cookies for publishing the site.

There's a starter file for each chapter, with the name CookieKingASP11_1.edf, CookieKingASP12_1.edf, and CookieKingASP13_1.edf, as well as a final site file, CookieKingASP_Final.edf. (If you're using the JSP version, substitute **JSP** for ASP in the filename.)

The site uses images that are in the Images folder, located under the CookieKing folder. To see the images, you may have to update the media paths to point to this folder. With the default installation of Drumbeat and the ASP samples files, the correct media path is

C:\Program Files\Drumbeat.2000\ASPSamples\CookieKing\Images

(If you're using the JSP version, substitute **JSP** for ASP in the path.) Refer to the section in Chapter 8 about changing media folders and updating paths.

MovieMaven

The MovieMaven site illustrates different ways to search and filter a database. The examples in Chapter 14 use the MovieMaven database and site file.

To set up the site:

  ✔ Set up the DSN moviemaven pointing to the moviemaven.mdb database.

  ✔ Set up a publish folder in your C:\inetpub\wwwroot folder named movies for publishing the site.

The folder also contains .CSV files for each of the database tables so that you can import them into your own database program and set up your own database. Also included are the exported query files (.dql) that you can import into your own site after you've set up the database. To take the easy road, however, just open the starter file (MovieMaven_ASP_Start.edf or MovieMaven_JSP_Start.edf) and follow the examples. Or, just take a look at the finished file (MovieMaven_ASP_Final.edf or MovieMaven_JSP_Final.edf) to see how it's all done.

The MovieMaven site uses images that are included in one of the clip art folders included with Drumbeat. By default, the folder is located at C:\Program Files\Drumbeat 2000\Media\Watercolors. If you installed Drumbeat to a location that's different from the default, you have to update the media paths. Refer to the section in Chapter 8 about changing media folders and updating paths.

ThePsychiatristIsIn.com

The purpose of this site is to illustrate using session information to personalize content on a web site. Examples in Chapter 16 use the PatientRecords database and Drumbeat site file.

To set up the site:

- ✔ Set up the DSN "Patients" pointing to the PatientRecords.mdb database (for Microsoft Access).
- ✔ Set up a publish folder in your C:\inetpub\wwwroot folder named therapist for publishing the site.

The site uses images in the Media folder, located under the Psychiatrist folder. To see the images, you may have to update the media paths to point to this folder. With the default installation of Drumbeat and the ASP samples files, the correct media path is C:\Program Files\Drumbeat 2000\ASPSamples\Psychiatrist\Media. (If you're using the JSP version, substitute **JSP** for ASP in the path.) Refer to the section in Chapter 8 about changing media folders and updating paths.

Microsoft Internet Explorer 5.0.

At the time this book was printed, Version 5.0 (commercial version) was the latest Internet Explorer incarnation, which supports CSS style sheets and a full range of dynamic HTML. Look in the PROGRAMS\MS_IE folder. The minimum version of Internet Explorer we recommend using with Drumbeat is 4.0 (throw Version 3 on the trash heap), but if you want the latest hot product, take this one and run.

Netscape Communicator 4.5

Netscape Communicator is an old friend we first met by the name of Mozilla. (We've all been around the block a few times since then.) The latest incarnation of Netscape at the time this book was printed, Communicator 4.5 (commercial version) also supports style sheets and dynamic HTML. Look in the PROGRAMS\NETSCAPE folder. You can use any version of Netscape with Drumbeat. Sites designed for Netscape with Drumbeat can be targeted at either Navigator 3 or 4.0 and later.

Chili!ASP (ChiliSoft)

The Chili!Asp 3.0 add-on (trial version) lets non-Microsoft web servers use Active Server Pages technology. Look in the PROGRAMS\CHILIASP folder. Chili!ASP works with Netscape Fast Track and Enterprise servers, WebSite (from O'Reilly), GO (from Lotus), and Apache, running on Windows NT, Sun Solaris, and IBM AIX. Other web servers and platforms may also be available. More information is available at the ChiliSoft web site, at www.chilisoft.net.

ASP hosting services

If you're in the market for an Internet Service Provider that supports the publishing of Active Server Pages, we've collected a few links for you to explore, where you can find ISPs with ASP hosting services in many areas of the world.

Adobe Acrobat Reader 4.0

Use Acrobat Reader (evaluation version) to view the Drumbeat documentation that's included in the installation package. Look in the PROGRAMS\ACROREAD folder. The Drumbeat documentation includes a Quick Start tutorial you can use to familiarize yourself with the program in addition to the entire Drumbeat User's Guide (more than 700 pages), in PDF format.

After you've installed Drumbeat, you can find the Quick Start tutorial in the folder C:\Program Files\Drumbeat 2000\QuickStart.pdf.

If you're new to Drumbeat, we highly recommend that you go through the Quick Start tutorial first to familiarize yourself with the program's main features. It takes only a couple of hours, and then you're ready to rock 'n' roll with this book. The Drumbeat Users' Guide is in the folder C:\Program Files\Drumbeat 2000\Documentation\DrumbeatUserGuide.pdf. If you've installed the program in a different drive from drive C, choose that drive first and find the Drumbeat 2000 folder.

Paint Shop Pro 5.03

Paint Shop Pro (evaluation version) is an easy-to-use image editor with which you can create buttons and other graphics for your web site. An evaluation version of this popular Windows image editor is included on the CD so that you can customize any artwork you find on the CD or in the Drumbeat program files. Look in the PROGRAMS\PSP folder. Check the Media folder (C:\Program Files\Drumbeat 2000\Media) to find an assortment of themed image folders, many of which include blank buttons you can customize. (If your installation folder is different, just substitute the path for C:\Program Files.) Also, in the Starting Points folder (C:\Program Files\Drumbeat 2000\StartingPoints), under each Starting Point is a Media folder that contains the images used in that Starting Point.

Interland Web Remote Control

Arrange for ASP web hosting services through Interland and you can use this easy remote-connection software (commercial product) to manage your site. Look in the folder PROGRAMS/INTRLAND. See the Interland web site for details: www.interland.com.

If You Have Problems (Of the CD Kind)

The two likeliest problems are that you don't have enough memory (RAM) for the programs you want to use, or you have other programs running that are affecting installation or running of a program. If you get error messages like Not enough memory or Setup cannot continue, try one or more of these methods and then try using the software again:

- ✔ Turn off any anti-virus software that you have on your computer. Installers sometimes mimic virus activity and may make your computer incorrectly believe that it is being infected by a virus.

- ✔ Close all running programs. The more programs you're running, the less memory is available to other programs.

- ✔ Have your local computer store add more RAM to your computer. This is, admittedly, a drastic and somewhat expensive step.

If you still have trouble with installing the items from the CD, please call the IDG Books Worldwide Customer Service phone number: 800-762-2974 (outside the U.S.: 317-596-5430).

Index

• D •

IDG Books Worldwide, Inc., End-User License Agreement

READ THIS. You should carefully read these terms and conditions before opening the software packet(s) included with this book ("Book"). This is a license agreement ("Agreement") between you and IDG Books Worldwide, Inc. ("IDGB"). By opening the accompanying software packet(s), you acknowledge that you have read and accept the following terms and conditions. If you do not agree and do not want to be bound by such terms and conditions, promptly return the Book and the unopened software packet(s) to the place you obtained them for a full refund.

1. **License Grant.** IDGB grants to you (either an individual or entity) a nonexclusive license to use one copy of the enclosed software program(s) (collectively, the "Software") solely for your own personal or business purposes on a single computer (whether a standard computer or a workstation component of a multiuser network). The Software is in use on a computer when it is loaded into temporary memory (RAM) or installed into permanent memory (hard disk, CD-ROM, or other storage device). IDGB reserves all rights not expressly granted herein.

2. **Ownership.** IDGB is the owner of all right, title, and interest, including copyright, in and to the compilation of the Software recorded on the disk(s) or CD-ROM ("Software Media"). Copyright to the individual programs recorded on the Software Media is owned by the author or other authorized copyright owner of each program. Ownership of the Software and all proprietary rights relating thereto remain with IDGB and its licensers.

3. **Restrictions on Use and Transfer.**

   (a) You may only (i) make one copy of the Software for backup or archival purposes, or (ii) transfer the Software to a single hard disk, provided that you keep the original for backup or archival purposes. You may not (i) rent or lease the Software, (ii) copy or reproduce the Software through a LAN or other network system or through any computer subscriber system or bulletin-board system, or (iii) modify, adapt, or create derivative works based on the Software.

   (b) You may not reverse engineer, decompile, or disassemble the Software. You may transfer the Software and user documentation on a permanent basis, provided that the transferee agrees to accept the terms and conditions of this Agreement and you retain no copies. If the Software is an update or has been updated, any transfer must include the most recent update and all prior versions.

4. **Restrictions on Use of Individual Programs.** You must follow the individual requirements and restrictions detailed for each individual program in the "About the CD" section of this Book. These limitations are also contained in the individual license agreements recorded on the Software Media. These limitations may include a requirement that after using the program for a specified period of time, the user must pay a registration fee or discontinue use. By opening the Software packet(s), you will be agreeing to abide by the licenses and restrictions for these individual programs that are detailed in the "About the CD" section and on the Software Media. None of the material on this Software Media or listed in this Book may ever be redistributed, in original or modified form, for commercial purposes.

5. **Limited Warranty.**

   (a) IDGB warrants that the Software and Software Media are free from defects in materials and workmanship under normal use for a period of sixty (60) days from the date of purchase of this Book. If IDGB receives notification within the warranty period of defects in materials or workmanship, IDGB will replace the defective Software Media.

   (b) **IDGB AND THE AUTHOR OF THE BOOK DISCLAIM ALL OTHER WARRANTIES, EXPRESS OR IMPLIED, INCLUDING WITHOUT LIMITATION IMPLIED WARRANTIES OF MERCHANTABILITY AND FITNESS FOR A PARTICULAR PURPOSE, WITH RESPECT TO THE SOFTWARE, THE PROGRAMS, THE SOURCE CODE CONTAINED THEREIN, AND/OR THE TECHNIQUES DESCRIBED IN THIS BOOK. IDGB DOES NOT WARRANT THAT THE FUNCTIONS CONTAINED IN THE SOFTWARE WILL MEET YOUR REQUIRE-MENTS OR THAT THE OPERATION OF THE SOFTWARE WILL BE ERROR FREE.**

   (c) This limited warranty gives you specific legal rights, and you may have other rights that vary from jurisdiction to jurisdiction.

6. **Remedies.**

   (a) IDGB's entire liability and your exclusive remedy for defects in materials and workman-ship shall be limited to replacement of the Software Media, which may be returned to IDGB with a copy of your receipt at the following address: Software Media Fulfillment Department, Attn.: *Drumbeat 2000 For Dummies,* IDG Books Worldwide, Inc., 7260 Shadeland Station, Ste. 100, Indianapolis, IN 46256, or call 800-762-2974. Please allow three to four weeks for delivery. This Limited Warranty is void if failure of the Software Media has resulted from accident, abuse, or misapplication. Any replacement Software Media will be warranted for the remainder of the original warranty period or thirty (30) days, whichever is longer.

   (b) In no event shall IDGB or the author be liable for any damages whatsoever (including without limitation damages for loss of business profits, business interruption, loss of business information, or any other pecuniary loss) arising from the use of or inability to use the Book or the Software, even if IDGB has been advised of the possibility of such damages.

   (c) Because some jurisdictions do not allow the exclusion or limitation of liability for conse-quential or incidental damages, the above limitation or exclusion may not apply to you.

7. **U.S. Government Restricted Rights.** Use, duplication, or disclosure of the Software by the U.S. Government is subject to restrictions stated in paragraph (c)(1)(ii) of the Rights in Technical Data and Computer Software clause of DFARS 252.227-7013, and in subparagraphs (a) through (d) of the Commercial Computer–Restricted Rights clause at FAR 52.227-19, and in similar clauses in the NASA FAR supplement, when applicable.

8. **General.** This Agreement constitutes the entire understanding of the parties and revokes and supersedes all prior agreements, oral or written, between them and may not be modified or amended except in a writing signed by both parties hereto that specifically refers to this Agreement. This Agreement shall take precedence over any other documents that may be in conflict herewith. If any one or more provisions contained in this Agreement are held by any court or tribunal to be invalid, illegal, or otherwise unenforceable, each and every other pro-vision shall remain in full force and effect.

CD Installation Instructions

1. **Insert the CD into your CD-ROM drive.**

2. **In Windows Explorer, navigate to your CD drive and click the drive to display the files on the CD.**

3. **To read the CD license agreement, double-click the file License.txt.**

4. **Double-click the file index.html to open the file in your browser.**

   The four linked web pages contain all the information you need for installing the software and using the related material on the CD. For more information, also see Appendix B.

5. **To install Drumbeat 2000, choose the version you want to install. Just click the link on the index.html page for the version you want. The program's installer walks you through the installation process.**

   Two versions of Drumbeat are provided on the CD, one for ASP and one for JavaServer Pages. You cannot install both versions on the same machine. See Appendix B for more information.

To ensure that you have the latest updates to Drumbeat, after you install the program it's a good idea to go to the Drumbeat web site (www.drumbeat. com) and check for service packs that contain updates you can download and install.

IDG BOOKS WORLDWIDE
BOOK REGISTRATION

We want to hear from you!

Visit **http://my2cents.dummies.com** to register this book and tell us how you liked it!

- ✔ Get entered in our monthly prize giveaway.
- ✔ Give us feedback about this book — tell us what you like best, what you like least, or maybe what you'd like to ask the author and us to change!
- ✔ Let us know any other ...*For Dummies*® topics that interest you.

Your feedback helps us determine what books to publish, tells us what coverage to add as we revise our books, and lets us know whether we're meeting your needs as a ...*For Dummies* reader. You're our most valuable resource, and what you have to say is important to us!

Not on the Web yet? It's easy to get started with *Dummies 101*®: *The Internet For Windows*® *98* or *The Internet For Dummies*®, 6th Edition, at local retailers everywhere.

Or let us know what you think by sending us a letter at the following address:

...*For Dummies* Book Registration
Dummies Press
7260 Shadeland Station, Suite 100
Indianapolis, IN 46256-3917
Fax 317-596-5498

BESTSELLING BOOK SERIES